*Invention and Discovery
of Reality*

Invention and Discovery of Reality

The Acquisition of Conservation of Amount

E. J. PEILL
Lecturer in Psychology,
University of Southampton

JOHN WILEY & SONS
London · New York · Sydney · Toronto

Library of Congress Cataloging in Publication Data:

Peill, E. J.
Invention and discovery of reality.

Bibliography: p.
1. Conservation of substance (Psychology)
2. Child study. 3. Piaget, Jean, 1896–
4. Bruner, Jerome Seymour. I. Title.

BF723.C68P44   155.4'13   74–10243
ISBN 0 471 67795 7

Text set in 11/12 pt. Photon Times, printed by photolithography, and bound in Great Britain at The Pitman Press, Bath.

Preface

The literature on conservation acquisition is often disappointing; loose thinking and weak methodology are common. Piaget's writings on the subject have been superficially read and inappropriately criticized, but Piaget's replies have not been illuminating. My hope is that this book will help to sort out some of the muddles which need never have occurred had there been greater concern for precision. Vague statements may offer protection against criticism, but they are unlikely to lead to progress. In the first part of the book I have tried to point out important conceptual distinctions which have been ignored, to pin down the routes to conservation proposed by Piaget and Bruner in particular, and to specify plausible routes which do not at present have names attached to them. The second part of the book (Chapters 7–11) contains a series of experiments designed to find out which of these routes are taken by children, and the book finishes by suggesting how the concept of conservation of amount could be acquired.

In showing why the problem of conservation acquisition is an interesting and important one, I have introduced a distinction between 'discoveries' and 'inventions' about reality. I have been warned that this gets me into 'deep epistemological waters'. Certainly my analysis is a superficial one, but I have found it useful as far as it goes, and it may provoke others to produce a more refined one. In this, as in my interpretations of existing theories of conservation acquisition, the intention has been to make suggestions, disagreement with which could lead to greater understanding of conservation acquisition in particular, and of cognitive development in general. The following passage from Popper (1963) reflects an attitude which I would like to adopt:

'... if you are interested in the problem which I have tried to solve by my tentative assertion, you may help me by criticizing it as severely as you can; and if you can design some experimental test which you think might refute my assertion, I shall gladly, and to the best of my powers, help you refute it.'

(Popper, 1963, p. 27)

Acknowledgments

I would like to thank Dr. A. R. Jonckheere, University College London, and Professor W. P. Robinson, Macquarie University, Sydney. Both of them helped me a good deal, Dr. Jonckheere with the earlier stages of the work reported here, and Professor Robinson with the later stages.

March 1974   *Elizabeth Peill*

Contents

CHAPTER 1

Introduction

Summary

The aim of both the child and the scientist is to understand the world. Among the products of scientific enquiry we can distinguish discoveries (e.g. generalizations from particular events) and inventions (e.g. theories explaining events by means of hypothetical constructs which cannot be observed directly). Both the processes of discovery and invention might play a role in the intellectual development of the child. Since discovery seems intuitively to be the simpler process, we might first of all consider the child to be primarily a discoverer rather than an inventor. According to Piaget's theory, however, concepts which it appears could be discovered are in fact better conceived as inventions on the part of the child. A search is made for a concept which must be considered an invention and not just a discovery; the concept of conservation of amount seems a suitable one for study. An explanation of conservation acquisition would increase our understanding of the process of invention, and make more acceptable the view that such a process underlies all cognitive development.

1.1 Discovery and invention

'On Tuesday, the Prime Minister sang at 7.15 am and cried at 4.30 pm.'
'If you sing before breakfast, you'll cry before dinner.'
'A state of positive affect following sleep is produced by a state of high arousal, which leads to extreme sensitivity to environmental events, making it likely that depression will develop during the course of a normal day's interaction with others.'

These are three statements which might be made by a person interested in understanding human behaviour. The first describes a particular event, the second expresses a generalization, and the third accounts for the generalization in terms of 'arousal', a variable which it will be assumed cannot be measured directly. It is the difference between the means of arriving at the second statement and the third which is of interest here. Both statements indicate that an active organization of events has taken place, but the third goes further beyond what is directly observable.

If the person arrived at the second statement after observing sequences of singing and crying shown by individuals, then he will be described as *'discovering'* the generalization. The account in terms of arousal could not be discovered from such observations; the person will be described as *'inventing'* it. Direct observation of the effects of a state of high arousal could allow the account to be discovered, but it is being assumed that such observation is impossible. Despite this difference in the means of arriving at the two statements, the same events could show them both to be inappropriate: if on Wednesday, Thursday and Friday the Prime Minister sang continuously throughout the day, the third as well as the second statement might be considered an inaccurate account of reality. That is, both the discovery and the invention are constrained by events in the 'real' world; the concern here is not with the invention of arbitrary notions, but with the invention of ideas about the real world.

The person who, we are supposing, made the three statements, was trying to understand what goes on in the world. He had the aims of a scientist. So has the child; it would not be surprising to find the same three levels of account, although we would not expect him to be aware of the distinction between the three.

'When Mummy put the cushion over the bear, and then took the cushion away, I could see the bear again.'
'Whenever an object is hidden by a cover, the object can be made to reappear by moving the cover.'
'Objects continue to exist in their locations in space when they are out of sensory contact.'

A young child of about three years might make these statements if only his language were sufficiently developed, but an infant of a few months would, it seems, make only the first statement. As we shall see in section 1.2, children only a few months old do not behave as if they assume object permanence; this concept seems to develop over the first two years or so of life.

The second statement expresses an idea which the child could discover about the world, whereas it seems that he must invent the idea of object permanence expressed in the third statement. He is not shown directly that objects continue to exist when they are out of sensory contact, although if objects frequently disappeared after being hidden the assumption of object permanence might be considered inappropriate. As in the example of an adult's invention, the invented idea is tightly constrained by reality.

This example suggests that if we are to explain the development of the child's understanding of the world, we must account for the two processes which have been called discovery and invention. Although both involve an active interpretation of experience, rather than a mere passive registration, discovery seems intuitively to be the simpler process; a more complex organization of experience would seem to be involved in the case of invention. If so, then we should first of all try to explain the development of the child's understanding of reality in terms of discovery, and only resort to invention if absolutely necessary. Perhaps an idea invented in the first instance by an abnormal individual becomes embedded in the culture and is then taught to children growing up in that culture. Maybe adults tell children, explicitly or implicitly, that objects have a permanent existence. The normal child's understanding of reality might not involve any invention on his part.

The major theorist of intellectual development, however, takes a quite different view. Piaget argues that concepts which it appears at first sight could be discovered by the child, are actually better construed as inventions or constructions. Piaget writes of '. . . this inventive construction which characterizes all living thought' (Piaget, 1970, p. 714). For example, it appears reasonable to assume that the child could *discover* that the number of elements in a set remains the same however they are arranged. As we shall see in section 1.4, however, such an assumption may be misleading; it may oversimplify the process whereby the concept is acquired.

It was first suggested above that since discovery seems to be a simpler process than invention, when trying to explain the development of ideas about reality, we should exclude as far as possible explanations in terms of invention. Now it is being suggested that concepts which appear to be capable of being discovered by the child are more accurately construed as inventions. To see whether this latter view is justified, we could first consider whether any one idea about reality cannot be considered a discovery and must really be considered an invention on the part of the child. If we find one clear example of invention, then we must reject the view that invention plays no role in the normal child's understanding of the world, and we must accept that a theory of intellectual development should account for the process of invention. It may even become simpler to consider the child as primarily an inventor rather than a discoverer.

In searching for a clear example of invention by the child, it seems sensible to begin by looking at development in the young infant, since ideas developed by an older child might rest on those developed earlier. Let us begin by considering the concept of object permanence.

1.2 Object permanence

To find out whether a child has the concept of object permanence, we can give him the opportunity of searching for a desired hidden object. If he assumes that the object still exists, then we would expect him to search for it. In 'The Construction of Reality in the Child' (Piaget, 1954; French edition, 1937), Piaget describes his testing of his own three children in this way for object permanence, and Décarie (1965; French edition, 1962) has developed a scale based on Piaget's work. The seven items in Décarie's scale are of increasing difficulty and the responses to them illustrate the development of the baby's search for hidden objects.

Only a few of the items will be described here. In the third item, the baby is shown an object, he reaches out for it, and before he touches it the object is hidden under a cloth. Does the baby lift the cloth to find the object? A baby who fails to do this may nevertheless pass the preceding item, in which part of the object is pulled from under the cloth to give the baby a clue. A baby who searches without any such clue may still fail the fourth item. In this, two cloths are used. The object is hidden under one of them, and the baby finds it; this is repeated once. Then, while the baby watches, the object is hidden under the second cloth. Where does he search? A common error is to look under the first cloth—the baby looks where he looked last time, rather than where he has just seen the object hidden. Older babies, however, are not tricked in this way; they locate objects accurately in space. In Décarie's sample of ninety children, none of the babies younger than nine months passed this fourth item, while most of those aged sixteen to twenty months did pass it.

Two questions arise from this account of testing for object permanence.

(a) Does the young baby's failure to search indicate that he lacks the concept of object permanence? A baby may be perfectly aware that the object is still located under the cover, but be unable to coordinate his movements well enough to stretch out and lift the cover. We can test this. Does the baby who fails to lift the cover from a hidden object nevertheless lift the object if this is uncovered? Does he lift a transparent cover under which the object has been placed?

Bower and Wishart (1972) tested sixteen twenty-one week-old infants. They measured each child's delay in picking up a pink manikin (the free capture time), and in picking up a transparent or an opaque plastic cup. All the children succeeded in the tasks, the mean time for the manikin being forty-five seconds and that for the cup, fifty-five seconds. Each child was next tested with the manikin hidden by the opaque cup, then by the transparent cup, and finally by the opaque one again. Bower and Wishart counted the number of children who, when the manikin was covered, removed the cover and then picked up the manikin, with the time between picking up the cover and picking up the manikin less than the free capture time. When the manikin was covered with the transparent cover, eight of the children succeeded; only two of them did so when the manikin was covered with the opaque cup.

It seems from these results that motor skill problems alone cannot account for the baby's failure to search for the hidden object. The results of other experiments, however, suggest that babies who fail to search for a hidden object may nevertheless assume object permanence. Bower and Wishart (1972) dangled the pink manikin on a string in front of the baby. Before he reached for the manikin, the lights were put out, leaving the baby in darkness. Infra-red cameras showed that all twelve of the twenty-week-old infants who were tested did reach out accurately for the manikin, although all of them failed the usual search tests. Maybe the babies were simply unable to inhibit a movement programmed while the manikin was visible, or maybe they really assumed that the manikin still existed although they could not see it.

Support for the latter interpretation is provided by Bower, Broughton and Moore (1971), who measured eye movements of twenty week-old babies and found that they anticipated the reappearance of an object that had moved behind a screen. Eight- to twelve-week-old babies, in contrast, made various errors suggesting that, for them, an object could exist in a place or could move continuously, but an object was not considered the same object if, having been stationary, it began to move.

These results suggest that we cannot identify one particular time in development when the baby begins to assume that objects have a permanent existence. There seems to be gradual development spread out over many months; maybe the assumption is present in primitive form at birth. However, although it is difficult to identify the beginning of the development of object permanence, maybe we can specify clearly when the concept is completely developed. This point leads to the second question.

(b) If the baby does search for a hidden object, does he necessarily assume that objects have a permanent existence? Maybe the baby has simply discovered that a hidden object can be made to reappear by removing the cover. On one occasion the baby may have accidentally knocked the cover off, or he may have considered it an object of interest in itself and picked it up for examination. He could then see that the hidden object reappeared. Generalization from this event would be a case of discovery rather than invention. The baby may not fill the gap between the object's disappearance and its reappearance; it is assuming the object's existence while it is out of sensory contact which constitutes invention.

If the object permanence test can be passed as a result of simple learning of the kind suggested, then maybe animals could be trained to pass it. Etienne (1973) discusses the responses of various animals to an object's disappearance. In their natural habitats, jays, crows, monkeys and apes do search for hidden objects, but pigeons, rabbits and chicks do not. An animal which does not naturally search may nevertheless be capable of learning to do so. Etienne tried to teach chicks to search for worms which they saw being pulled through a glass tube until the worms disappeared behind either of two screens. The chicks could move behind the screen to reach the worms. Under certain circumstances, some chicks did learn to search behind the correct screen. These chicks had learned to make a specific searching response. The acquisition of this response can be seen as an example of instrumental learning; we would not speak of the chick's 'inventing an assumption about reality'. Unfortunately, Etienne does not report whether, with experience of a wider variety of searching tasks, the chicks would have acquired the generalized search response which in the human infant is taken to indicate the concept of object permanence.

It seems possible, then, that a baby could search for a hidden object without having invented the assumption that the object existed while out of sensory contact. He may simply have discovered how to make objects reappear. What would be a stricter test of object permanence? Maybe we can be sure that a child has the concept only if he verbalizes it; if so, then we can hardly hope to say that a child of eighteen months to two years possesses the concept, since his speech will not be sufficiently well developed. Yet by about this age the child can succeed at rather complex search tasks which may indicate true object permanence.

This discussion suggests that if we are interested in investigating the child's invention of some idea about reality, object permanence is not a good idea to work on. Development seems to occur while the child is learning to coordinate sensorimotor responses, so there is a risk that the child may know something without being able to give a clear indication of his knowledge. Discovery may play a role in the early stages of development of the concept, and we cannot be sure at what point the child assumes continued existence of an object, that is, at what point invention occurs. Perhaps it would be more fruitful to look at concepts which develop rather later in life, when the child's responses can more confidently be interpreted as reflecting his knowledge.

1.3 Qualitative identity

The development of object concepts continues, according to Piaget, with acquisition of the idea that an object maintains its identity despite changes in appearance. Piaget calls this the concept of qualitative identity. As a person or a plant grows, we are prepared to consider it to be still the same thing. When a ball of plasticine is rolled into a sausage, it is considered still the same piece of plasticine.

Piaget (1968a) outlines a study by Voyat, in which the child watched the growth of a 'chemical garden'. A piece of potassium ferrocyanide was added to copper sulphate solution, and a growth rather like seaweed was produced. The child made drawings of the 'seaweed' at various stages in its growth: A, B, C, etc. Young children accepted the identity of the seaweed at successive stages, A and B or C and D, but denied the identity between widely different stages such as A and H. Voyat found that by about seven or eight years, children readily accepted that it was the same seaweed throughout.

Can the development of qualitative identity be considered an invention on the part of the child? Certainly the general idea that objects maintain their identity despite changes in appearance cannot be discovered. Neither can particular instances of the concept. No demonstration could show us that a piece of plasticine is 'still the same stuff' when it is rolled into a sausage. In this respect, the concept of qualitative identity resembles the examples of invented ideas given in section 1.1. However, in the case of both those examples, the ideas could be shown to be inappropriate by events in the real world. This is much less so in the case of qualitative identity. Whether or not we choose to label an object as the same or different from itself in another guise depends on the task in hand. From the point of view of a customer, a crystal vase is no longer the same thing if he drops and breaks it on his way to the cash desk; from the point of view of the shopkeeper, however, it is the same thing.

The process of deciding whether to consider an object the same or different from itself at another time is perhaps better construed as the development of a useful classification, than as the invention of an idea about reality. We can study the development of the general concept of qualitative identity only by looking at its application to particular cases. Yet we see that particular applications of the concept are only loosely constrained by events in the real world. For this reason, the concept of qualitative identity is not a suitable focus for our study of the invention of an idea about reality.

1.4 Quantitative identity: conservation of amount

(a) Introduction

When a ball of plasticine is rolled into a sausage, we do not only classify it as 'the same plasticine'; we also believe that the amount of plasticine remains exactly the same. The assumption that amount remains the same unless material is added or subtracted is called conservation of amount. The concept of conservation is also applied to other quantities, such as number, length, weight, volume and area.

To an adult, it is perfectly obvious that the amount of plasticine remains exactly the same when only the shape is changed. Yet the young child seems not to assume conservation of amount. Here are the responses of three typical children in a test of amount conservation. All three were in the same class of a London school and were aged seven years.

The child is seated at a table beside the experimenter. On the table are two identical balls of plasticine.

Experimenter: 'Here's one for you, and one for me. Let's pretend it's toffee. So this is your toffee and this is my toffee. Have we both got the same to eat, or have you got more, or have I got more (pointing)?'

Julie: 'Both the same.' (Had Julie thought one ball had more to eat, adjustments would have been made until she agreed they were both the same.)

Experimenter: 'We've both got the same to eat. Now I'm going to roll mine like this. (Rolls her ball into a sausage.) Have we both got the same to eat, or have you got more, or have I got more (pointing)?'

Julie: 'You've got more because yours is long and mine's only a ball.'

Experimenter: 'If you were very, very hungry, and you wanted to eat as much as you could, which one would you choose, that one or that one, or wouldn't it matter which one?'

Julie: 'That one (sausage).'

Susannah begins by answering in the same way as Julie, but then changes her mind.

Experimenter: (Rolls her ball into a sausage, and asks the amount question.)

Susannah: 'You've got more. It's longer.'

Experimenter: 'If you were very, very hungry . . .?'

Susannah: 'It wouldn't matter, 'cos if they were both the same before, they would be the same afterwards. Yours is just a different shape.'

Catherine answers as an adult might.

Experimenter: (Rolls her ball into a sausage, and asks the amount question.)

Catherine: 'We've got the same. When you had it in a ball it was the same, but it doesn't matter if you roll it, it's the same, but if you take a bit off then it won't be the same.'

Experimenter: 'If you were very, very hungry . . .?'

Catherine: 'No, it wouldn't matter.'

While Catherine answered in much the same way as an adult would, Julie appeared to think that rolling increased the amount of plasticine. Susannah at first judged that there was more in the sausage than the ball, but later corrected herself. Did Susannah and Julie simply misunderstand the question? It may well be the case that some children give nonconserving judgments simply because they do not understand the question but, as will be shown in Chapter 2, such superficial factors certainly cannot account for all nonconserving judgments. The young child really does seem to think that rolling changes amount, at least in the situation described above.

(b) Definition of the concept: the NAS criterion

Before considering how the concept of conservation of amount might be acquired, let us first define the concept more precisely. The concept can be defined as equivalent to a criterion for judging amount, on the basis of which everything except addition and subtraction are considered irrelevant to amount changes. The criterion can be formulated thus: 'If Nothing is Added or Subtracted, amount remains the same'. In later chapters, this will be referred to as the *NAS criterion*. Only if a person's amount judgments are consistent with the NAS criterion can we conclude that the person has the concept of conservation of amount; if they are not consistent with the NAS criterion, we have no reason to conclude that he has the concept. We can think of a conserver as 'using' that criterion, as long as we are careful not to assume that he is simply applying a verbal formula. Although we can define the concept of conservation as logically equivalent to the NAS criterion, this does not mean that psychologically conservation acquisition involves merely the development of a verbal rule.

How are we to decide whether a person is using the NAS criterion? Certainly Catherine, who said '. . . it doesn't matter if you roll it, it's the same, but if you take a bit off then it won't be the same', made a good attempt at verbalizing the NAS criterion. But what if she had said 'It's the same because if you roll it back it will be the same again' or 'It's the same because you just rolled it'? These reasons are commonly given by children. Some children judge that the amounts are still equal after one of the pieces has been rolled, but give no reason. The problem of deciding when a child can be deemed 'a conserver' is considered in Chapter 2.

Children who fail to judge consistently with the NAS criterion generally seem to be judging amount on the basis of appearance. Both Julie and Susannah judged that there was more in the sausage than the ball, and gave as their reason 'because it's longer'. Their nonconserving judgments can be considered to have derived from perceptual criteria. More evidence for such a view is discussed in Chapter 4.

(c) Possible modes of development

How might the child acquire the concept of conservation of amount? Could it be discovered? Let us consider the possibilities:

(i) We cannot *see* or otherwise sense that amount is conserved when a ball of plasticine is rolled into a sausage. Even an adult, if shown only the ball and the sausage, and not the change from one to the other, would be unable to do better than say 'They could be the same amount'. In order to be sure that the amounts are exactly equal, it is necessary to know that one was rolled into the other without any addition or subtraction of material.

(ii) People who come across the child's nonconservation for the first time commonly suggest that if the sausage were rolled back into a ball, amount conservation would be demonstrated to the child. There are two reasons why rolling back could not provide a demonstration of conservation. Firstly, there is no reason why amount should not increase with rolling and then decrease by the same amount with rolling back. Hence demonstrating that the sausage can be made into a ball again is logically insufficient to allow the conclusion that amount remained the same throughout. Secondly, many children who judge, like Julie, that there is more in the experimenter's sausage than in their ball, nevertheless know that the amounts would be equal if the sausage were rolled into a ball again. Psychologically, as well as logically, knowing about rolling back is insufficient for conservation. This point is discussed further in Chapter 3.

(iii) Even if conservation of amount cannot be demonstrated, the conservation of other quantities can be. Number, weight, length and volume conservation can all be demonstrated. Maybe the child discovers that these quantities are conserved, and then generalizes the concept to amount. There are several difficulties with this suggestion.

Amount conservation is acquired *before* conservation of weight and volume. Weight conservation is tested in a way similar to amount conservation, simply by asking the child 'Do they still weigh the same?' rather than 'Are they still the same to eat?'. Alternatively, the child may be shown how to work a balance and how to establish the initial equality of weight of the two balls of clay by means of this, and then predict what the scales would show after one of the balls had been changed in shape. To test volume conservation, the child is shown that the level of water in a glass rises if a ball of plasticine is placed in it. The child is asked to judge whether the liquid will rise to the same height when the shape of the plasticine is changed, into a sausage perhaps: 'Will this take up just as much room as the ball? Where will the water come to?'

It is well substantiated that for any one material, such as plasticine or clay, amount, weight and volume conservation are nearly always acquired in that order. Laurendeau and Pinard (quoted by Piaget and Inhelder, 1961) found only twelve inversions of that order after testing four hundred and forty-one children. Uzgiris (1964) found eight inversions out of a hundred and twenty children. Those few children who did not show the normal order of development may simply have failed to attend during part of the testing; they may really have developed in the normal way. Age norms quoted by Piaget and Inhelder (1961) show that when these conservation concepts were applied to clay, around seventy-five per cent of children conserved amount at eight years, weight at nine to ten years, and volume at eleven to twelve years. This being the case, amount conservation could not be acquired by generalization from weight or volume.

Conservation of number, however, is acquired some time before conservation of amount. To test number conservation, two rows of perhaps seven beads are laid out one above the other, so that each bead in one row is clearly paired with one in the other row. The child agrees that there are just as many beads in each row, then the experimenter rearranges the beads in one row, either spreading them out or squashing them up, so that the one-to-one correspondence between the rows is no longer obvious. Just as in the test of amount conservation, the young child denies that the two rows contain just as many beads. Usually the longer row is judged to have more. The Piagetian norms show that number conservation is acquired by age six by about seventy-five per cent of children, about two years earlier than amount conservation.

It is possible, then, that the child discovers that number is conserved when the elements are only rearranged, and then generalizes the concept of conservation to amount. But simply to say that the concept generalizes would not explain what was happening during this time. Perhaps the child must come to think of the continuous material (plasticine) as composed of a fixed number of units which can be rearranged. Support for this comes from the fact that amount of discontinuous quantity is conserved earlier than is amount of continuous quantity. For example, Smedslund (1961a) found that conservation of amount of linoleum squares was acquired before that of plasticine. Each of his subjects was tested for conservation using both materials. Five children conserved only the continuous material, whereas twenty conserved only the discontinuous material. Although the order of acquisition of different conservation concepts may give clues about how conservation is acquired, it is not helpful merely to label as 'generalization' the successive acquisition of conservation of number, discontinuous quantity and continuous quantity.

In any case, even if we could account for 'generalization' of the concept of conservation from number to continuous quantity, it seems not to be the case that the acquisition of number conservation is merely a matter of discovery. It is logically possible that the child could learn to conserve number by counting the beads in each row, discovering that it remains the same however the rows are rearranged. However, it is not uncommon to find children who can count but who do not conserve number. If asked to count the beads in each row after giving a nonconserving judgment, they may even distort their counting to agree with their judgment that there are more beads in the longer row. The ability to count, therefore, seems not sufficient for conservation of number, although it may help the child to acquire conservation.

Wohlwill and Lowe (1962) investigated the relationship between counting and conservation of number. Their subjects were seventy-two children whose mean age was five years, ten months. Firstly, the children were given several counting tasks. They were asked to give the experimenter six chips from a pile. All but one of the children did this correctly. Then, the experimenter made a row of seven chips, and the child was asked to make a row with just as many chips. All but four of the children managed to do this. However, the great majority of the children failed the number conservation tasks. For example, when the seven chips in one of two equal rows were spread out, only nine of the children said there were still the same number in each row. We see that many children could count, but did not conserve.

Eighteen of the children then underwent training. A single row of six, seven or eight stars was presented. Above the row were three windows, each covered with a card displaying the figures 6, 7 or 8. The child was told to count the stars in the row, and to lift the card showing the corresponding figure, to find a chip. The row of stars was then lengthened or shortened, and the child was again required to lift the card showing the number of stars, but he was not allowed to count. If he responded incorrectly, he was told to count, and he was shown the correct card. After eighteen training trails, the children were tested again. There was virtually no improvement in conservation test performance. Whereas two of the eighteen children had given conserving judgments in the pre-test mentioned above, three did so in the post-test. The counting was clearly an ineffective training procedure.

It seems, then, that number conservation cannot be considered to be simply a discovery. To attempt to explain the acquisition of amount conservation in terms of generalization from a discovered concept of conservation seems not to be appropriate.

(iv) If experience of the physical world is not sufficient for the child to discover that amount is conserved, maybe learning from the social environment is sufficient for conservation acquisition. A social learning theory cannot account for the first appearance of the concept of conservation, but if we are concerned with the development of the normal child rather than that of an abnormal innovative individual, this is not a problem. It is unlikely that all children are told directly about conservation of amount. All children may, however, observe that adults behave as if changing the shape of an object is irrelevant to its amount. This could merely serve to make the child aware of a problem, to encourage him to develop as he would without such social stimulation, but to develop more quickly. Observation of adult behaviour may, however, have a more direct effect on conservation acquisition.

Waghorn and Sullivan (1970) showed nonconservers a film of an adult being given a test of conservation of amount of liquid. The adult gave conserving judgments. One week later, the children were post-tested for conservation of amount of liquid and of clay. The children who had seen the films performed significantly better in these post-tests than did children in the control group who had merely conversed with the experimenter while the others were being trained. This result suggests that children are prepared to imitate adult conserving behaviour; Waghorn and Sullivan suggest that the children learned the meanings of the words 'same', 'more' and 'less' by watching how adults used them.

A related view is that of Berko and Brown (1960), who suggest that the child's vocabulary training may be responsible for changes in judgments given in conservation tests. At first, they suggest, the child will be taught the words 'more', 'less' and 'same' in simple situations from which he is likely to make inappropriate generalizations. In the case of liquid, for example, he might be taught the meanings of quantity words when the liquid is in identical glasses, so that it is appropriate to judge amount on the basis of level. When the child is presented with a conservation test, in which liquid is poured into a thinner glass and the level rises, he will judge that there is now 'more', i.e. he will give a nonconserving judgment.

While it is likely that such social factors play a role in the acquisition of conservation, it is hard to see how such a social learning theory could be sufficient to account for all the facts of conservation acquisition. We have already seen that the concept of conservation is applied to different quantities at different times: number conservation is acquired some time before amount conservation, and weight and volume conservation are much later to develop. The order of acquisition of these concepts is nearly always found to be the same. If social factors were solely or primarily responsible for conservation acquisition, much greater variability in the order of development of the various conservation concepts would be expected.

(v) If learning from the physical or social world is not sufficient for the acquisition of amount conservation, maybe it is simply a matter of maturation. A maturation theory would hold that as long as the child had an environment adequate for normal development of his nervous system, he would acquire conservation. No specific experience with liquid, beads, etc., would be necessary. Such a theory would find it difficult to account for the fact that some conservation concepts are acquired before others, since presumably what would mature would be a concept which could be applied generally. Nor could it explain specific accelerating or retarding effects of certain environments. There is some evidence of such effects.

Price-Williams, Gordon and Ramirez (1969) tested fifty-six Mexican children aged between six and nine years, for conservation of amount, number, weight and volume. They compared children from pottery-making families with children matched for age, sex, schooling and socio-economic status whose families were not pottery-makers. They found that the pottery-makers' children acquired amount conservation significantly earlier, but were only slightly (not significantly) better on other conservation tasks. This result suggests that experience with manipulating clay had helped the children to acquire amount conservation; it could not be accommodated by a maturation theory of conservation acquisition.

So far, we have failed to account for the acquisition of amount conservation. Perhaps we must resort to the process of invention. Certainly the concept of conservation is not merely an arbitrary idea; it is consistent with the real world. We can specify conditions under which an assumption of conservation of amount could be considered inappropriate. If amount is assumed to be conserved over changes in appearance, then a ball of clay of a particular size can be labelled as containing 'amount X', and it will be possible to list uses for this amount: it might be just enough to make a water-jug of standard size, or four standard drinking cups. If it turned out that on some occasions a ball of the size labelled 'amount X' could be made into four drinking cups, while on other occasions only two could be produced, then the assumption of amount conservation could be questioned. That is, an assumption of quantity conservation implies that measurement is possible; if it proves impossible, then the assumption may be called into question.

If we wish to study a concept which can be considered an invention on the part of the child, then amount conservation seems a good choice: it develops when the child is verbally quite adept and can give us reasons for his amount judgments; the concept can be defined precisely; amount conservation is not commonly taught in schools and we can be confident that at least some children are not directly informed about the adult assumption of conservation of amount—these children, we assume, invent the concept for themselves.

(d) What would be the value of an explanation of the acquisition of amount conservation?

We cannot assume that all quantity conservation concepts are acquired in precisely the same way. Discovery may well play a more important role in the case of number conservation, for example, than in the case of conservation of amount. Hence an explanation of the acquisition of amount conservation may not be applicable in detail to the acquisition of other conservation concepts. Such an explanation would, however, be of general value. As indicated in section 1.1, the major theory of cognitive development, that of Piaget, assumes that the child is primarily an inventor rather than a discoverer. Although Piaget's general framework is now widely accepted among both research workers and educationalists, Piaget's theory does not provide one full explanation of any aspect of cognitive development. None of the cognitive acquisitions studied by Piaget are completely explained by his theory. We do not understand the process of invention. This is not to deny the immense value of Piaget's theory, but if we could provide a full account of any one invention, then the general idea that a process of invention underlies all cognitive development would be much more clearly acceptable. In trying to explain the acquisition of amount conservation, the aim is to understand a general process which has been called invention.

It may be helpful to outline Piaget's general theory to provide a background for the more detailed account of his theory of conservation acquisition to be considered in later chapters. A second theory which will figure prominently in the discussion of conservation acquisition is that of Bruner; he, too, provides a general theory of intellectual development. Both Piaget and Bruner view the child as an active organizer of experience, who is constructing an internal representation of the world which allows him to deal with it effectively. There are, however, important differences between the two theories, as will become clear.

1.5 Piaget's theory of intellectual development

The purpose of this section is merely to acquaint the reader with some of the general properties of Piaget's theory of intellectual development. Many introductions to Piaget's theory are available, but two brief accounts which complement each other quite well are those by Inhelder (1962) and Piaget (1970). The account below provides a superficial impression which can easily be refined and corrected by further reading.

Piaget conceives of intellectual development as a process of adaptation to the environment. The child becomes increasingly capable of dealing with the world in an effective way. The theory can be divided into two aspects: a description of intellectual development in terms of stages, and an account of the way the child moves through these stages. Let us first consider the description.

Each stage is described in two ways: in terms of symptoms, or things the child does, and in terms of structures inside the head, supposedly responsible for the symptoms. There are four stages of development: the sensorimotor stage, lasting from birth until about eighteen months; the preoperational stage (from eighteen months until about seven years); the concrete operational stage (about seven to eleven years); and the formal operational stage, which begins at about eleven years and lasts during adulthood. The ages given are approximate; it is accepted that environmental and genetic factors can cause variations. The order, however, is considered invariant. No child should develop any of the symptoms of the formal operational stage until he has shown all those of the preceding stages. Although

Piaget describes the stages as having distinct properties, it is not supposed that the child suddenly acquires a whole new set of symptoms as he moves to the next stage. In section 1.4, it was shown that various conservation concepts are acquired between the ages of about six and eleven years; these are all symptoms of the concrete operational stage. Within each stage, it is not until the child is ready to move on to the next one that all the symptoms are fully developed.

Some of the symptoms of the stages have already been mentioned. During the sensorimotor stage, the child constructs a world composed of permanent objects located in time and space. By the end of the stage, he searches for hidden object without making the mistake of 'looking where he looked last time' (see section 1.2), and he moves round a barrier to obtain an object which he cannot go to directly.

During the preoperational stage, the child develops symbolic processes: language, imagery and imitation of absent models. Concepts of qualitative identity also develop (see section 1.3). The child comes to accept that a piece of plasticine is 'still the same stuff' after it has been rolled.

The beginnings of logical thinking appear at the concrete operational stage. The concepts of quantity conservation (see section 1.4) have already been described. The child also begins fully to understand the concept of classes. If asked 'Are there more lions in the world, or more animals?' the preoperational child, knowing that lions are animals, will say 'I don't know, I'd have to count them'. The concrete operational child, however, knows that the including class cannot be smaller than the included class.

Finally, at the formal operational stage the child can think scientifically. If asked to find out what factors affect the period of a pendulum, he is able to specify the possibilities, test them, and draw valid conclusions from the results. A less mature child, in contrast, is likely to vary two factors at once and conclude that one of them was responsible for a change in period. His observations may even be distorted by his prior belief about the relevant factors.

The internal structures supposed to be responsible for these symptoms are described in terms of logical models. These are most fully worked out for concrete and formal operational thinking. If the child knows that there must necessarily be more animals than lions, then he must in some sense be manipulating the equations:

'The class of lions = the class of animals − the class of animals which are not lions'

and

'The class of animals = the class of lions + the class of animals which are not lions'.

That is, he must be performing the operations of combining one class, A, with another, A′, to form class B, and also dissociating A′ from B to leave A. A set of such operations, interrelated so as to form a structure, constitutes concrete operational thinking. A more complex structure constitutes formal operational thinking.

The concrete operational structure is supposed to develop separately for different attributes, such as number, amount, weight and volume, although one particular structure is held to be responsible for conservation of the same attribute applied to different materials, e.g. for conservation of amount of both liquid and plasticine. To accommodate the fact that conservation of amount of different materials (e.g. liquid and plasticine) is not acquired simultaneously, Piaget speaks of material as differing in their 'resistance' to the child's operations. A similar phrase is used to account for the 'décalages' between conservation of different attributes: number, amount, etc. Piaget admits that he cannot yet provide an explanation of the 'décalages'; the 'resistance' account is post hoc.

How are the structures developed? As a result of his actions upon the world, the child extracts generalizations, or 'schemes'. These can be thought of as rules or assumptions used for understanding events. Understanding an event involves two processes—assimilation, or integration of the event into existing schemes, and accommodation, or adjustment of the scheme to fit the event more closely. Piaget (1970) gives the following example:

'For example, the infant who assimilates his thumb to the sucking schema will, when sucking his thumb make different movements from those he uses in sucking his mother's breast. Similarly, an eight year old who is assimilating the dissolution of sugar in water to the notion that substance is conserved must make accommodations to invisible particles different from those he would make if they were still visible.' (Piaget, 1970, p. 708)

Sinclair (1973) describes how these processes lead to the development of new schemes:

'... new patterns of thought grow out of the combinations of already existing patterns. ... By assimilating more and more varied contexts a certain pattern of thought or action will encounter an obstacle to which it cannot accommodate; the subject will then search for a different but allied pattern which is already established and will find a new combination to deal with the situation, thereby creating a new, more powerful, pattern. In this way, each new acquisition opens up possibilities for conflicts, whose resolution leads to new structures of thought.' (Reproduced with permission from H. Sinclair in *Constraints on Learning*, Academic Press, London, 1973, pp. 399–400)

Whereas at the sensorimotor stage, the schemes are only utilized in external actions, objects are known as things to be sucked or things to be grasped, at later stages the child no longer has to perform actions in order to 'know' objects. Piaget then speaks of operational schemes, or operations. It is not until the concrete operational stage, however, that the operations are fully developed and organized into complete structures. The mechanism of development as it applies to the acquisition of concrete operational thinking should become clearer in Chapter 5, in which Piaget's account of conservation acquisition is discussed.

1.6 Bruner's theory of intellectual development

Piaget has worked on his theory of intellectual development for nearly a lifetime; Bruner's theory is not nearly so fully developed. The main account appears in

'Studies in Cognitive Growth' (Bruner *et al.*, 1966). Bruner acknowledges the great influence of Piaget on his own work and thinking and, as we saw above, both theories are based on similar general assumptions.

Bruner describes development in terms of modes of representation of knowledge. Knowledge can be represented enactively (in terms of action), ikonically (in terms of images) or symbolically (e.g. in the form of language). In the adult, a particular piece of knowledge may be represented in any or all of these ways, but there are developmental changes in the use of the various forms.

In infancy, knowledge is represented enactively: '. . . the identification of objects depends not so much on the nature of the objects encountered as on the actions evoked by them'. (Bruner, 1966a, p. 12). Bruner's account of infancy is very like Piaget's. By the end of the first year, the child becomes capable of ikonic representation: '(he) . . . is finally able to represent the world to himself by an image or spatial schema that is relatively independent of action'. (Bruner, 1966a, p. 21). The last mode of representation to be acquired is the symbolic mode. This is characterized by properties such as categorial and hierarchical organization, that is, the properties of language.

The child develops language long before thought has the same organizational properties. This is likely to be due to an innate predisposition to develop grammatical rules. Quite independently of language use, something happens to the organization of thought, the beginnings of symbolic representation appear, and then the child can become aware of a mis-match between what he says and how he organizes his thinking. Awareness of this conflict leads him to refine his thinking so that it acquires all the properties of symbolic systems. The child's use of language is, then, considered necessary but not sufficient for him to represent the world symbolically. One of the tasks which requires symbolic representation is the conservation test. In Chapter 5, we shall see how the change from ikonic to symbolic representation is supposed to come about.

From these superficial accounts of the two theories, it may appear that Bruner is simply emphasizing a different aspect of development from Piaget, and that the two theories are really compatible. There is, however, rather a fundamental difference between them. In Piaget's theory, the process of thinking involves the operations. While the world may be represented in the form of symbols, or images, these themselves are only 'known' through the operations. In Bruner's theory, in contrast, thinking involves only manipulation of representations; Bruner's theory has no equivalent of Piaget's operations. What Piaget's child achieves through concrete and formal operational thinking, Bruner's child achieves through symbolic representation. An implication of this is that Bruner's child is much more directly influenced by the symbols which occur in the culture which surrounds him:

'Our point of departure is, then, a human organism with capacities for representing the world in three modes, each of which is constrained by the inherent nature of the human capacities supporting it. Man is seen to grow by the process of internalizing the ways of acting, imaging and symbolizing that "exist" in his culture, ways that amplify his powers. He then develops these powers in a fashion that reflects the uses to which he puts his own life.' (Bruner, 1966b, p. 320–321)

This difference between the two theories appears clearly when each is applied to conservation acquisition, as will be shown in Chapters 3 and 5. Piaget's view of 'representation' and how it differs from that of other psychologists is discussed by Furth (1968, 1969).

1.7 Outline of the book

In this chapter, a distinction has been made between the processes of 'invention' and 'discovery', using examples rather than formal definitions. Although both processes involve an active organization of experience and cannot be considered to require only passive registration of events, invention seems intuitively to be the more complex process. An attempt has been made to establish that at least one idea about the world must be considered an invention on the part of the child—the concept of conservation of amount. The aim here is to understand this process of invention.

An important preliminary to the discussion of conservation acquisition is a consideration of methodological issues. Widely different methodologies and techniques have been used by researchers tackling the problem of conservation acquisition; are they equally acceptable, or are some more appropriate than others? This is discussed in Chapter 2.

Having suggested suitable ways of investigating conservation acquisition, three questions are raised: 'What are the origins of the concept of conservation?'; 'What is the role in conservation acquisition of changes in perceptual criteria?'; and 'What is the mechanism by which conservation is acquired?' The extent to which these questions have been answered by the existing literature on conservation acquisition is discussed in Chapters 3, 4 and 5.

This discussion results in the development of four models of conservation acquisition, which are specified in Chapter 6. The models differ in the proposed route to conservation acquisition. In particular, they differ in the role ascribed to changes in perceptually based judgments of amount. Is the problem for the non-conserving child simply to ignore the change in appearance as a ball of plasticine is rolled into a sausage, or must he interpret the appearance in a new way? Predictions are derived from the models and these are tested in experiments described in Chapters 7–11.

Chapter 12 summarizes and synthesizes the findings, suggesting how amount conservation seems to be acquired. Our understanding of the general process of invention is reconsidered in the light of this suggestion.

CHAPTER 2

Questions of Methodology

Summary

The chapter begins by considering whether nonconserving judgments are simply an artifact of the test situation. Having concluded that young children do indeed fail to conserve amount in standard Piagetian tests, techniques for distinguishing between children at various stages of conservation acquisition are discussed. By using these techniques a description can be developed of the sequence of responses given as conservation is acquired; such a description can be obtained by either longitudinal or cross-sectional methods. Any adequate theory of conservation acquisition must explain this sequence. Supplementary evidence is necessary to test such a theory, and this may be obtained from either observation or training studies. The advantages and disadvantages of each are discussed.

2.1 Introduction

This chapter has two aims. The first is to consider whether the young child's non-conserving judgment is really indicative of a belief that amount can be changed by means other than addition and subtraction of material. Maybe he has simply misunderstood the question, or is unable to express his thoughts accurately in verbal form. Maybe we are presenting him with a task which is not a pure test of conservation, which he fails only because he does not possess the other necessary abilities. The first aim then is to answer the question 'Is conservation acquisition a phenomenon worth investigating as an invention, or can it be reduced to a mere procedural artifact?'.

Secondly, on the assumption that conservation acquisition is a phenomenon of substance, ways of investigating it will be discussed. A wide variety of techniques have been used to study the acquisition of conservation. Are some more appropriate than others?

In connection with the first aim, it is important to recognize that we can never be completely sure that the child does not possess the concept of amount conservation. In a particular test we may, after thorough questioning, become convinced that a child firmly believes that the amount of plasticine after rolling is greater than it was at first. When tested in a quite different situation, however, this child might demonstrate that he can conserve amount of plasticine. Failure to find such a situation is not sufficient grounds for concluding that the child does not possess the concept. Of course, neither can we assume that he does possess the concept in the absence of any demonstration of his use of it. Frank's screening experiment (Bruner *et al.*, 1966) illustrates the point that tests of conservation may differ considerably in difficulty. The screening experiment purports to show that when protected from seeing the change in level as liquid is poured into a wider or a narrower container, the young child does conserve amount. He fails to do so, however, when the change in appearance is visible. The conclusion drawn from Frank's results is that children as young as four years do possess the concept of amount conservation, although they apply it only under certain circumstances.

Bruner's theory of conservation acquisition, which the screening experiment is used to support, is discussed in Chapters 3 and 5. In this chapter the question of the child's use of the concept of conservation in different situations will be ignored. Here, the concern is with procedural factors which may cause any one test of conservation to be an invalid indicator of the child's real amount judgment. Although the focus will be on the standard Piagetian conservation test, many of the points to be made are applicable to any test of conservation.

2.2 The validity of Piagetian conservation tests

The standard paradigm will be outlined first, then some criticisms of it will be considered.

(a) The standard paradigm

The conservation tests described in Chapter 1 followed the standard Piagetian paradigm. Tests of this kind are the most commonly used. Although the tests differ in the attribute to be judged (e.g. number, amount, weight or volume) and in the material used (e.g. beads, plasticine, sand or water) fundamentally they are the same. A typical test of amount conservation using plasticine is as follows.

(i) The child first agrees that two identical pieces of plasticine, A and B, have the same amount (perhaps 'The same to eat').

(ii) Then, one of the pieces, B, is deformed in some way—broken into little bits, or squashed into a pancake, or rolled into a sausage, B'.

(iii) The child is again asked to judge the amounts, this time to compare A with B'.

A child using the concept of conservation judges that there is still necessarily the same amount in A and B', and may give a reason such as 'You didn't add any on or take any away'. If, on the other hand, the child judges that A is not the same amount as B', then he is not using the concept of conservation.

In future, a 'conserving judgment' will mean a judgment that A and B' are equal in amount (although the child may make such an equality judgment without using the concept of conservation. That he gives a conserving judgment is necessary but not sufficient evidence that he is using the concept of conservation.) A 'nonconserving judgment' will mean a judgment that A and B′ are not equal in amount.

Conservation of amount can be tested in a similar way by pouring liquid, sand or beads from one of two equally full identical beakers, into a wider or narrower beaker, or into a number of tiny beakers. In a test of length conservation, two equally long sticks are first aligned one above the other, than one of them is displaced so that it extends beyond the other at one end. In a test of number conservation, two equal rows of beads are placed in one-to-one correspondence, then one row is extended or collapsed.

The paradigm in all these tests is to begin with two entities which are identical in appearance and which are agreed to be equal in quantity. Then one of them is deformed in some way that is to an adult irrelevant to quantity changes, but which to a young child may not be irrelevant.

Further details of the testing procedure, refinements of the basic test, are given later. First, some criticisms of this basic procedure will be considered. These focus on the comparison the child is asked to make—A with B′ rather than B with B′—and on the test's reliance on verbal interaction between the child and the experimenter. This latter aspect can be attacked at three levels: the child may fail to understand the words used, he may be influenced by the particular form of the question, and he may be misled by ambiguity in the question; it may refer to real or to apparent amount.

(b) Does the child understand the words used?

Perhaps the child gives a nonconserving judgment simply because he does not understand what 'same amount' or 'more' mean. This point has been put strongly by Braine (1962):

> 'It would seem to be intrinsically impossible to study how a concept *develops* with methods which employ verbal cues to evoke the concept. For, if the child understands the verbal cue, he must already have developed the concept.' (Braine, 1962, p. 46)

Braine is not referring to conservation tests in particular, but to Piaget's methods in general. As an illustration of his point, Braine takes an imaginary study of the development of the child's concept of 'table', in which the child is asked about a variety of objects 'Is this a table or not? Why?'. Braine points out that unless the child responds more or less appropriately, the experimenter learns very little about the child's concept. Yet, if he does respond appropriately, he must have already developed the concept.

This situation is not, however, analogous to an investigation of the development of quantity concepts in the child. In the case of amount, for example, we can distinguish between the child's understanding of 'same' and 'more', and his criterion for judging whether or not two amounts are equal. The subjects in an experiment on conservation acquisition can be pre-tested for their understanding of these words. For example, Curcio et al. (1972) pre-tested their subjects in the following way. Three identical containers were used. Two were filled with birdseed to the same level, and the third was filled to a higher level. The child was told to 'Point to the jars that have the same amount of seeds to eat' and 'Point to the jar that has more seeds to eat'. The jars were then rearranged and the questions repeated. Curcio *et al.* do not report how many of their subjects failed this pre-test, but forty-seven passed it although they failed to conserve.

In studies of conservation acquisition, we are trying to understand the changes in the child's criteria for judging quantity. When verbal tests are used, it is assumed that important changes occur after the child has learned the words 'more' and 'same' applied to quantity. The results of two experiments suggest that children learn these words at quite a young age.

Griffiths, Shantz and Sigel (1967) tested fifty-four children aged four to five years for their understanding of 'more', 'less' and 'same' applied to number, length and weight. In each of the tests, the child was asked to compare a standard stimulus with one which was either identical to it, or which differed from it only in the attribute to be judged. For example, in the number tests, the standard stimulus was a set of three lollipops glued to cardboard, and the comparisons comprised an identical set, a set of two, and a set of four lollipops. For each of these, the child was asked 'Does this set have more lollipops, less lollipops, or the same number of lollipops as this set (standard)?'. The percentage of children giving correct judgments was high. All the children correctly applied 'more' to length judgments, and virtually all did so to weight judgments. Success was by far the lowest in the case of 'same' applied to weight, when only fifty-nine per cent of the children answered correctly. There was no difference in difficulty between the words 'more' and 'less' when applied to one particular attribute. When the correct answer was 'same', the children made more errors than when the correct answer was 'more' or 'less', but only when the attribute to be judged was length or weight. One might conclude that the children had difficulty in understanding 'same'. However, only in the case of number could the child be sure that the stimuli were exactly the same; the children were possibly unsure how accurate their judgments of length and weight were supposed to be. This problem of interpretation of 'same' does not really arise in conservation tests, since the initial equality of two quantities is established to the child's satisfaction, and for a conserver the equality judgment after deformation is logically necessary, and not based on a perceptual comparison.

While Griffiths *et al.* found no difference in difficulty between 'more' and 'less', this result is contrary to the findings of Donaldson and Wales (1970). The children they tested were aged three and a half to five years. They used model apple trees, and asked the child 'Does one tree have more/less apples on it than the other?'. If the child answered 'Yes', he was asked to indicate which tree had more/less apples. If he answered 'No', he was asked 'Is there the same number of apples on each tree?'. This kind of questioning, in which the child was asked a series of short questions rather than one long one, and in which testing of understanding of 'more' was separated from testing of 'less', may well produce more reliable results than the more complex questioning used by Griffiths *et al.* Donaldson and Wales found that the children's main difficulty was with 'less'—they often used this to mean 'more'. There was, however, no real difficulty with 'more' or 'same'.

Except when the experimenter is interested in quantity judgments in very young children (e.g. Mehler and Bever, 1967; Bever, 1970; Gelman, 1972), the subjects in conservation experiments are generally at least five to six years old. The results of the two experiments just described suggest that among these children there should be little difficulty with the words 'more' and 'same', although it might be advisable to avoid the word 'less' unless pre-testing has shown this to cause no difficulty.

It is quite possible, though, that some children who take part in conservation experiments do not understand quantity words such as 'amount', 'length' or 'area'. But this need not be a problem, since such words can usually be avoided, and the attribute to be judged can be made clear in a picturesque way. The child might, for example, be asked to judge whether two lengths are 'just as far to walk, so that two people, one on each road, would be just as tired' (Inhelder and Sinclair, 1969, p. 8). In the case of amount, the child can be asked to judge whether there is 'the same to eat' or 'the same to drink'.

Although it seems unlikely, then, that the words used should present difficulties for the child, the precaution can be taken of giving each subject a pre-test for understanding of these words. However, if the child is to be given thorough conservation testing of the kind described later in this chapter (section 2.3), then children who simply do not understand what is required of them should be detected without recourse to a pre-test.

(c) Is the child influenced by the form of the question?

Even if the child does understand the words used, the particular form of the question may influence him. If the child is asked 'Is one more than the other?', he may feel obliged to agree and hence be more likely to give a nonconserving judgment than if he is asked 'Are they both the same?'. This problem was investigated by Pratoomraj and Johnson (1966). Using clay, blocks and sand in conservation tests, they asked four- to seven-year olds questions framed around the phrases 'Are they the same?', 'Are they different?', 'Is there more?' and 'Is there less?'. They analysed the number of conserving judgments given to each kind of question, and found no significant differences between them. This suggests that the children were not particularly sensitive to such differences in the question asked.

However, Hall and Kingsley (1968), in a study of length conservation, found that the particular question asked did seem to influence the child's judgment. In one series of tests, they simply moved two equal lines further apart, and asked the child first 'Is the one I moved longer or shorter or the same length as the other piece?', and then 'If we measured them, which would be longer and which would be shorter or would they be the same length?'. Forty per cent of the children changed their initial judgment in their answer to the second question. This led Hall and Kingsley to conclude: 'Clearly, the instructions were just as important as the visual appearance of the objects' (p. 202). It could simply be, though, that the nonconservers, trying to judge on the basis of appearance, were unable to make confident judgments of the lines after they had been moved eight to twelve inches further apart. The children might well have changed their judgments if they had been asked the same question twice; this was not checked. Hall and Kingsley's conclusion is not, therefore, acceptable.

In trying to avoid the possible bias of a short question such as 'Are they both the same to eat?', the experimenter might use a complex one like Hall and Kingsley's 'Is the one I moved longer or shorter or the same length as the other piece?' Such a question may well be too difficult for the child. Rothenburg (1969) sees the solution in asking a series of single-part questions. In a test of number conservation, Rothenburg asked children 'Does this bunch (i.e. row of blocks) have the same number of blocks as this bunch?' Whether the child answered 'Yes' or 'No', he was then asked 'Does one bunch have more blocks?' This procedure has the advantage that children can be classified as inconsistent responders, who presumably do not understand the task. But a possible disadvantage of Rothernburg's technique is that children who are confident in their judgment will grow impatient with such persistent questioning, and, if several tasks are given, will lose interest and cease to answer.

What then is the best form of question to use? There is no evidence to suggest that a short question such as 'Are they both the same to eat?' does bias the child's response, although it seems less risky to make explicit the full range of choices. A question such as 'Are they both the same to eat, or is this one more, or is this one more?' can be asked slowly and can be accompanied by pointing to each object as it is mentioned. Such a question seems acceptable, as long as the experimenter is careful not to influence the child's judgment by means of nonverbal cues, and is vigilant for signs that the child does not understand.

(d) Does the child assume the question refers to apparent, rather than real, amount?

Attacking verbal assessment at a more general level, Braine and Shanks (1965a, b) argue that some children who really can conserve may fail to do so in a standard Piagetian test because they interpret the question as referring to phenomenal, rather than real, quantity. Braine and Shanks' evidence comes from a series of experiments using illusions. For example, (1965a), they used a 'ring segment' illusion. Each trial involved a pair of segments, one of which was really bigger than the other, as was clear when the segments were superimposed. When they were placed one above the other however (juxtaposed), the bigger segment looked the smaller. Pairs of segments were presented superimposed, then juxtaposed, and so on in a series of items. In each item, the child was asked either 'Which is really the big one?' or 'Which looks bigger?'. Braine and Shanks found that seventy-eight per cent of the children, who were aged from four to seven and a half years, always selected the segment which looked bigger; they interpreted both questions as referring to phenomenal size.

While this could have been because they could not make a distinction between reality and appearance, Braine and Shanks think that was true only of the youngest children (younger than about five years). Support for this claim came from the results of experiments in which feedback was given; the child was rewarded for a correct answer with chips which could later be exchanged for sweets, and penalized for an incorrect answer by losing a chip. He was also given demonstrations that the 'really bigger' segment was the one which looked bigger in the superimposed position. Whereas young children (three to four years) generally failed to learn to answer correctly 'Which is really the big one?', the majority of the older ones learned quickly. Because learning was so fast, and because there was no learning in a similar task in which nonsense words replaced 'looks' and 'really' (see below), Braine and Shanks concluded that the older children required the feedback only to make clear to them the meaning intended by the experimenter, and that they already understood the distinction between reality and appearance.

The implication is that to make an accurate assessment of whether or not a child can conserve, feedback should be given to ensure that he does not assume he is to judge whether the two quantities *look* the same. To this methodological point, Braine and Shanks add a theoretical one, that conservation acquisition can be seen as one symptom of the ability to make a distinction between reality and appearance. This will be mentioned again in Chapter 3.

It is not really clear from Braine and Shanks' results that the children who learned from feedback did understand the reality–appearance distinction. In the training in responding to 'really bigger' and 'looks bigger', the child was shown that when asked 'Which is really bigger?', he should choose the segment which looked bigger when the segments were superimposed. It is possible that the child could learn this in a mechanical way without really understanding that an adult considers the 'really bigger' segment still to be bigger in the juxtaposed position. As mentioned above, Braine and Shanks tested for the possibility that only mechanical learning was taking place, but they did so in rather a strange way. Two rectangles, one bigger than the other, were presented in superimposed and juxtaposed positions. When asked 'Which one kivils bigger?', the child was rewarded for choosing the bigger rectangle. When asked 'Which is tarmly, tarmly bigger?', he was rewarded for choosing the bigger rectangle in the superimposed position, but the smaller one in the juxtaposed position. Since there was no illusion, there was no possibility that the child could learn that when asked which was 'tarmly' bigger, he should choose the one which looked bigger in the superimposed position. The nonsense word task may therefore have required more complex learning than the illusion tasks, and the fact that there was no learning in the nonsense word task cannot be taken as demonstrating that learning in the illusion tasks was not simply mechanical.

Despite this criticism of their work, Braine and Shanks may be correct in suggesting that the child is likely to interpret a question about quantity as referring to appearance rather than reality. Feedback need not be nonverbal, however. It will be argued below (section 2.3b) that countersuggestion should be used in conservation testing—if the child gives a nonconserving judgment, for example, he can be told 'Somebody else said they're both the same to eat still, because I didn't add any on or take any off. Do you think that was right or wrong?'. Suggesting an alternative judgment to the child in this way could make him aware that the experimenter may be referring to reality rather than appearance. He might even indicate this to the experimenter by saying 'They don't look the same to eat, but they are really.'.

Acceptance of Braine and Shanks' point does not mean that nonverbal techniques must be introduced into the testing.

(e) Do nonverbal tests produce the same results as verbal ones?

In this discussion of the validity of verbal tests of conservation, the experiments considered so far have investigated directly the child's understanding and use of language. Nothing has yet suggested that the reliance of Piagetian tests on verbal interaction presents any real problems. However, more powerful evidence against the view that verbal tests are invalid would be to show that verbal and nonverbal tests yield the same results. Unfortunately, many experimenters who have used nonverbal tests of conservation have not made comparisons with verbal tests. Three experiments which do include such comparisons will be described.

The first of these is not strictly a nonverbal test, but the child was not directly asked to judge quantity. Silverman and Schneider (1968) showed the child two identical jars containing different amounts of little sweets. They then poured the smaller amount into a thinner jar so that the level was higher than that of the greater amount of sweets. The child was asked which jar of sweets he would like, and why. Most children chose the jar they thought had more sweets. If this was the reason for their choice, and they chose the jar which by adult standards had more sweets (but in which the level was lower) then they were classified as conservers. The results are presented in terms of the percentages of children who conserved at each age. Fifty per cent conserved at ages six to seven years, sixty per cent at seven to eight years, and seventy-three per cent at eight to nine years. Silverman and Schneider state that these results 'conform very closely' to those obtained by Piaget and others who have used standard verbal tests, and they conclude that '. . . Piaget's criteria are valid measures of conservation, independent of the child's capacity for verbal distinction.' (p. 289.)

In fact, the Genevan data on a comparable conservation task, beads in glasses, indicate that fifty-four per cent of their subjects conserved at six years, and ninety-six per cent did so at seven years (Piaget and Inhelder, 1969, p. 163; French edition, 1963). The large difference at age seven between the two sets of results renders Silverman and Schneider's conclusion invalid. If we can draw any conclusion from Silverman and Schneider's results, it is that the nonverbal test seems to have been rather more difficult than the verbal one. The experiment could have been conducted by testing each child by both verbal and nonverbal means, or by comparing matched groups of children. Either of these designs would have avoided the problems of comparing performance in the nonverbal test with norms obtained from children of quite different background.

The second experiment on nonverbal assessment of conservation avoids the design flaw of Silverman and Schneider's study. Mermelstein and Shulman (1967) did give each child both a nonverbal test and conventional verbal tests. Groups of six- and nine-year-old children were tested for conservation of liquid and of discontinuous quantity by verbal methods, and a nonverbal test of conservation of liquid amount was also given. In this test, the child poured one of two equal amounts into a large jar. By means of a hidden tap, the poured liquid was made, apparently, to fill the large jar. The child was classified as a 'conserver' if his face or comments indicated surprise. Mermelstein and Shulman found that children 'conserved' (i.e. showed surprise at the liquid's filling the large jar) on this test without conserving on either of the verbal tests. Of a hundred and twenty children, twenty-six 'conserved' in only the nonverbal test, while four conserved in only the verbal test of conservation of discontinuous quantity. Since discontinuous quantity is conserved about a year earlier than continuous quantity (liquid) when both are tested by verbal means, it seems particularly impressive that liquid conservation was acquired first when this was tested nonverbally. Mermelstein and Shulman conclude from their results that

> '... the presence or absence of language itself significantly affects performance ... Clearly then Piaget's clinical approach is deficient in the sense that it does not take into account the language variable. It is entirely possible, then, that children who possess the concept of conservation but cannot verbalize it escape Piaget's detection.' (Mermelstein and Shulman, 1967, p. 50)

However, Mermelstein and Shulman are not justified in their assumption that their nonverbal test assessed conservation. There is no reason to suppose that a surprise reaction to liquid behaving in strange ways is indicative of a nonverbal conservation concept. Experience of liquids leads the child to have expectancies about how they will behave, as is demonstrated by the common finding that nonconservers predict that liquid will rise to a higher level if poured into a thinner glass (e.g. Piaget and Inhelder, 1971; French edition, 1966). It is not therefore at all surprising that children who did not conserve in Mermelstein and Shulman's verbal tests knew that the liquid they were pouring could not fill the large jar. It would be much more interesting to discover that children conserved in verbal tests without being surprised by liquid behaving in strange ways, since this would suggest that knowledge of those empirical laws was not necessary for conservation.

Although their nonverbal test did not assess conservation, the intention of Mermelstein and Shulman was a reasonable one: to provide a demonstration of apparent nonconservation and see whether the child was surprised by it. A demonstration of apparent nonconservation of weight is given to the child in Smedslund's extinction test. Although intended as an indicator of the child's understanding of the logical necessity of conservation, the extinction test might be adapted to test conservation nonverbally. However, Miller (1973) found very few facial or verbal expressions of surprise when he gave conservers demonstrations of apparent nonconservation of weight, suggesting that indication of surprise may not be a very useful nonverbal response. Extinction tests are discussed in more detail in section 2.3c.

The inadequacies of the two experiments described so far do not allow us to conclude whether nonverbal assessment of conservation produces the same results as verbal assessment. An experiment by Schwartz and Scholnick (1970) is only slightly more satisfactory. In their experiment, the child was first given a verbal test of conservation of discontinuous quantity (M. & M. candies). This test consisted of two tasks: the sweets were poured into a narrower glass, and into a wider one. This verbal test was repeated after the nonverbal testing.

The nonverbal tests involved some pre-training. The child was presented with two cards on which sweets were stuck. One card was the experimenter's and the other was 'Billy's'. Billy was represented by two drawings, one of which showed a happy face and the other a sad face. The child was told to choose Billy's happy face if Billy had as much to eat as the experimenter, but to choose the sad face if he had less. The child was rewarded with a sweet if he chose the correct face. After being trained to criterion, conservation tasks were introduced. Only one of these was comparable to the verbal test. In this, two identical glasses were presented; they contained equal amounts of little sweets. If the child chose Billy's sad face, indicating that he thought Billy's glass contained less, sweets were added until the child agreed that 'Billy would be happy'. Then the contents of Billy's jar were transferred to a wider glass, and the child again selected one of Billy's faces. There were four tasks like this one. It seems that the child was considered to have a given a conserving judgment if he chose Billy's happy face.

Out of forty children, whose mean age was five and a half years, seven passed all four verbal tasks, and six passed the nonverbal ones. Four children passed both kinds of test, thirty-one failed both, two passed only the nonverbal test, and three passed only the verbal test. These results suggest that the two kinds of test were about equal in difficulty, although the numbers of children who passed them are too small to allow a confident conclusion.

A problem with Schwartz and Scholnick's nonverbal test is that no distinction was made between the judgments 'Billy has more' and 'Both the same to eat'. A child would have been classified as a conserver if he judged that the amount of sweets in the wider glass was more than that in the experimenter's glass. Such a judgment could have been based on the width of the glass. It is more common for nonconservers to judge liquid amount on the basis of level, however, therefore not many errors of classification would be expected.

Schwartz and Scholnick's technique seems to have no advantages over a verbal test. A child trained to select Billy's happy or sad face could easily have been trained to say 'same' or 'more'. Pre-training may not even have been necessary if a verbal response had been required. As we shall see in section 2.3a, a verbal test has the advantage that the child's verbally stated reasons for his judgment can be taken into account. In contrast with Schwartz and Scholnick's, Silverman and Schneider's nonverbal test could have yielded interesting results. A child could possibly have an intuitive understanding of amount conservation which influenced his choice of food or drink, but which was not verbalized. Silverman and Schneider's results suggest that this is unlikely, although for the reason indicated above no firm conclusions can be drawn from them.

The above account of nonverbal tests of conservation has added little to the argument concerning the validity of standard Piagetian tests. From the results of direct investigations of the child's understanding of questions about quantity, it was concluded that children of the ages normally used in conservation tests would probably understand the words 'same' and 'more' applied to quantity, and that use of a pre-test could ensure that all subjects understood the words used. The particular form of the question asked has not been shown to bias the child's judgment, although presumably the experimenter's nonverbal cues could do so. While there may be a risk that the child assumes we are asking 'Do they *look* the same to eat?', thorough testing of the kind to be described below would be expected to make the experimenter's meaning clear to a child who understands the distinction between reality and appearance. Careless questioning could, of course, lead to invalid results, but there is no reason to suppose that verbal tests of conservation need be invalid.

(f) Should identity rather than equivalence tests be used?

Now, a quite different reason will be considered, as to why children who really can conserve might not be detected in standard Piagetian tests. The conservation concepts apply to changes within one object, and testing could be carried out using only one object instead of the customary two. Elkind (1967) suggests that Piaget uses a comparison object because he wants to be sure that the child remembers the initial appearance. According to Elkind, Piaget thinks that the child might achieve 'pseudo-conservation' by remembering a ball of clay as larger than it was, to compensate for an apparent increase in amount when it is rolled into a sausage. Use of a comparison object ensures that the child is aware of any illusion of change in amount when the shape is changed.

Support for Elkind's account of Piaget's views can be found in Piaget (1968b). He writes:

'The natural tendency of young children, evidently, is to conserve as long as they are not confronted by facts which they do not expect, and whose inexplicability leads them to change their opinion.'

and

'In general, children expect conservation . . .' (Piaget, 1968b, p. 978)

A possible implication of Piaget's statements is that the child's memory of the initial appearance could become distorted to conform more closely to his expectancy that the amount remains the same. This would be less likely to happen if a comparison object were used.

However, Elkind himself (1967) makes a distinction between 'identity' and 'equivalence' conservation tests. Standard Piagetian tests (equivalence) involve a comparison object, A, as well as an object B which is deformed to B'. Elkind suggests that the giving of a conserving judgment logically requires performance of the deductive sequence:

$$B = B'$$
$$A \text{ was equal to } B$$
$$\text{Therefore, } A = B'$$

Elkind predicted that because of this deduction, equivalence tests would be more difficult than identity tests, in which there is no comparison object and the child has simply to judge $B = B'$. Elkind assumes that there are some children who can conserve but cannot deduce. If this is true, it follows that children who conserve in an identity test may fail to do so in an equivalence one, just because they cannot perform the deduction.

Equivalence tests of conservation have indeed been found to be more difficult than identity ones by Elkind and Schoenfeld (1972) (number, amount and length); Hooper (1969) (discontinuous quantity); McManis (1969) (discontinuous quantity and amount); Moynahan and Glick (1972) (length); Papalia and Hooper (1971) (discontinuous quantity); and by Schwartz and Scholnick (1970) (discontinuous quantity).

With one exception, these experiments do not show whether identity tests were easier merely because the child did not see the pre- and post-deformation appearances simultaneously, and so achieved 'pseudo-conservation'. The exception is Hooper's (1969) experiment, in which this possibility could be tested. Hooper designed an equivalence test which was similar to an identity test in terms of perceptual cues, but which still required the deduction. In this test, which was called equivalence conservation I, a comparison container, A, was used, but it was hidden behind a screen just before the contents of container B were transferred to B'. The child was then asked to compare the amounts in A and B' without being able to see A. Hooper compared performance in this test with performance in a conventional equivalence test (II) and in an identity test. Each child was given three tasks under one of three conditions: identity, equivalence I or equivalence II. Children were classified as conservers if they gave at least two conserving judgments justified by an adequate reason; otherwise they were scored as nonconservers. The results showed that there was no significant difference between performance in the two kinds of equivalence test, but that the identity test was significantly easier than these. That is, the equivalence test was more difficult than the identity test even when the comparison object was hidden before the deformation. These results suggest that the identity test was not easier merely because the child was unaware of the extent of the change in appearance after deformation. Possibly it was the deduction which made both kinds of equivalence test more difficult. Hooper concluded that

'... it is clear that the equivalence conservation task format is not the most appropriate means of valid identity conservation assessment.' (Hooper, 1969, p. 245)

However, Koshinsky and Hall (1973) repeated Hooper's experiment, making a within-subjects rather than a between-subjects comparison between the identity, equivalence I and equivalence II tasks. This was a more powerful test than Hooper's but they found no sign of the identity tasks being easier. Other experimenters have also failed to find a difference in difficulty between identity and equivalence tests of conservation. In view of the prevailing tendency not to publish failures to find significant differences, it is not surprising that this list is shorter than the one above: Moynahan and Glick (1972) (number, amount and weight); Northman and Gruen (1970) (amount); Papalia and Hooper (1971) (number); and Teets (referred to by Papalia and Hooper, 1971) (weight).

Why is the difference not always obtained? Maybe it appears only in the case of certain attributes or certain materials. However, although discontinuous quantity is not represented in the list of failures, number, weight and amount of liquid (continuous quantity) appear in both lists. It has been suggested that the effect appears only among young children, and some of the results listed above can be cited to support this suggestion (Elkind and Schoenfeld, 1972; Hooper, 1969). Papalia and Hooper (1971) suggest that this could be due simply to a ceiling effect; older children may be so advanced that they pass both tests. However, Elkind and Schoenfeld (1972) argue that preoperational children (in Piaget's sense) can give conserving judgments simply by calling upon 'accumulated past experience'. This experience is not sufficient for them to conserve in an equivalence test because they cannot perform the deduction. They state that

> 'Identity conservation is not truly quantitative and involves only figurative aspects of perceptual processes (i.e., global quantity judgments comparable to those used when a child judges a cluster of 10 pennies as more than a cluster of 6—because of the perceptual impression of numerosity).' (Elkind and Schoenfeld, 1972, p. 532)

How this argument can be applied to conservation of continuous quantity (e.g. liquid or plasticine) remains a mystery.

Elkind, along with other experimenters, apparently assumes that the difference in difficulty between identity and equivalence conservation tests is due to competence factors—that the child is *unable* to perform the deduction in the equivalence test. Two questions arise:

(i) Does the conserver in an equivalence test perform a deduction? Although logically the equivalence test does involve a deduction, this need not mean that psychologically a deduction is performed. The child might apply the following strategy:

Make initial amount judgment on the basis of appearance.
Observe the deformation.
Since nothing has happened that is relevant to amount changes, repeat the initial judgment.

None of those who found a difference in difficulty between identity and equivalence tests demonstrated that the child's failure to perform the deduction was responsible. Support for the view that a deduction need not be performed in equivalence tests comes from results obtained by Smedslund (1964). He found that equivalence conservation tests were passed by children who failed tests of transitivity. In these, they learned that A was more than B, and that B was more than C, and they had to deduce that A was more than C. In the case of discontinuous quantity (linoleum squares), thirty-one children failed to perform this deduction although they did conserve; only four children passed the transitivity test but failed to conserve. Unless it is assumed that deductions are easier to perform when they are hidden in an equivalence test of conservation than when they are directly requested, Smedslund's results suggest that children may conserve in equivalence tests without performing a deduction.

If this is true, then why should equivalence tests ever be more difficult than identity ones? Two reasons will be suggested. The identity test might be easier simply because the child is asked to judge the *same* piece of material before and after deformation; the concept of conservation might be less obviously relevant when the child is asked to judge two separate pieces of material. The second reason is related to this. The child may actually confuse the question 'Is there still the same amount?' with 'Is it still the same stuff?'. He may give a conserving judgment when all he means is 'It's still the same stuff'. Such a confusion cannot arise in an equivalence test. Children may be misclassified as conservers more commonly in identity tests than in equivalence tests.

(ii) Are competence factors involved? Whether or not a deduction is psychologically necessary in the equivalence test, performance rather than competence factors may be responsible for its being more difficult than the identity test. The difference might disappear if the child were given a chance to think again about his judgment. If so, this would not have been noticed in any of the experiments listed above, since in none of them was conservation testing at all thorough.

An experiment by the author (Experiment A) was designed to test the suggestion that the difference in difficulty between identity and equivalence tests is only superficial. Each of seventy-two children, aged between six and seven and a half years, was given three tests of conservation. Two were equivalence tests, and the third was an identity test. The identity test was given either first or second to control for order effects. Each test involved the rolling of a short fat plasticine sausage into a long thin one. After the rolling, the child was asked for an amount judgment, and for his reason. He was then given a countersuggestion which was intended to encourage him to think again about his judgment. If he had given a conserving judgment, the countersuggestion was 'Well, somebody else said there's more to eat now/(I've got more to eat) because it's /(mine's) longer. Do you think that was right or wrong?' A child who had given a nonconserving judgment was told 'Well, somebody else said it's still the same to eat/(we've both got the same to eat still) because I just rolled it/(mine), I didn't add any on or take any away. Do you think that was right or wrong?' The amount question was then repeated, to see if the child had accepted the suggested judgment.

It was predicted that although analysis of the first judgments given might show a difference between identity and equivalence tests, this difference would disappear when the responses after contersuggestion were taken into account. In fact, the results showed no differences at all between performance in the identity and equivalence tests. It was expected that a difference would be most likely to appear in the first test given, but those given the identity test first performed no differently in their first, second or third tests, from those given an equivalence test first. Neither was there any difference between these two groups in the change in performance between the first and second tests. Well over half the children gave nonconserving judgments, so the failure to find any differences cannot have been due to a ceiling effect. Since no differences were found between identity and equivalence tests, the hypothesis that any differences were merely superficial ones could not be tested.

We have seen in this account of identity and equivalence tests that some studies show equivalence tests to be slightly more difficult, although it is not clear why this is, nor how superficial the difference may be. On the one hand, there is not sufficient reason to conclude that equivalence tests are an inappropriate means of assessing the child's conservation level. On the other, there is no evidence that identity tests lead to children being mistakenly classified as conservers, although there is reason to suppose that this might be the case. It seems, then, that neither kind of test is obviously preferable. Both have possible risks attached, but the extent of these has not been established.

(g) Conclusions

In this section, the aim has been to decide whether or not the standard Piagetian test of conservation is fundamentally valid. It has been criticized for its dependence on verbal interaction between the child and the experimenter. We have seen that, if care is taken with the questioning, it should be possible to identify children whose verbal skills are inadequate, and to obtain valid data from the others. The standard Piagetian test has also been criticized on the grounds that in order to give a conserving judgment, it is necessary to perform a deduction, which the child may be unable to do. There is, however, no evidence which convincingly shows that children fail to conserve in the standard Piagetian test merely because they cannot perform the deduction. Although the deduction is logically necessary, it may not be psychologically necessary. We can conclude that the standard test has not been shown to be unsatisfactory, and that no alternatives have been shown to be clearly preferable.

An additional justification for using the standard Piagetian test is that it leads to meaningful data. When children's performance in these tests is compared with their performance in other, theoretically related, tests the results can be interpreted as evidence either for or against particular theories. This should become clear in later chapters. If this did not happen, we would have to look again at the possibility that the standard Piagetian test is fundamentally unsuitable for assessing the child's conservation level.

2.3 Refinements of the basic Piagetian test

It could have been that amount conservation was acquired suddenly, that the child either showed no trace of conservation, or else gave every indication of possessing a fully developed adult concept. In practice, however, it is easy to show more gradual development. Assuming that the standard Piagetian test is fundamentally valid, we can consider refinements of the basic test which allow finer discriminations to be made between children whose conservation concepts are at different stages of development.

It is useful to be able to discriminate between children at various stages of conservation acquisition, since much of the evidence both for and against theories of conservation acquisition consists of analyses of relationships between performance in conservation tests and performance in tests of supposedly related abilities. If children were classified only into two gross categories of conservers and nonconservers, then a very close relationship between conservation and another ability might be obscured, and might not be discriminable from a more distant relationship.

Throughout this discussion, children who seem to be at later stages of conservation acquisition will be described as having a more stable, or a better established, concept of conservation. Although appropriate at a superficial level, in that children labelled in this way behave as if they are more convinced of conservation, the description may have implications of which we should be wary. It might imply that all children acquire conservation by a single route; this will be discussed later in this chapter (section 2.5). A second possible implication is that the nonconserver develops a conservation concept which at first is weak and easily overwhelmed, but which gradually grows stronger until it is fully established. It may well be inappropriate to think of conservation acquisition in this way, as will be shown in later chapters.

Five bases for discriminating more finely between children will be considered: the ability to give certain kinds of reasons for conserving judgments; resistance to countersuggestion; resistance to extinction; performance in a series of similar items; and performance in an amount construction test. The focus will be on differentiating between children all of whom show some sign of conserving in standard Piagetian tests. It is much more difficult to distinguish between children at different distances from showing their first signs of conservation. It might be assumed that children who are most responsive to conservation training are nearest to developing the concept but, as will be shown later in this chapter (section 2.5c), the results of training programmes can be difficult to interpret. If there existed a generally accepted theory which specified the necessary prerequisites for conservation, this might allow discriminations to be made among nonconservers: the more prerequisites a child possessed, the nearer he would be to developing conservation. However, such a theory does not yet exist. The problem of discriminating between nonconservers will be left aside, therefore, and only children who show signs of conserving in standard tests will be considered.

(a) Reasons for conserving judgments

Children who give conserving judgments are often also able to give reasons for these judgments. Commonly given reasons are 'It was the same at first', 'You didn't add any on or take any away', 'If you rolled it back it would be the same', 'If I rolled mine it would be like yours' and 'Yours is long and thin, mine is short and fat'. These are examples which occur in a test of amount conservation using plasticine sausages, but similar reasons are given in other conservation tests.

In Chapter 1, conservation was defined as being equivalent to the NAS criterion: 'If nothing is added or subtracted, amount remains the same'. Only if a child judges consistently with this criterion, can we conclude that he has the concept of conservation. The reason most clearly related to the NAS criterion is 'You didn't add any on or take any away'. We might decide that no child is to be called a conserver unless he gives that reason for his conserving judgment. The problem of deciding when a child is to be labelled a 'conserver' is discussed in the next section. Here, our concern is with ways of distinguishing between children at different stages of conservation acquisition. We might find that children who say 'It's the same because you didn't take any off or add any on' appear, on the basis of other evidence, to be more advanced than other children. However, the author has found that rather few children give that reason. In one experiment (Experiment B), forty-six children gave conserving judgments, and thirty-eight of them gave reasons like those listed above. Only four of these referred to the absence of addition and/or subtraction. Perhaps because of their rarity, children who give this kind of reason have not been singled out for particular attention.

Smedslund (1962) classified the reasons given for both conserving and non-conserving judgments into three groups.

Symbolic: defined as reasons referring either directly or indirectly to previous events in the same task, e.g. 'If we squeeze it they will become equally big again'.

Perceptual: reasons referring either directly or indirectly to observable features of the present situation, e.g. 'It is bigger'.

Ambiguous: those which could not be put into either of the other two categories, e.g. 'I don't know'.

As would be expected, nearly all the symbolic reasons justified conserving judgments. There were, however, many conserving judgments justified by only perceptual or ambiguous reasons. Smedslund tested the stability of the child's conservation concept by giving him a countersuggestion. In this experiment, piles of small linoleum squares were used to test conservation of amount. One of two equal piles was changed into a ring or some other shape. If the child gave a conserving judgment, he was given a countersuggestion: 'Are you sure there is the same amount in both? In another nursery there were many boys/girls who said there is more in the ring.' Out of forty children who had not given symbolic reasons for their conserving judgments, eighteen accepted the countersuggestion, but only one of the twenty-seven conservers who had given a symbolic reason accepted the countersuggestion.

Assuming that resistance to the countersuggestion indicated a better established conservation concept than did acceptance, it seems that giving a symbolic reason for a conserving judgment also indicates a better established concept than does failure to give such a reason. There may, however, be reservations about accepting that countersuggestion can be used to assess the stability of a conservation concept. This is discussed below.

(b) Countersuggestion

'Countersuggestion', means a judgment suggested by the experimenter, which is different from the child's own judgment. Various arguments can be made against the use of countersuggestion: when given a countersuggestion, the child could feel he was being told his judgment was wrong, and may therefore accept the suggested judgment without really understanding how it could apply. Acceptance of the countersuggestion may reflect a desire to please the experimenter, a respect for authority, or some such characteristic, rather than uncertainty in one's own amount judgment. But the value of using countersuggestion to assess the stability of a child's conservation concept will be defended in three ways.

(i) We can analyse the child's performance in a series of tasks, each of which involves a countersuggestion. In an experiment by the author (Experiment A), seventy-two children were each given three conservation tasks, involving the rolling of a short fat plasticine sausage into a long thin one. If the child gave a nonconserving judgment, then he was given a conservation countersuggestion: 'Well, somebody else said we've both got the same to eat still, because I just rolled mine, I didn't add any on or take any away. Do you think that was right or wrong?' If the child gave a conserving judgment, then he was given a nonconservation countersuggestion: 'Well, somebody else said I've got more to eat, because mine's longer. Do you think that was right or wrong?' After being given the countersuggestion, the child was again asked for an amount judgment, to see whether he had accepted or resisted the suggested judgment. The results were as follows:

44 children never accepted the countersuggestion;

18 children accepted the conservation countersuggestion in one or two tasks, then in subsequent tasks they spontaneously conserved and resisted the nonconservation countersuggestion;

7 children accepted the countersuggestion in one or two tasks, but showed no clear improvement or decline in performance over the series of tasks;

3 children always accepted the countersuggestion.

We see that the majority of children did not accept whatever was suggested to them. There were no children who converged on nonconservation although eighteen converged on conservation. These results suggest that children were influenced by a suggested judgment only if they thought it was reasonable.

(ii) Conservation performance can be related to performance in another test in which countersuggestion is not used. Suppose a certain theory of conservation acquisition predicts a specific relationship between conservation level and performance in some other test, e.g. a test involving addition and subtraction of material. In order to test this prediction, children might be classified into three groups on the basis of their performance in conservation tasks. Children who accept the countersuggestions may be classified as intermediate conservers; those who always give conserving judgments and resist the nonconservation countersuggestion may be classified as conservers; and those who always give nonconserving judgments and resist the conservation countersuggestion may be classified as nonconservers. If, using such a classification, the predicted relationship occurs, then it can be concluded both that the classification was an appropriate one, and that the theory is supported. If, on the other hand, the predicted relationship does not occur, then the conclusion is that either the theory is wrong, or the conservation classification was inappropriate, or both. In several of the experiments by the author which are described in later chapters, the assumption that those who accept countersuggestions can be classified as intermediate conservers leads to sensible, interpretable results; the use of countersuggestion is validated by an external criterion.

(iii) Perhaps the best way of showing that children who accept countersuggestions are not simply responding to social pressure is to ask the child to give a reason for the suggested judgment. In another experiment by the author (Experiment B), fifty-eight children aged six to seven and a half years were given three conservation tasks only the first two of which are relevant here. In each task, one of two identical short fat sausages was rolled longer. After the rolling, the child was asked to give an amount judgment, and a reason, and he was then given a countersuggestion. If he had given a conserving judgment, this was 'Somebody else said I've got more to eat (i.e. more in the longer sausage). Why do you think they said that?'. A child who had given a nonconserving judgment was told 'Somebody else said we've both got the same to eat still. Why do you think they said that?' After the child had given any reason he could, the amount question was repeated, to see whether he had been influenced by the countersuggestion. A child was considered to have accepted the countersuggestion if he gave the suggested judgment when the amount question was repeated.

The results clearly showed that children did not accept the suggested judgment unless they had been able to give an appropriate reason, e.g. 'Because it's longer' in the case of the nonconservation countersuggestion, or 'It was the same at first' in the case of the conservation one. In the first task, only one child accepted the countersuggestion without giving an appropriate reason, and in the second task one other child did so. This contrasts with nine children who accepted the suggested judgment after giving an appropriate reason in the first task, and nine who did so in the second. In the first task, thirty-four children resisted the countersuggestion and failed to give an appropriate reason; in the second task, there were also thirty-four who did so. These results suggest that children do not generally accept a countersuggestion unless they understand the reasoning behind it; they do not merely accept whatever the experimenter suggests.

A second interesting result, not strictly relevant here, was that of the nonconservers who could give an acceptable reason for the suggested conserving judgment (ten out of thirty-four in the first task; eight out of twenty-seven in the second), most did then accept the suggested judgment (eight in the first task; eight in the second). In contrast, most of the conservers who gave a reason for the nonconservation countersuggestion, did not accept it (twelve out of thirteen in the first task; fourteen out of fifteen in the second). It seems that if a nonconserver can think of a reason for a conserving judgment, then he thinks that conservation is 'better' than nonconservation. A conserver, on the other hand, may realize that one could judge 'It's more because it's longer', while believing this to be an incorrect judgment.

We can conclude from this discussion that use of countersuggestion does seem to be a good way of distinguishing between children at different levels of conservation acquisition.

(c) Extinction

Smedslund (1961b) suggested another way of testing the stability of conservation. In a so-called 'extinction' procedure, he gave the child a demonstration of apparent nonconservation, and asked him to explain it. He also tested the child to see if he would predict conservation or nonconservation in subsequent tasks. If a child believes in the logical necessity of conservation, then he should deny the validity of the apparent nonconservation.

This kind of procedure can be used only for attributes which can be measured in a way that is understood by the child. Smedslund used weight demonstrations on a balance. He began with two balls which weighed the same, then he surreptitiously removed a piece from one of the balls while changing its shape. He showed the child that the weight had changed, and asked him to explain this. The child was then asked to predict what would happen to the weight of another piece of plasticine when its shape was changed. There were two criteria for resistance to extinction: explaining the weight change in terms of necessary loss of material, and predicting conservation in the next task. Smedslund does not make clear how these two were related in the results, whether children tended to extinguish on both or neither criteria. He reports that out of thirteen conservers who had given symbolic reasons for their judgments, only six resisted extinction. It might be argued from this that the extinction test provides a way of distinguishing between those with a complete 'logically necessary' concept of conservation, and those who do not have such a fully developed concept although they can give reasons for their conserving judgments. Alternatively it could be that the extinction test is not a valid means of assessing the level of development of a conservation concept.

Although Smedslund's use of a demonstration of nonconservation seems to be sensible, his criteria for resistance to extinction may not be the most appropriate. Both his criteria will be considered. If the extinction test has been properly carried out, then the child should be convinced that no addition or subtraction occurred. He may, therefore, be more likely to think of other reasons for the nonconservation, such as 'The scales have gone wrong'. Other experimenters (e.g. Hall and Kingsley, 1968; Miller, 1973; Smith, 1968) have indeed found that, among both child and adult conservers, it was rarely suggested that material must have been added or subtracted. It may therefore be unreasonable to assume that any child who appreciates the logical necessity of conservation will give an addition/subtraction reason for the nonconservation. However, such a child would not be expected to explain the nonconservation by referring to the change in appearance: 'It's less because you squashed it down'. Maybe it would be better to use the giving of such a perceptual reason as a criterion for extinction, instead of the addition/subtraction criterion for resistance to extinction. But this perceptual criterion for extinction may not be satisfactory either. It was mentioned above that in Experiment B by the author, it was found that when conservers were told 'Somebody else said I've got more to eat. Why do you think they said that?', many of them suggested 'Because it's longer' although they did not accept the nonconserving judgment; they repeated their conserving judgments when asked to judge the amounts again. That is, children who gave conserving judgments were frequently able to give a reason for a rejected nonconserving judgment. More details of these results were given in section 2.3b. In the extinction test, the child is asked to give a reason for the apparent nonconservation. On the basis of the results just mentioned, we might expect children to give perceptual reasons just to satisfy the experimenter, even though they do not believe that the nonconservation is possible.

There are also doubts about Smedslund's other criterion for extinction, prediction of nonconservation in a subsequent task. Suppose a child who believes in the logical necessity of conservation is mystified by the demonstration of nonconservation, or decides that the scales must have gone wrong. He would be quite justified in expecting the same thing to happen in a subsequent identical task. Such a child would not, however, be expected to predict nonconservation if a different pair of scales and a different material were introduced. An experiment by Miller (1973) included some tasks which were different from the extinction tasks. In one, the scales were used as in the extinction tasks, but cardboard squares were weighed in place of clay. In another item, the scales were removed and the child used his hands to estimate the weights of pieces of clay. In these tasks, between fifty and eighty per cent of the conservers did predict nonconservation of weight. These did seem to be generalization to different situations. Most experimenters, however, have not tested their subjects in situations different from the extinction test.

Although Smedslund's criteria for extinction have commonly been used, in many cases the data is given in enough detail to allow its re-interpretation with different criteria.

If the extinction test is to be used as a means of assessing the level of development of the child's conservation concept, then one requirement that ought to be met is that adults, who presumably have a fully developed 'logically necessary' concept, do resist extinction. Hall and Kingsley (1968) found that only one out of forty-eight adults gave perceptual reasons for the apparent nonconservation, although hardly any of them gave addition/subtraction reasons. Miller, Schwartz and Stewart (1973) also found that only one of their thirty-six adult subjects gave a perceptual explanation in any one of three extinction tasks. These authors do not specify how many addition/subtraction reasons were given. It seems, then, that adults only rarely extinguish if the perceptual criterion for extinction is used, rather than the addition/subtraction criterion for resistance to extinction.

A second way of validating the extinction test is to compare the performance of older, presumably more advanced, conservers with that of younger conservers. Miller (1973) made such a comparison. Children were classified as conservers if they gave correct judgments in all of four weight conservation tasks. The mean age of the young conservers was eight years, ten months, and that of the older group was eleven years. After the conservation test, the children were given three demonstrations of apparent nonconservation (extinction test), followed by a series of tasks in which objects were not actually weighed after deformation, but in which the children made predictions about their weights. These were equivalent to ordinary conservation tasks. In the extinction tasks, the children were asked to explain the nonconservation. Reaction times were also taken: the child was required to press one of three buttons to indicate the relative weights of the two objects as demonstrated by the balance. Reaction times would be expected to be longer if the child's expectancies were violated. In addition, the session was video-taped so that facial expressions of surprise could be identified.

In the extinction test, there were no significant differences between the young and the old conservers in the extent to which they extinguished: fifty-seven per cent of the young, and fifty per cent of the older conservers gave at least one 'denial' reason for the nonconservation (e.g. statements that the scales were wrong), although ninety-one per cent of the young and eighty-three per cent of the older conservers gave at least one perceptual reason. There were, however, slight differences in the kind of 'denial' reasons given: eight of the young, but none of the older, conservers gave addition/subtraction reasons; the older children were more likely to refer to malfunctioning of the scales.

Facial and verbal expressions of surprise were rare in both groups. However, the reaction times did indicate that the children's expectancies were violated in the extinction test. The reaction times in the extinction tasks were compared with those in 'base-line' trials in which the objects weighed were enclosed in opaque bags so that the child presumably had no expectancy about their relative weights. The reaction times in the extinction trials were about twice as long as those in the base-line trials. In these behavioural measures, the only significant difference between the young and the older conservers was in the verbalizations of surprise: five of the young conservers gave such responses, but none of the older ones did.

In the conservation tasks following the extinction test, it was common for children to be influenced by the demonstrations of nonconservation. In the first task, about eighty per cent of the young conservers and about seventy per cent of the older ones predicted nonconservation. These levels fell in subsequent tasks to between fifty and sixty per cent. However, there was no overall difference between young and old conservers in the extent to which they predicted nonconservation.

Miller's results, then, show hardly any differences between young and old conservers in their responses to demonstrations of apparent nonconservation. Even the differences which did occur were not always in the expected direction: it was the younger group, for example, who gave more verbalizations of surprise. Moreover, if the perceptual criterion for extinction is used, most of the children in both groups did extinguish.

This account of extinction tests leads to the conclusion that they have not been shown to be a valid means of differentiating between children with a complete 'logically necessary' concept of conservation, and those who give conserving judgments but do not have such a fully developed concept. Whether the extinction test could provide a useful means of distinguishing between children at lower levels of conservation acquisition seems not to have been investigated.

Extinction tests have most commonly been used in training experiments—the resistance to extinction of the trained children is compared with that of 'natural conservers', i.e. those who have acquired conservation without help from the experimenter. The assumption seems to be that if there were no difference in the extent to which the groups extinguished, this would support a conclusion that the trained concept was equivalent to a naturally acquired one. Such a comparison between trained and 'natural' conservers seems a strange one, since if the extinction test is valid, then the extent to which the 'natural' group extinguishes should vary with their level of conservation acquisition. Performance in the extinction test of the trained group alone should demonstrate whether or not the children acquired a 'logically necessary' concept during training.

A rather different so-called 'extinction' procedure has been used by Brison (1966). Liquid was poured from one of two identical glasses into a thinner glass, as in a normal test of conservation of liquid amount. Then it was poured back into what appeared to be the original glass, but was in fact a glass with a thick bottom. The liquid level in this new glass was then higher than that in the comparison (apparently identical) glass. If the child judged that there was more liquid in the thick-bottomed glass than in the comparison one, he was classified as having given an extinction response. Brison's subjects were twelve conservers who were aged from five years, four months to six years, four months. Most of them had given at least four correct judgments and reasons in a five-task conservation test. Only two of the twelve extinguished both times, while six of them resisted extinction both times.

In Brison's test, the child simply had to believe that the pouring operations were a more reliable indicator of amount than was the final appearance of the liquid. However, in the extinction test devised by Smedslund, the child was led to believe that the balance was a reliable indicator of weight; if he said 'The scales are wrong', he was denying the validity of an indicator which the experimenter had encouraged him to use. It would not therefore be surprising if Brison's extinction procedure was easier to resist than Smedslund's. There is not as yet sufficient evidence to decide whether Brison's test is a better means than Smedslund's of assessing a child's conservation level, since it has been much less widely used.

(d) Responses in a series of similar tasks

A more obvious way of distinguishing between stable and unstable conservation concepts is simply to give the child a series of similar tasks. In the case of amount conservation using plasticine, one of two equal balls might be rolled into a sausage, then squashed into a pancake and finally broken up into little pieces. For certain purposes, the series of tasks could involve repetitions of one particular deformation, e.g. rolling. A child could conserve in one or two of these tasks, but give a nonconserving judgment in a third task. Even if three tasks were used, there could be a risk that a child who showed no sign of conservation would demonstrate a weak conservation concept in a fourth task, or that a child who appeared to be a perfect conserver would show signs of nonconservation. An investigation could show how many children are likely to change their responses in this way after a certain number of tasks.

Such an analysis was made of the results of Experiment A by the author. Seventy-two children were each given three conservation tasks involving the rolling of a short fat plasticine sausage into a long thin one. In each task, a countersuggestion was given: if the child had given a conserving judgment, he was given a nonconservation countersuggestion, and if he had given a nonconserving judgment, he was given a conservation countersuggestion. After being given the countersuggestion, the child was again asked to give an amount judgment, to see whether he had accepted or resisted the countersuggestion. In each task, therefore, the child gave two amount judgments after the rolling.

Children were classified as conservers if they always gave conserving judgments, as nonconservers if they always gave nonconserving ones, and as intermediate conservers if they gave both kinds of judgment.

25 children were conservers in the first task; they all remained conservers throughout the three tasks. That is, none of them would have been classified differently had only one or two tasks been given.

21 children were intermediate conservers in the first task. The rules for classifying children determined that they remained intermediate conservers whatever their performance in subsequent tasks.

26 children were nonconservers in the first task. Seven of these improved in the second task: they either spontaneously conserved or they accepted the conservation countersuggestion. These seven, who would have been classified as nonconservers had only one task been given, could be classified as intermediate conservers when two tasks were given. Of the remaining nineteen, two improved in the third task, and could then be classified as intermediate conservers.

We see that, of those who would have been classified as nonconservers had only one task been given, twenty-seven per cent could be classified differently when two tasks were given. Of those who would have been classified as nonconservers had only two tasks been given, eleven per cent could be classified differently when a third task was included.

These results suggest that over a series of tasks, more and more children show that they can conserve. Children who conserve in a single task, however, are unlikely to decline in performance over a series of similar tasks. It appears that experiments in which only a single conservation task is given run the risk of including children who really can conserve among the 'nonconservers'.

(e) Amount construction

In a test of conservation, the child is asked to judge amounts which the experimenter presents. A variation of this is to ask the child to construct an amount which bears a certain relationship to a given amount. For example, the child might be asked to pour liquid into a glass until the amount is equal to that in a given wider or narrower glass. Such a test will be called an amount construction test.

It is unreasonable to expect anyone to pour out an amount which is really equal to that in a wider or narrower glass. However, an adult would know that the liquid in a thinner glass must come to a higher level than that in a wider glass, if the amounts are to be equal.

There is no logically necessary connection between amount construction and conservation—knowing that liquid does not change in amount when it is poured into a container of different width is not logically equivalent to knowing that if the amount in a thinner container is to be equal to that in a wider container, the level in the thinner one must be higher. However, Piaget (1968a) argues, on the basis of his theory of the psychological operations underlying the concept of conservation, that a child cannot be a true conserver unless he can pass the amount construction test. He recommends that a child be given an amount construction test in order to see whether he is really a conserver. If it became clear that his theory was untenable, Piaget would presumably no longer make this argument.

However, use of the amount construction test to assess conservation level could be justified on other grounds. Suppose a group of children at different stages of conservation acquisition were given both a conservation test and an amount construction test. If performance in the two tests were very highly correlated, this evidence alone could allow the amount construction test to be used as a test of conservation, even without any theory relating the two tests. But such evidence does not at present exist.

(f) Conclusions

The above discussion of the amount construction test shows that there are different ways of justifying, or validating, a particular test of conservation. Three ways will be identified. They can be called logical, empirical and theoretical.

A test is justified on *logical* grounds if it appears to be a concrete realization of the concept being assessed. Both identity and equivalence tests of conservation are justified on these grounds. Similarly, if we make certain assumptions about the nature of a concept, and ignore psychological factors such as 'desire to please the experimenter', it is logically necessary that a child who resists a countersuggestion, or who denies the validity of a demonstration of nonconservation, has a more adequate conservation concept than a child who does neither or only one of these. In contrast, there is no logical justification for using the amount construction test as a test of conservation. Neither is Mermelstein and Shulman's nonverbal test of conservation (section 2.2e) justified on logical grounds.

A test which is logically valid might nevertheless be shown to be inappropriate for psychological reasons. *Empirical* justification takes into account these psychological factors. A test would be empirically justified if it were found that children known or believed to be at different stages of conservation acquisition performed differently in this test. The giving of certain kinds of reasons, and resistance to countersuggestion, were justified on empirical grounds as indicators of a more highly developed concept of conservation. The extinction test, however, seemed not to be justified on empirical grounds.

In the above account of the amount construction test, it was stated that a *theoretical* justification alone is not sufficient. In the case of the amount construction test, it was suggested that empirical justification was necessary. However, once a theory is itself backed by sufficient empirical evidence for it to be accepted, then tests justified on the basis of this theory could be used.

Cohen (1967) apparently failed to see the difference between conservation and amount construction; she assumed that both kinds of test assessed the concept of conservation. On the basis of children's performance in amount construction tasks, Cohen concluded that conservation could be elicited in children who failed to conserve in standard tests of the concept.

Experimenters such as Cohen, and Mermelstein and Shulman (1967), concluded, inappropriately from their results, that the standard Piagetian conservation test could lead to a misleading assessment of a child's conservation level. They would not have made their mistakes if they had analysed more carefully their justifications for using particular tests of conservation.

2.4 Criteria for classifying children

In section 2.3 a discussion of refinements of the standard Piagetian test was presented, which could allow discriminations to be made between children at different stages of conservation acquisition. Now, the problem of deciding when a child can be deemed 'a conserver' will be examined. As indicated above, theoretical justifications play only a minor role in the ordering of children according to the level of development of their concept of conservation. However, in deciding at what point we can begin to call a child 'a conserver', theoretical reasons are much more important. In deciding who is to be called a conserver, the experimenter is making an assumption about what the concept of conservation is, both logically and psychologically. Hopefully, there would be agreement in the logical definition of conservation. Unfortunately we cannot be sure, because most experimenters define conservation only in terms of performance in the test used. However, let us assume that there is agreement that logically, to say a person uses the concept of amount conservation, is equivalent to saying that he uses the criterion 'If nothing is added or subtracted, amount remains the same'. We then have to decide what a person must do if he is appropriately to be described as using the NAS criterion.

A simple solution would be to classify as conservers only those who say in conservation tests 'It's the same because you didn't add any on or take any away'. However, this solution is based on an assumption that the child verbalizes his reasoning. It seems likely that many children do not do so. If we accept that simple solution, then, we will probably reject from our class of 'conservers', many children who use the concept of conservation. We must look for less direct indications of its use. Experimenters with different theoretical outlooks have arrived at different solutions to the problem. A comparison of Piaget's approach with that of Bruner will illustrate this point.

Piaget sees conservation as a symptom of a specified cognitive structure. The operation of identity (nothing added, nothing subtracted = the same amount) forms only one part of this structure. Hence the giving of reasons other than 'You didn't add any on or take any away' can indicate the child's possession of the structure, and therefore of conservation. The reasons which Piaget thinks indicate a judgment based on operational thinking are as follows.

Identity: 'It's the same plasticine', 'It was the same at first', 'You didn't add any on or take any away'.
Reversibility: 'If you rolled it back it would be the same'.
Compensation: 'The sausage is longer but it's thinner'.

According to Piaget, the operations of identity, reversibility and compensation underlie the concept of conservation. The giving of these reasons is taken as evidence that the child's thought is operational; a child who gives none of these reasons is not considered a true conserver.

Bruner, however, does not accept Piaget's theory of conservation. He sees identity as the basis of conservation, and denies that conservation is based on reversibility and compensation. Furthermore, Bruner holds that the concept of identity is present in the child long before he gives conserving judgments in the standard Piagetian test. Hence the ability to give identity, reversibility or compensation reasons has no significance for Bruner. In his experiments, a child can be labelled a 'conserver' simply on the basis of his amount judgment, even if he does not give a reason.

Although Piaget seems to use a much stricter criterion than many other conservers for labelling a child a conserver, it is not clear exactly what his criterion is, since the reports of his experiments do not contain the details conventionally given by Anglo-Saxon psychologists. From Inhelder and Sinclair (1969) it appears that, for routine assessment purposes, Piagetians classify a child as a conserver if he answers correctly in two similar tasks, and gives acceptable reasons. More thorough testing is used, however, in the assessment of the results of training experiments. In such cases, Piaget recommends that the amount construction test be used. Inhelder and Sinclair (1969) advocate adding related tests, the use of countersuggestion, and testing the child again several weeks later.

This raises a commonly made criticism of Piaget's methodology, that of his flexible testing procedure. Let us compare the procedure used by Piaget and Inhelder (1941) with that used by Smedslund (1961c).

Piaget and Inhelder used several different questions when asking the child to compare the two amounts after one of them had been deformed, e.g. 'Elles sont encore la même chose de pâté?'; 'Il y a la même chose de terre dans les deux?'; 'Est ce qu'il y a la même chose à manger dans les deux?'. Any one child might be asked one or more of these questions. In addition, he might be asked some of the following questions: 'Les deux boulettes rondes avaient la même chose de pâté avant?'; 'Mais alors où a passé la pâte de celle-ci (boudin) qu'il y en a moins qu'avant?'; 'Et si je la roule et que je refrais une boulette avec?'.

Smedslund describes his procedure as follows:

'After each deformation the following standard question was asked: "do you think the (ring, cross, etc.) contains *more,* or *the same amount as,* or *less* clay than the ball?" After each answer the experimenter asked in a neutral but interested voice "Why do you think so?" ' (Smedslund, 1961c, p. 73)

Smedslund's procedure, like that of most non-Piagetians, is very rigid compared with Piaget's. One possible reason for this difference, suggested by Braine (1962), lies in the psychologist's conception of his task. Piaget is attempting to diagnose the child's cognitive structures, which are supposed to exist in some form inside the child's head:

'... the subject is not conscious of the existence of his cognitive structures ... He acts, he operates, he behaves. And from his behaviour we, the psychologists, detect the structures. But the structures are unconscious. They are expressed in regular forms of responses that we believe we are discovering in the subject's behaviour.' (Piaget, 1971, p. 3)

The most effective way of making such a diagnosis might well be to use flexible questioning gauged to suit each child.

An alternative view of the psychologist's task is that he is trying to develop theoretical constructs which allow the child's behaviour and development to be understood, but which need not be supposed to have any real existence. According to Braine (1962), this is the view taken by 'modern behavioural theory', which conceives of intellectual processes as hypothetical constructs. These are defined in terms of other constructs within the system, and also in terms of the procedures which elicit responses supposed to be indicative of the processes. Given this latter requirement, the experimental procedures must be rigid.

The implication of Braine's view is that one's conception of the psychologist's task determines whether one uses flexible or rigid methods. There is an alternative explanation of the difference between Piaget's approach and that of psychologists who have chosen to replicate and extend his investigations. The methods used for scientific enquiry change as progress is made. If one is trying to demonstrate the existence of nonconserving children, which perhaps was Piaget's intention in his early work in this area, then there is much to be said for using a flexible procedure, asking for the child's judgment in a variety of ways. Having established that the phenomenon is fairly robust, and does not disappear if the question to the child is rephrased, standard procedures can be developed. This, according to Inhelder (1962), is what the Piagetians are doing.

When trying to test theories of conservation acquisition, it is preferable to have clearly defined criteria for classifying children, and this necessitates the use of standard procedures. Unless these conditions are met, it is difficult to evaluate different theories and their supporting evidence. The particular criteria used, however, are to some extent arbitrary. For many purposes it does not matter whether a particular response pattern is labelled 'conserving' or 'intermediate' as long as the pattern is clearly specified. The problem of deciding whether a particular response pattern can be classified as 'conserving' does become important, however, when the results of conservation training experiments are being evaluated.

2.5 Kinds of evidence useful for testing theories of conservation acquisition

In the account of conservation testing given in section 2.3, it was assumed that children could be ordered according to the level of development of their conservation concepts. This implies that different responses are given in conservation tests as the concept is acquired. It is this sequence of responses which a theory of conservation acquisition must explain.

In this section, two ways of obtaining the sequence will be examined, by longitudinal or cross-sectional methods, and an outline given of the kinds of evidence which can supplement this description to support or disprove theories of conservation acquisition. This supplementary evidence may arise from observation or from training studies; the advantages and disadvantages of each of these will be considered.

(a) Longitudinal and cross-sectional methods

One way of arriving at a description of the stages of conservation acquisition would be to test each of a number of children on several occasions as they developed conservation. This longitudinal method is hardly ever used, perhaps because it takes a long time to complete a study. There is also the more important problem that repeated testing might interfere with normal development. Piaget and Inhelder (1961) refer to a longitudinal study by Inhelder and Noelting, in which children were followed up over a period of five and a half years as they acquired concrete operations. Few details are given, but Piaget and Inhelder imply that the results support Piaget's interpretations of cross-sectional data.

Cross-sectional methods are much more commonly used in experiments on conservation acquisition. Groups of children assumed to be at different stages in conservation acquisition are tested, and an attempt is made to interpret their responses in terms of a sequence. Usually the independent variable is age, and children of the same age are assumed to have developed at comparable rates along one particular route. Older children, it is assumed, will be further along the route than younger ones. In practice, it is found that conservation tests are not perfectly age-related, i.e. two children of the same age may be at different points on the route, so the additional assumption is made that children who are developing at different rates are all progressing along the same route. In the case of extreme groups, this assumption may itself become the object of study. One might, for example, enquire whether children with very low IQs are progressing along the same route as those of normal IQ, but at a slower rate (e.g. Woodward, 1961).

Having used either a longitudinal or a cross-sectional method to arrive at a description of the stages of conservation acquisition, we are ready to gather other evidence which can be used for testing explanations of these stages. The kinds of evidence used can be divided into two categories: observation and training studies.

(b) Observation studies

These have been so called because there is no attempt to interfere with the normal course of development; the experimenter presents his subjects with situations which will allow him to observe this course.

Suppose each child is given conservation tasks and a set of theoretically related tasks, e.g. tasks in which material is either added or subtracted and the child is asked to judge the effect on amount. It would be assumed that all children who responded in the same way in these tasks would be at the same point on the developmental route to conservation acquisition. It should be possible to build up a scale ranging from complete failure on all the tasks to complete success. The order of difficulty of the various tasks could provide evidence for or against particular theories of conservation acquisition. For example, Smedslund's theory (1961d) holds that conservation is a symptom of a fully developed addition–subtraction schema. This theory predicts that tasks in which material is added or subtracted should be easier than conservation tasks, and it could be disproved if it were found that some addition–subtraction tasks were more difficult than a test of conservation,

Problems arise if a perfect scale of difficulty is not found: test A might be easier than test B for some children, but more difficult for others. The experimenter might well abandon his approach in search of one leading to clear-cut results, but Flavell and Wohlwill (1969) discuss possible interpretations of such woolly data.

They argue that the competence/performance distinction made in psycholinguistics is useful in studies of cognitive development.

'The competence model gives an abstract, purely logical representation of what the organism knows or could do in a timeless, ideal environment ...'

The performance, or automaton, model

'... represents the psychological processes by which the information embodied in competence actually gets assessed and utilised in real situations.' (Flavell and Wohlwill, 1969, p. 71)

Flavell and Wohlwill apply this distinction to the behaviour of children at three levels in the acquisition of a particular cognitive ability. In the case of conservation, they suggest that the nonconserver may be thought of as not having the competence for conservation, whereas the intermediate conserver has the competence but has difficulty in realizing this in performance, and the conserver can always realize his competence in performance.

If a child fails a particular test, this failure might be due either to his not having the competence required, or to a performance error. If it were found that test A was harder than test B for some children, but easier for others, this variant order of difficulty could be accounted for in terms of performance difficulties, and the two abilities involved could still be thought of as entering competence in a fixed order.

Flavell and Wohlwill identify various possible psychological relationships between abilities. They suggest that the kind of relationship which is of most interest to the developmental psychologist is the one they call nonimplicative mediation. If two abilities X and Y have such a relationship to each other, then there is no logically necessary relationship between them, but psychologically one of the abilities helps in the development of the other. As an example of two abilities which could have such a relationship to each other, Flavell and Wohlwill take coordination of dimensions and conservation. (A child can coordinate dimensions if he can, for example, take into account both the increase in length and the decrease in width as a plasticine sausage is rolled.) It is not logically necessary that a child who conserves coordinates dimensions, but coordination of dimensions might be psychologically necessary for conservation acquisition. The relationship of nonimplicative mediation is distinguished from implicative mediation, in which the two abilities concerned are logically related. For example, the ability to coordinate two dimensions presupposes the ability to take into account each dimension separately. If we found a child who could do the first but not the second, we would have to conclude there was something odd about the tests used to assess these abilities. Flavell and Wohlwill also identify nonmediation relationships, in which one ability does not help the other to develop. They go on to consider complicated types of mediation—for example, ability X might help in the development of Y in some, but not all, children. It would be interesting to discover whether such relationships exist; whether there are alternative routes to the development of a particular concept.

This valuable analysis by Flavell and Wohlwill leaves unsolved the problem of interpreting a particular set of data in terms of one or more of these relationships. If there were found to be a variant order of difficulty between two tests then, according to their scheme this could be interpreted as due to:

    (i) performance difficulties which obscure an invariant competence relationship of a mediation kind, or

    (ii) of a nonmediation kind;

    (iii) a variant competence relationship of a mediation kind—one ability helps in the development of the other among some children only, or

    (iv) a variant competence relationship of a nonmediation kind.

Suppose the theory being tested holds that X does help in the development of Y. Whether or not an observed variant relationship between X and Y were interpreted as evidence against the theory (i.e. interpretations (ii) or (iv)) would depend largely on the theory's plausibility. That is, this particular set of results would need to be considered within the context of other evidence.

Smedslund's theory of conservation acquisition provides an example of this, The results of Smedslund's early experiments on the relationship between addition/subtraction tasks and conservation tasks were consistent with the theory (e.g. 1961c). In a later experiment, however, the relationship was much less clear-cut. Certain tasks involving addition and subtraction were more difficult than conservation tasks. Smedslund (1964) suggests that performance difficulties could account for this. He points to the fact that in the earlier experiments the additions and subtractions were carried out on visible collections, whereas in the later experiment the collections were hidden. There was also a difference between the earlier and later conservation tests: in the former, a collection of linoleum squares was deformed into a ring, whereas in the latter it was merely spread out. Such hypotheses about performance difficulties could be investigated in further experiments. However, had there been an alternative theory which could accommodate all the results without recourse to a performance–competance distinction, presumably this would have been preferred.

This account of the interpretation of results of observation studies suggests that they may not be a very powerful means of testing theories of conservation acquisition. As an alternative or an additional method, many experimenters have preferred to use training experiments. At first sight these provide a more powerful way of investigating development because it becomes possible to be more confident about specifying causal relationships.

(c) Training studies

If a training experiment is being used to test a prediction about how conservation is acquired naturally, then it is necessary for the experimenter to be able to identify when a trained conservation concept is the same as a 'natural' concept. In section 2.4 we saw that experimenters do not all use the same criteria to classify a child as a conserver. These differences cause problems in evaluating the results of training experiments.

According to Piaget, conservation is a symptom of the concrete operational structure. If we train a child to give conserving judgments, then he may simply acquire an isolated response. If so, this is not equivalent to 'natural' conservation, and from our experiment we may draw inappropriate conclusions about how conservation is acquired naturally. Piagetians make recommendations about how to distinguish between children who have acquired a truly operational concept, and those who have merely acquired an isolated response. Both pre- and post-testing should be thorough. The particular concept to be trained should be tested using several tasks, and there should also be post-tests of generalization (see below). Attention should be paid to the child's reasons for his judgments, and he should be given countersuggestions. There should be a delayed post-test several weeks after the training, since an operational concept would not be forgotten, whereas an isolated response might well be.

Unless both pre- and post-testing are thorough, the experiment is open to the criticism that children who appeared to be nonconservers before training had in fact begun to acquire the concept, and that children who appeared to be conservers after training really acquired only a narrowly applicable rule.

One of the most important of the Piagetian bases for evaluating the results of training experiments is the degree of generalization of the trained concept. Since Piagetians believe that successful training results in the acquisition of an operational structure, Inhelder and Sinclair (1969) recommend that the post-test should include 'at least one item pertaining to the same structure but touching a different problem (for example, conservation of weight—transitivity of weight).' (p. 5) (Transitivity is the ability to deduce the relationship between A and C when given that between A and B and between B and C. It is one of the symptoms of operational thinking.) There are problems with Inhelder and Sinclair's recommendation. Even among children who have developed naturally, the relationship between conservation and transitivity is far from perfect (Smedslund, 1961c; 1964). In Chapter 1, other examples were given of the décalages between symptoms of concrete operational thinking. Given these décalages, it is difficult if not impossible to specify precisely what generalization there should be from a trained concept of conservation.

Whether or not we could specify the generalization expected by Piaget's theory, degree of generalization might not be accepted by a non-Piagetian as a valid criterion for evaluating training procedures, for the following reason. If there were evidence (in fact there is none) that all children who have acquired conservation of amount of plasticine have also acquired conservation of amount of liquid, and vice versa, this finding could be interpreted in one of two ways.

(i) The same cognitive structure is responsible for both conservations.
(ii) The two concepts are acquired independently, but normally the child has experience which allows him to acquire both at the same time.

Suppose a child were trained to conserve amount of plasticine, and succeeded in all the recommended tasks of conservation of amount of plasticine, but failed to generalize the concept to liquids. Only if interpretation (i) were held would this child's failure to generalize be taken as evidence that the trained concept was different from the naturally acquired one. The results of this hypothetical experiment might even be taken as support for interpretation (ii) by those who prefer this interpretation of the evidence.

It seems, therefore, that even if the pre- and post-testing is extremely thorough, whether or not a training programme is accepted by an individual as successful depends to a large extent on his criteria for classifying a child as 'a conserver'. This situation arises because of the lack of an accepted theory about the psychological nature of the concept of conservation.

The value of training programmes can also be questioned on other grounds. If the aim of research is to discover how the child acquires conservation naturally, then the procedure used in a training experiment must involve experiences which the child would be expected to get in his normal everyday life. It is hard to know what such experiences would be in the absence of an ethological study of the young child's everyday experiences of judging quantity. It is, however, easier to specify what they are unlikely to be for most children. In many training experiments the child is actually told the acceptable answer in the conservation test, perhaps by teaching him a rule such as 'Whenever we start with a length like this one, and we don't add any sticks to it or take any sticks away, but only move it, it stays the same length even though it looks different.' (Beilin, 1965). Waghorn and Sullivan (1970) trained nonconservers by showing them films of an adult giving conserving judgments in a conservation test. Some children may be given direct training in their natural environment, but many must have acquired conservation without such direct teaching, although they may be rarer now that some infant school teachers include conservation training in the curriculum. Even if it could be shown that the trained concept in a direct teaching experiment such as this was equivalent to the 'natural' concept, this would not necessarily mean that the way it was acquired was in any way the same.

This discussion of training experiments is based on the assumption that the experimenter is interested in conservation as an example of an invention. The fact that the child can acquire conservation as a result of direct teaching by an adult is only of minor interest if the aim is to understand invention by the child. However, conservation training experiments might be of interest for other reasons. The experimenter might be investigating how children respond to various training procedures, with the aim of understanding the processes of learning. If so, then it may be unimportant whether or not a particular procedure has any parallel in the child's everyday life. Whether the trained concept is equivalent to the naturally acquired one may also be of little interest.

If, however, conservation is being studied as an example of an invention by the child, then it could be concluded from this discussion that the problems associated with training techniques outweigh the advantages, and that although there are some difficulties with interpreting results of observation studies, it is these which are more useful for testing theories of conservation acquisition. Certainly a theory supported by observational data will make predictions about how conservation can be taught, and should training in the predicted way prove totally unsuccessful, then the theory would lose credibility. The theory would be quite unharmed, however, if a quite different training procedure proved much more effective. The quickest route to conservation acquisition may not be the route taken by the child in his natural setting.

CHAPTER 3

What are the Origins of the Concept of Conservation?

Summary

The problem can be expressed as 'How does the NAS criterion become available to the child?' He cannot discover that if nothing is added or subtracted, amount remains the same. The evidence suggests that the concept of qualitative identity may be a psychological prerequisite of conservation, but there is no theory which specifies adequately how the one helps in the development of the other. The child could discover certain constraints between addition, subtraction and deformation on the one hand, and appearance and amount on the other. Such discoveries could be necessary for invention of the NAS criterion.

3.1 Introduction

In Chapter 1, conservation of amount was defined as equivalent to application of the criterion 'If nothing is added or subtracted, amount remains the same' (the NAS criterion). Only if the child's judgments are consistent with the NAS criterion can we say that he has the concept of conservation of amount. Because of the precision of this definition, it is useful to describe the conserver as 'using' the NAS criterion, as long as care is taken not to assume that the child applies a verbal formula. The problem can then be expressed as a search for the origins of the NAS criterion.

We know that in standard Piagetian tests the young child does not judge amount in accordance with the NAS criterion, but seems to judge on the basis of appearance. We do not know, however, whether the young child is capable of using the NAS criterion and for some reason fails to use it in standard tests. Perhaps he does use the NAS criterion, but only in other tests. If he does, this merely directs us to looking at much younger children to find the origins of the NAS criterion; the problem of accounting for its origin remains.

It is assumed that the child does not simply *discover* that if nothing is added or subtracted, amount remains the same. Perhaps, then, the idea of conservation of amount is an elaboration of the concept of qualitative identity. If so, then what is involved in this elaboration? Perhaps the child discovers various facts about the effects of addition, subtraction and deformation on appearance, facts which direct him towards the invention of the NAS criterion, or at least which remove impediments from his invention of it. In this chapter, these possibilities will be discussed.

3.2 Qualitative identity and conservation

When we roll a ball of plasticine into a sausage, we can ask the child 'Is there still the same amount to eat?' or we can ask him 'Is it still the same plasticine?'. The former question asks the child about conservation of amount, while the latter asks him about qualitative identity. It is possible that a child could say either 'It's still the same plasticine but there's more of it', or 'It's not the same plasticine now you've rolled it, but there's still the same amount'. In fact, children who give the first answer are quite common, but children who give the second are rare. In psychological development, qualitative identity seems to precede conservation.

Bruner (1966c) describes an experiment by Nair which demonstrates this. Five-year-old children poured water from one container into differently shaped ones, and were asked 'Is this the same water . . .?' and 'Is there as much, more, or not as much water . . .?'. From the data given, it seems that out of a total of a hundred and sixty sets of responses from forty children, fifty-six indicated qualitative identity without conservation, but only one indicated conservation without qualitative identity. Piaget (1968a) reports that he has obtained similar results. However, Papalia and Hooper (1971) did not obtain such a clear-cut developmental relationship between qualitative identity and conservation, particularly when the child was required to give a reason for his judgment before being deemed to have passed a particular task.

In their experiment, sixty children aged from four to six years were given tests of number conservation (using poker chips) and of amount conservation (using seeds in glasses). Both identity and equivalence tests of conservation were given. Identity tests, in which no comparison object is used, are more directly comparable with tests of qualitative identity: in both, the child is asked to compare an object with itself before deformation. The performance in the equivalence tests will be ignored here. In addition to the conservation tests, a test of qualitative identity was given with each of the two materials. Each test consisted of five tasks. Scalogram analyses were performed on the results. When the giving of a correct judgment was sufficient for passing a task, qualitative identity was easier than conservation in the case of both seeds and poker chips. The difference in difficulty was not, however, as dramatic as that found by Nair. The mean number of tasks passed in the qualitative identity and in the conservation tests were not significantly different in the case of either material. Furthermore, when a satisfactory reason was required, qualitative identity was more difficult than conservation for both seeds and poker chips, although again the mean numbers of tasks passed were not significantly different.

Despite the discrepancy between Nair's results and Papalia and Hooper's, the evidence suggests that very few children conserve without possessing the concept of qualitative identity. These few may be intermediate children who are unsure of both judgments. The evidence is not inconsistent with the view that qualitative identity is necessary for conservation. If it is, what role does it play in conservation acquisition?

It could be that conservation arises directly from qualitative identity, that conservation is nothing but an elaboration of qualitative identity. Qualitative identity could, however, be merely a necessary condition for conservation, not its direct source. These alternative views of the developmental relationship between the two concepts have been expressed by Bruner and Piaget respectively.

Bruner (1966c) holds that conservation arises directly from qualitative identity, that children who fail to conserve in standard Piagetian tests already have the concept of conservation and are merely 'seduced' by the immediate appearance, and that they can resist seduction only if they represent the situation symbolically. The results of Frank's screening experiment are given in support of this view. Ten children at each of the ages four, five, six and seven years were given a two-task conservation pre-test, followed by a screening test, and a conservation post-test identical to the pre-test. A simplified account of the screening test will be given.

The child was shown two containers, one of which (the standard) contained water. The containers were either the same or different in width, and the same or different in height. We shall consider the case of a pair of containers equal in height, with the comparison wider than the standard. After showing the pair to the child, both glasses were placed behind a screen so that the water level was hidden and only the tops could be seen. The water was poured from the standard into the comparison. The child was asked whether there was still the same amount of water, and to give a reason. In the next stage of the test, the screen was not used, and the child was simply asked to predict whether there would still be the same amount of water if the contents of the standard were poured into the comparison; he was also asked to predict the liquid level. In the third stage, the screen was introduced again, and the child made both level and amount judgments. Finally, the screen was removed and the child was again asked whether there was the same amount of water as there had been before pouring.

One of the hypotheses tested in this experiment was that if the nonconserver was screened from the post-deformation appearance, he would represent the situation symbolically rather than ikonically, and so would give a conserving judgment based on identity. The second hypothesis was that experience of the screening would help the child to conserve when the screen was removed. This aspect, concerned with the mechanism by which conservation is acquired, is discussed in Chapter 5. In this chapter, only the results relevant to the first hypothesis will be considered.

When the liquid was screened, the number of equality amount judgments was higher than in the pre-test. None of the ten four-year-olds had conserved in the pre-test, but nine of them gave equality amount judgments when the liquid was first screened. Two of the ten five-year-olds conserved in the pre-test, but seven did so when the liquid was first screened. Half of the six- and half of the seven-year-olds conserved in the pre-test, and all but one of them did so during screening. During screening, quality amount judgments were most often justified by qualitative identity reasons, e.g. 'It's only the same water'. These results apparently support Bruner's view that the nonconserver has an ability to conserve which is based on identity, but which he does not normally reveal because he is misled by changes in appearance.

However, it could be that what appeared to be conserving judgments during screening were really perceptually based judgments—the children may have assumed that nothing had changed, and that the level of the liquid was the same after pouring as before. If so, they could have made equality amount judgments based on level. This suggestion is supported by the results in the second stage of the experiment. Nine of the four-year-olds, six of the five-year-olds and three of the six- and seven-year-olds failed to guess correctly that the level in the wider comparison would be lower than that in the standard. Almost all the errors consisted of saying that the level would be the same. That is, although most of the four- and five-year-olds gave equality amount judgments during screening, most of them assumed that the levels in the two glasses were the same. Their amount judgments could have been based on appearance. Because of this, they do not provide a clear indication that the young children could conserve.

A further problem with the screening experiment is that the results are not consistent across the three stages of the screening test. In the third stage, for example, only five of the four-year-olds gave equality amount judgments during screening, whereas nine of them had done so in the first stage. On the other hand, three of them gave correct level judgments in the third stage, although only one had done so in the second stage. Correct level judgments among the five-year-olds rose from four in the second stage, to seven in the third. Such instability means that interpretations of the results must be treated with suspicion. Unless the child gave as his reason for an equality amount judgment during screening 'because you didn't add any on or take any away', it may not be valid to conclude that he was conserving.

Replications of the screening experiment have focused more on its training aspect than on the judgments given during screening, and they will be considered in Chapter 5.

Piaget (1967, 1968a) does not accept that nonconservers give conserving judgments during screening, for the following reasons.

(i) He finds Frank's assessment of the child's conservation level inadequate. Some of the children classified as nonconservers on the basis of the pre-test may really have had some grasp of conservation which would have been detected had the testing been more thorough.

(ii) He reports that in his own screening experiments, nonconservers who gave equality amount judgments during screening also judged that the liquid level in the screened container was the same as it had been before pouring. Piaget calls these children pseudo-conservers; they were just assuming that nothing had changed as a result of the pouring. Unfortunately, in Piaget's full account of his screening experiments (Piaget and Inhelder, 1971; French edition, 1966), the relevant data are not given.

There is, then, insufficient evidence to be sure whether nonconservers use the NAS criterion when they are protected from seeing the post-deformation appearance. Nevertheless, it is worth considering further the theory that conservation originates in qualitative identity.

Bruner describes the way qualitative identity supposedly becomes elaborated into conservation. He sees that process of development as one of

'. . . translating "primitive" identity into a more conceptually refined form . . . The child . . . can say, for example: "They are the same water, but they do not look the same". Finally, this can be translated into the linguistic equivalent: "They are the same amount".' (Bruner, 1966c, p. 192)

This quotation suggests a similarity between Bruner's view and that of Braine and Shanks (1965a; 1965b), who hold that the ability to make a distinction between reality and appearance is necessary for conservation, and that in some cases, including amount conservation, it is sufficient. However, the ability to distinguish between reality and appearance is not logically sufficient for judging that in reality amount remains the same unless material is added or subtracted. Hence it is not clear why Bruner states that 'They are the same water but they do not look the same' is equivalent to 'They are the same amount'. Certainly adult use of language would not allow us to say the first without implying the second, but that is only because adults have the concept of conservation of amount; the equivalence is different from that between 'A is more than B' and 'B is less than A'.

Bruner does, however, accept that linguistic development is not sufficient for conservation acquisition. He states that the nonconserver

'. . . does not have the structure built for dealing with perceived identity in a way appropriate for using language in this complicated way . . . He is operating . . . with one "moment" or one event at a time. . . When the child develops the sort of hierarchical structures that permit him to organize a series of experiences into variants of a base form . . . He then finds means for verifying and checking and extending his simple conception of identity: through an appeal to reversibility, through compensation, through measure and so forth.' (Bruner, 1966c, p. 205)

(Bruner's view that reversibility is merely a justification for conservation, and not a component of it, is discussed in section 3.4; his view of compensation, which is similar, is discussed in Chapter 4.)

Piaget (1968a) criticizes Bruner's interpretation of the relationship between qualitative identity and conservation on the grounds that Bruner fails to make a clear distinction between qualitative and quantitative identity. Bruner uses the single term 'identity' to mean both 'the same stuff' and 'the same amount of stuff', although the latter is also called on occasions 'equivalence'. Piaget, however, prefers to make a much clearer distinction between the two types of identity, since he believes that a child at the pre-operational stage of development can possess a qualitative identity concept, while quantitative identity develops only with operational thinking:

'(Qualitative identity) can . . . be acquired by the dissociation of a perceptive quality from other perceptive qualities: e.g., with liquids if $a =$ colour, $b =$ the quality of being a liquid and $c =$ shape, then abc stays 'the same water' for the subject because a and b have not changed and only c is modified.' (Piaget, 1967, p. 533)

Quantitative identity, on the other hand, is logically sufficient for conservation: it is defined as 'Nothing added, nothing subtracted = the same quantity', i.e. it is equivalent to the NAS criterion. As far as the author knows, Piaget does not point out that quantitative identity is logically sufficient for conservation; psychologically, he believes, quantitative identity is acquired only along with the operations of reversibility and compensation:

'It is, then, the total system or grouping which is responsible for the formation of the conservations, and not identity. Identity is but one element of the system, and an element which has been transformed by the system itself, rather than being the source of the system.' (Piaget, 1968a, p. 37)

Evidence from a longitudinal study by Inhelder and Noelting (referred to by Piaget and Inhelder, 1961) supports Piaget's argument that identity, reversibility and compensation form a single cognitive structure; it was found that all three kinds of reason developed contemporaneously rather than in succession. No data are given. If, as Bruner holds, identity were the sole basis of conservation, and reversibility and compensation merely justifications, then identity reasons would be expected to appear first. It is interesting that as examples of identity reasons, Piaget gives both qualitative and quantitative types: 'C'est la même pâté' and 'On n'a rien ôté, rien ajouté'. Maybe he thinks that if a qualitative identity reason is given for a conserving judgment, then the child must be using operational reasoning; a child who had only pre-operational identity would not give a conserving judgment.

Results contrary to those reportedly obtained by Inhelder and Noelting arose in an experiment by the author (Experiment B). Each child was given three conservation tasks using plasticine. Each task included a countersuggestion, although no reasons were given for the suggested judgments. Forty-six children gave at least one conserving judgment. Of these, thirty-two gave at least one identity reason, i.e. 'It was the same at first' or 'You didn't add any on or take any away'; 'It's the same plasticine' was not accepted. Only four of the identity reasons referred to lack of addition and/or subtraction. Eight children gave compensation reasons for conserving judgments, and three gave reversibility reasons. These results are more as expected by Bruner's theory than as expected by Piaget's: identity reasons were by far the most common.

Although the evidence presented here does not allow us to conclude whether conservation originates in qualitative identity, Piaget's criticisms of Bruner's view do seem valid. The distinction between qualitative and quantitative identity is an important one, and Bruner does tend to merge the two concepts. However, having made this point, Piaget does not go on to suggest how quantitative identity develops. In his most detailed account of conservation acquisition, 'Logique et Equilibre dans les Comportements du Sujet' (1957), he does not mention quantitative identity at all. Neither is it clear what Piaget considers to be the role of qualitative identity in conservation acquisition.

We have, then, no satisfactory account of why qualitative identity should be a necessary prerequisite of conservation; perhaps it is merely incidental that qualitative identity develops first. Other factors which could play a role in the development of the concept of amount conservation will now be considered. Conservation acquisition involves coming to believe that certain transformations are irrelevant to quantity change; perhaps learning about those which are relevant, addition and subtraction, plays an important role. This possibility will be discussed in the next section.

3.3 Addition and subtraction and conservation

Let us assume that the child begins by judging amount only on the basis of appearance. He might observe that the amount looks more when material is added, and looks less when some is subtracted. He might eventually judge that the amount is increased by addition and decreased by subtraction, even without seeing the change in appearance. Such a child might still be basing his judgments on appearance—he might be assuming that addition had made the amount look more, and that subtraction had made it look less. Nevertheless, it is not completely inconceivable that the child could acquire from direct experience the criteria 'If material is added, then there is more' and 'If material is subtracted, then there is less'. But it is not obvious why the child should go on to think that amount is changed *only* by addition and subtraction. Smedslund suggests how this development could take place.

Smedslund (1961d) describes conservation acquisition in terms of increasing dominance of an addition–subtraction schema over a deformation schema. 'Schema' is not defined, but it seems that when fully developed the addition–subtraction schema is sufficient for adult conserving behaviour. The deformation schema is presumably responsible for judgments that amount changes as a result of rolling, pouring, etc. It seems Smedslund describes a child as using the deformation schema if he gives a perceptually based judgment in a conservation test. We cannot assume that the deformation schema is equivalent to perceptual criteria, however, since Smedslund writes of the deformation schema as eventually disappearing completely; the child does not completely abandon perceptual criteria. Hence the status of the deformation schema is not clear.

According to Smedslund, a conflict mechanism is responsible for the increasing domination of the deformation schema by the addition–subtraction schema. The child is supposedly confronted by situations in which both schemata are activated in equal strength. For example, if a ball of plasticine is rolled into a sausage, and a piece taken off, then the conflicting judgments might be 'More in the sausage because it's longer' (deformation schema) and 'Less in the sausage because you took some off' (addition–subtraction schema). Since the addition–subtraction schema has

'. . . greater clarity, simplicity and consistency, it will gradually or suddenly begin to dominate, whereas the deformation schema with its high degree of ambiguity, complexity and internal contradiction will be weakened and will eventually disappear completely, even in pure deformation situations without addition/subtraction.' (Smedslund, 1961d, p. 157)

Smedslund carried out two kinds of experiment to support his theory.

(i) Experiments to show that use of the criteria 'If some is added then there is more', and 'If some is subtracted then there is less' preceded conservation.

(ii) Experiments to show that a conflict mechanism is responsible for the acquisition of conservation.

The second kind of experiment, concerned with the mechanism of conservation acquisition, is discussed in Chapter 5.

In the experiments intended to investigate the nonconserver's use of addition and subtraction criteria, the child was given a series of conservation tasks, and also a set of tasks in which there was addition and subtraction of material. In one such experiment (1961a), balls of plasticine were used. At first they were equal in amount, then a small piece was removed from one of them, then put back again, a piece was added to the other ball, and then removed. At each stage, the child was asked for an amount judgment. In the conservation tasks, one of two equal balls was changed into a ring, or a cross. Children were scored as passing the addition–subtraction test if they gave correct judgments and explanations throughout; a similar criterion was used in the conservation test.

Smedslund found that children did indeed seem to use the criteria 'If some is added then there is more' and 'If some is subtracted then there is less' before using the NAS criterion. Twenty-nine children passed the addition–subtraction test but failed the conservation test, whereas only nine children conserved but failed addition–subtraction. Smedslund considers that 'momentary distractions' could have been responsible for these nine failures of the addition–subtraction test, and that data more clear-cut than these cannot be expected.

The results are interpreted as supporting the view that:

'The concepts of conservation are symptoms of an additive composition of the objects. Development in this area consists in a progressively more structured and balanced organization of the operations of addition and subtraction (equilibration). This equilibration is accompanied by an increasing resistance to perceptual disturbance.' (Smedslund, 1961a, p. 207)

In later experiments, however, Smedslund found that some addition–subtraction tasks were more difficult than the conservation test. For example, Smedslund (1964), using sets of linoleum squares, found that tasks in which a square was added to one set and then removed tended to be more difficult than the conservation test, although tasks in which subtraction preceded addition were easier. Smedslund identifies various procedural factors which could have been responsible for the increased difficulty of the addition–subtraction task. These results suggest, however, that the development of the addition–subtraction schema, culminating in the acquisition of conservation, cannot be described in such a simple way as had at first appeared.

Hall and Kingsley (1968) provide evidence which they interpret as counter to Smedslund's theory. Adult and child conservers were given demonstrations of apparent nonconservation in an extinction test: the experimenter surreptitiously removed some plasticine from one of two equal balls while changing its shape, and then demonstrated on a balance that the two pieces no longer weighed the same. The subject was asked to explain this. Hall and Kingsley argue that if conservation were a symptom of an addition–subtraction schema then the subjects should explain the nonconservation in terms of loss of material. In fact, it was rare for subjects to give such reasons, and other experimenters have also found this (Miller, 1973; Smith, 1968). Smedslund himself, however, implies that addition/subtraction reasons were common in his own extinction test (1961b).

Hall and Kingsley's argument is not a strong one. Since apparently nothing had been added or subtracted, it seems likely that the subjects would try to think of other possible reasons for the change in weight after deformation, e.g. 'The scales have gone wrong'. The rarity of addition–subtraction reasons does not provide convincing evidence against Smedslund's theory.

Other experimenters have taught children the effects on appearance and quantity of addition and subtraction, to see if this leads them to conserve (Feigenbaum and Sulkin, 1964; Smedslund, 1961c; Wallach, Wall and Anderson, 1967). These training experiments have not been successful. This is not evidence against Smedslund's theory, however, since he does not state that use of the criteria 'If some is added, then there is more' and 'If some is subtracted, then there is less' is sufficient for conservation, merely that it is necessary.

The evidence discussed in this section is rather inconclusive; it is not clear whether children learn to conserve through using the criteria 'If some is added, then there is more' and 'If some is subtracted, then there is less'. Further evidence relevant to Smedslund's theory is discussed in Chapter 5.

We have seen that the use of the criteria 'If some is added, then there is more' and 'If some is subtracted, then there is less' often (but not invariably) precedes use of the NAS criterion. This is consistent with the view that some factor leads to the development of all three criteria, but is not sufficient for the development of the NAS criterion and possibly is not sufficient for the development of the other two. At the beginning of this section it was suggested that the criteria 'If some is added, then there is more' and 'If some is subtracted, then there is less' might be discovered through observing the effects on appearance of addition and subtraction. Such observations could have a direct influence on the development of the NAS criterion, and not just an indirect influence via use of the criteria 'If some is added, then there is more' and 'If some is subtracted, then there is less'.

Let us again begin with a child who judges amount only on the basis of appearance. If he is to come to think of the transformation performed (addition, subtraction or deformation) as a relevant cue, then he must learn about the effects on appearance of these transformations. A child who thought that the same change in appearance (and therefore the same change in amount) could be brought about by addition or subtraction as by deformation would have no reason to consider transformations as possible bases for amount judgments. The transformation performed will remain an irrelevant cue until the child becomes aware that it bears a specifiable relationship to the change in appearance. This idea will become clearer as it is discussed further in relation to Piaget's operational reversibility and non-Piagetian interpretations of this.

3.4 Reversibility and conservation

Piaget commonly defines reversibility as the ability to perform a particular action in the reverse direction. For example, Piaget (1957) gives the following definition:

'... la capacité d'exécuter une même action dans les deux sens de parcours, mais en ayant conscience qu'il s'agit de la même action.' (Piaget, 1957, p. 44)

Piaget considers reversibility to be one of the characteristics of operational thought. Since the acquisition of conservation is one of the symptoms of having reached this stage of development, Piaget's account of conservation acquisition is in terms of the development of this system of operations, reversibility, identity and compensation, but the nature of the supposed relationship between the development of these three is difficult to ascertain.

Piaget's evidence for the role of reversibility in conservation seems to be that one of the reasons given for conserving judgments is 'If you rolled it back it would be the same'. This has led non-Piagetians to interpret reversibility as the knowledge that the pre-deformation appearance (and amount) can be obtained by reversing the deformation.

This particular interpretation of reversibility is, however, what Piaget calls empirical return or renversabilité. Empirical return can easily be discovered from experience of the physical world, and Piaget accepts that nonconservers have often done this. Piaget and Inhelder (1941) point out the differences between empirical return and reversibility. A child who knows about empirical return, but who has not yet acquired reversibility, sees the return to the initial state as possible, but not as necessary; this child is thinking in terms of a series of physical states rather than in terms of the deformation itself. In contrast, a child with operational reversibility sees the return to the pre-deformation appearance as necessary; he reasons in terms of the deformation performed and it is this which he conceives of as reversible.

Pinard (reported discussion in Inhelder, 1962) describes a way of distinguishing between reversibility and empirical return. A child who has given a nonconserving judgment when a ball of clay was rolled into a sausage, and then agrees that the amount is unchanged when the sausage has been rolled back into a ball, is asked 'How could you get more clay?' (assuming he said there was more in the sausage than the ball). If the child rolls the ball into a sausage again, this demonstrates that he has attained only empirical return. If, however, he adds some clay on, then he has true reversibility.

This is an odd test. It is based on the assumption that a child cannot have true reversibility if he thinks that amount can be changed by a change of shape, i.e. if he is a nonconserver. It does not provide a test of reversibility which is logically independent of conservation, yet this is just what is needed to test Piaget's theory.

Many non-Piagetians have ignored the distinction between reversibility and empirical return, and have attempted to test Piaget's theory by carrying out experiments on the relationship between conservation and empirical return. There have been demonstrations that nonconservers know about empirical return, accompanied by conclusions that Piaget is wrong to consider reversibility a component of conservation. There have also been demonstrations that teaching children about empirical return helps them to acquire conservation, interpreted as support for Piaget's theory. Although these experiments are irrelevant to Piaget's views about reversibility and conservation, they are of interest because they inform us about the possible prerequisites of conservation.

Many conservation training experiments have incorporated demonstrations of return to the pre-deformation appearance, e.g. Beilin (1965) and Smith (1968) (verbal rule instruction); Sigel, Roeper and Hooper (1966) and Rothenburg and Orost (1969) (multi-factor training); Braine and Shanks (1965a) (training to distinguish between reality and appearance); Wallach and Sprott (1964) (training in addition/subtraction and empirical return). All these experimenters thought that demonstrations of, or references to, return to the pre-deformation appearance might help the child to conserve. Brainerd and Allen (1971), after reviewing conservation training experiments, conclude that it is those which include demonstrations of empirical return (called reversibility by these authors) which tend to be the successful ones; they do not, however, specify how the success was supposed to have been achieved.

In none of the above experiments could the role of demonstrations of empirical return be evaluated independently of other elements in the training procedure. However, Wallach, Wall and Anderson (1967) carried out a number training experiment in which empirical return was less confused with other factors. The material used for training was dolls and beds: at the beginning there was a doll in every bed. Subjects in the empirical return training group saw the dolls rearranged so that the correspondence between dolls and beds was not apparent. The child was asked 'Do you think we can put a doll in every bed now?' and he was allowed to try and do that. Trials of this kind were repeated until the child answered correctly four times in succession. In fact the children, all of whom failed to conserve in the dolls-and-beds pre-test of conservation, nearly all answered the empirical return questions correctly from the beginning. The median number of training trials given was four. This suggests that it was not ignorance about empirical return which was preventing the child from conserving. It is surprising, therefore, that twelve of the fourteen children who underwent this training did give conserving judgments in the dolls-and-beds post-test. These results illustrate the general point that the child in a training experiment may not be learning exactly what the experimenter is teaching him.

Wallach et al. also carried out a similar training procedure using liquid. The child saw water from one of two identical containers being poured into a wider container, and he was asked 'If I pour this water back into the empty glass, will it be filled just like this one (comparison)?'. After the child had made his prediction, the water was poured back so that he could see whether he had been correct. It was again found that most nonconservers predicted correctly from the beginning, although in this investigation there was no increase in conserving judgments in the post-test.

Bruner (1966c) also found that nonconservers knew about empirical return of liquids: twenty-seven out of thirty-eight nonconserving four- and five-year-olds answered an empirical return correctly. Bruner argues from this that 'reversibility' (which he interprets as empirical return) is not a component of conservation as Piaget believes it is. Rather, Bruner suggests, 'reversibility' is used as a justification once the child gives a conserving judgment based on identity.

Those who interpret Piaget's reversibility as empirical return also attack his theory on logical grounds. Wallach (1969) points out that there is no reason why quantity should not change during deformation and then change back during reversal of the deformation; there is therefore no reason why the child should agree that quantity is conserved simply from a demonstration of empirical return.

A second criticism of Piaget's views about the relationship between reversibility and conservation arises from Berlyne (1965) and from Elkind (1969), who both interpret reversibility as empirical return. There are cases of reversible transformations to which conservation is not applied, such as the length of a rubber band during stretching, and also cases of nonreversible transformations to which conservation is applied, e.g. we judge that amount is conserved when an egg is cooked. It could be argued that since empirical return is not a distinguishing characteristic of situations to which conservation is applied, knowledge of empirical return cannot be necessary for conservation. This need not mean, however, that knowledge of empirical return is irrelevant to conservation acquisition. Maybe conservation is more difficult to apply to cases in which the deformation cannot be empirically reversed.

When deformations are reversible, it is true that a demonstration of return to the pre-deformation appearance cannot, logically, convince the child of conservation. It could nevertheless be that knowledge of empirical return is necessary for the acquisition of conservation in cases where empirical return is possible. Why this should be is argued below.

As mentioned in section 3.3, it is plausible that a child who uses only appearance as a basis for judging amount must know about the effects on appearance of addition, subtraction and deformation, if he is to conserve. A child who thought that the same change in appearance (and therefore in amount) could be achieved by addition or subtraction as by deformation, would have no reason to think of the transformation performed as a basis for amount judgments. Neither would a child who thought that deformation could cancel out the effect on appearance of addition or subtraction. Suppose we roll a ball of plasticine, B, into a sausage, B′, and then take a piece off, leaving B′−. To compare the amounts in B and B′−, an adult would apply the criterion 'If some is subtracted then there is less'. A young child, however, would judge on the basis of appearance. Why should he come to think of the subtraction as a suitable basis for his amount judgment? He may well fail to do so because he thinks B′− could equally well have been achieved just by rolling B, or that B could be obtained again by rolling up B′−. That is, the child may think that addition or subtraction and deformation are to some extent equivalent, in that a particular change in appearance can be achieved by either transformation. To a child who judges amount only on the basis of appearance, the transformation performed would be an irrelevant cue. It could become potentially relevant through his learning the constraints between addition, subtraction and deformation on the one hand, and appearance and amount (judged on the basis of appearance) on the other.

Knowledge of empirical return has generally been investigated for deformation, and not for addition or subtraction. Many nonconservers know that the pre-deformation appearance can be obtained by rolling/pouring back, but they may also think that rolling/pouring back would work even if material had been added or subtracted during the deformation. There is some evidence to suggest that nonconservers do think the effects of addition or subtraction can be cancelled by deformation. Rothenburg and Orost (1969) mention this in their number training experiment. After a deformation or an addition/subtraction, nonconservers were asked to change the blocks so that both rows had the same number. It was found that they generally tried to make the rows look alike without performing the necessary additions/subtractions. Unfortunately, no detailed results are given.

64

An experiment by the author (Experiment C) investigated this question. Children aged between four and eight years were given three conservation tasks, and a test in which material was subtracted during the deformation. In two of the conservation tasks, one of two plasticine sausages was rolled longer, and in the third, one of two plasticine balls was squashed into an irregular shape. In the 'deformation with subtraction' test, two equal balls were used, and a piece was subtracted from one of them just before it was rolled into a sausage. In all the tasks, children were given a countersuggestion to see how sure they were of their judgment, and they were also asked about empirical return: 'What if we roll mine (sausage) back again, will we both have the same to eat, or will you have more, or will I have more? Why?'.

It was found that virtually all forty children gave correct empirical return judgments in the conservation tasks; only a single error was made. However, ten children gave incorrect answers when there was subtraction as well as deformation, and nine of these thought the amounts would be the same again when the sausage was rolled into a ball. All but one of the children who gave incorrect empirical return judgments in the 'deformation with subtraction' test also gave incorrect judgments of the post-deformation amount in that test; they thought there was more in the sausage than the ball. However, five of them did give conserving judgments in the conservation test, although none of them performed perfectly in all three conservation tasks.

These results demonstrate that children who know that rolling can cancel out the effects of rolling sometimes believe that rolling can also cancel out the effects of subtraction. None of the children who judged consistently with the criterion 'If some is subtracted then there is less' made that error; neither did any of those who always judged consistently with the NAS criterion. The children who conserved in the conservation tasks on one but not on all occasions may not have used the NAS criterion, but that possibility will not be considered yet; it will be raised again in later chapters. The results of this experiment support the view that ignorance of the constraints between transformations and changes in appearance is an impediment to conservation acquisition; knowledge of these constraints may be necessary for conservation.

This brings us back to Piaget's reversibility. A definition given by Piaget (1960) is '... the possibility of making an operation correspond to one and only one reverse operation which cancels it out' (p. 93). Clearly, according to this definition, a child who thought rolling could cancel out the effects of subtraction could not have operational reversibility. The experiment just described may be getting nearer to providing a test of reversibility than the conventional empirical return studies. However, the effects of transformations on appearance may need to be specified even more closely before the child can be said to have true reversibility. Piaget (1957) writes:

'Le fait de pouvoir dérouler la même action dans les deux sens correspond ainsi en un sens à la définition physique de la réversibilité ..., tandis que la conscience de l'identité de cette action, malgré la différence des sens de parcours, confère à la réversibilité une signification opératoire ...' (Piaget, 1957, p. 44)

What might be meant by saying the child is aware of the 'identity' of the deformation with its reverse? In order to test for this awareness, a particular deformation must be put in a context of others. Absence of a sense of identity could be indicated by a belief that two different outcomes could be achieved by a particular deformation.

Let us devise a concrete realization of this idea. Suppose we present a child with a set of plasticine sausages, equal in width but differing in length: B', B'+, B'++, etc. We also give him a short fat sausage, B. If the child thought that B could be rolled to look just like more than one of the thin ones (perhaps B' and B'+) we could say his specification of particular deformations was not sufficiently precise for him to understand a one-to-one correspondence between a deformation and its reverse. He must have rather a blurred idea of the effects of rolling on appearance, and on amount (if he judges amount on the basis of appearance). A similar interpretation could be made if he thinks that more than one of the long thin sausages could be rolled back to look just like B. If the child is to be aware of an identity between the rolling of B to B', and the rolling back of B' to B, then he must not make either of these errors—he must not think that B could be rolled to look like both B' and B'+; he must not think that both B' and B'+ could be rolled back to look like B.

An analogy may make this clearer. Imagine a set of pairs of identical twins, A and A', B and B', etc. They divide into two groups, one group consisting of A, B, C . . ., and the other consisting of A', B', C' . . .. Our task is to pair the twins again, A with A', B with B', and so on, to indicate that we are aware of the identity between A and A', etc. If we cannot distinguish between A and B, or between A' and B', then we cannot hope to succeed. We are likely to pair A with B' and B with A'. We will be in a situation similar to that of the child who thinks B can be rolled to look like both B' and B'+, or that B' and B'+ can both be rolled back to B. He cannot hope to understand an 'identity' between rolling B to B', and rolling B' back to B.

We may be able to say, then, that a child understands reversibility only if he knows that the fat sausage can be rolled to look just like only one of the thin sausages, and that only one of the thin ones can be rolled back to look just like the short fat one. This knowledge may even be psychologically sufficient for the child to establish an 'identity' between the deformation and its reverse, although in the absence of a definition of what Piaget means by this, we cannot be sure. While it would be inappropriate to suggest too strongly that the situation described above provides a test of Piaget's reversibility, success in such a test does seem to be a necessary condition for saying a child understands reversibility. Furthermore, the knowledge specified bears a logical relationship both to conservation (as will be shown below) and to operational compensation as this is interpreted in Chapter 4. It is therefore useful knowledge to investigate in its own right, whether or not it corresponds to Piaget's reversibility. This knowledge that the fat sausage can be rolled to look like only one of the thin sausages, and that only one of them can be rolled back to look like the fat one, will be called 'the uniqueness of reversibility'; it is thus linked, but not necessarily identified, with Piaget's reversibility.

There is no logical reason why knowing about the uniqueness of reversibility should lead the child to conserve. The child could know that B can be deformed to look like B' only, and not like B'+ or B'−, without judging that B is the same amount as B'. However, a child who thought that B could be rolled to look like both B' and B'+ would probably not be assuming that rolling was irrelevant to changes in amount. Assuming that this child agrees that B'+ is not the same amount as B' (as he would just by judging on the basis of length), we could not describe him as using the NAS criterion: he thinks that rolling B can produce two amounts which are not equal. It has already been argued that we cannot call a child a conserver unless he judges amount consistently with the NAS criterion. We cannot, therefore, call a child a conserver unless he knows about the uniqueness of reversibility.

It is possible that in psychological development the child assumes that uniqueness of reversibility *because* he has acquired the concept of conservation; knowledge of the uniqueness of reversibility may be only a symptom of having acquired conservation. It seems much more likely, though, that the child's discovery of the uniqueness of reversibility removes an impediment to conservation acquisition: the child's assumption that B can be rolled to look like both B' and B'+ may prevent him from acquiring the concept of conservation.

The uniqueness of reversibility is similar to Halford's (1970a) interpretation of Piaget's compensation. For liquids in glasses, Halford suggests that 'basic to the idea of compensation' is the knowledge that

'... given that nothing has been added or subtracted, then a change in one dimension must be accompanied by one and only one change in another dimension.' (Halford, 1970a, p. 306)

Among glasses of equal width but different heights, only a glass with one particular height will exactly fill a standard glass. Halford assumes that recognition of this is equivalent to recognition of a perfectly compensating relationship between the dimensions (p. 309). That is, Halford fails to maintain a distinction between judgments about appearance and judgments about amount; this will be made clearer in Chapter 4, where Piaget's compensation is discussed.

Halford argues that by learning these and other constraints between deformation, addition and subtraction on the one hand, and changes in appearance on the other, amount judgments based on appearance can become consistent with those based on the NAS criterion: '... consistency can be achieved in the sense that all cues yield the same result' (p. 304). This is not the case. It is possible to judge on the basis of appearance that a particular long thin sausage *might* hold the same amount as a short fat one, and hence to accommodate an appearance-based judgment to an NAS-based one, but no appearance criterion could lead to the same judgment as the NAS criterion on all occasions.

Halford applies his theory to liquids in full containers, but it can also be applied to plasticine sausages. Halford states that if a child is to conserve, he must learn that B'− would be shorter than B if rolled to the same width, whereas B'+ would be longer, and only B' would be the same length as B. He assumes, however, that the child who has learned this also judges that the amount in B'− is less than the amount in B, and that B'+ is more than B. He argues that from here it is 'but a short step' (p. 306) for the child to conclude that B' is equal to B. Here, Halford is confusing predictions about appearance with judgments about amount. Logically, a child could know that B'— would be shorter than B (and less) if rolled to the same width, while continuing to judge that B'— is more than B because it is longer. If this situation does not occur, then an explanation is required. Once the child judges that B'— is less than B because it would be less if rolled to the same width, he is indeed well on the way to conservation acquisition, if not already there; the problem is to explain how he came to make that judgment. Hence, although Halford may be correct in assuming that knowledge of the uniqueness of reversibility is important in, and possibly necessary for, conservation acquisition, this knowledge cannot be given the central role assigned to it by Halford.

Evidence suggesting that conservers are more likely to know about the uniqueness of reversibility is provided by Halford's series of experiments (1968, 1969, 1970b, 1971). For example, Halford (1969) used two containers, O and I, equal in capacity but different in height and width, along with a set of containers the same width as I but either shorter or taller. The child was required to predict whether the contents of each of this set of full containers would over- or underfill O. The children in the experimental group were shown that the contents of the full container O exactly filled I. A child who was ignorant of the uniqueness of reversibility, i.e. who thought that containers other than I would exactly fill O, would make errors in this task. However, knowledge of the uniqueness of reversibility is not logically sufficient for correct performance, since the child also has to know, for example, that containers taller than I would over- not underfill O. It seems likely, though, that children who know about the uniqueness of reversibility also have this other knowledge, and so Halford's test may be assumed to assess knowledge of the uniqueness of reversibility.

In this and similar tasks, Halford demonstrates that conservers are likely to perform better than nonconservers; he also shows that training children in such tasks improves their performance in conservation tests. However, Halford divided his subjects into conservers and nonconservers on the basis of their performance in a single conservation task, and the scores of these two groups in the tests of the uniqueness of reversibility were compared. In all the experiments, the mean score of conservers was well below the maximum, and that of nonconservers was well above the minimum. For example, one set of results obtained under the conditions described above was:

conservers' mean score	:	27·4
nonconservers' mean score	:	24·7
maximum possible score	:	36
minimum possible score	:	0
score expected by chance	:	18

Without a more refined measure of conservation level, it is impossible to specify clearly the relationship between knowledge of the uniqueness of reversibility and conservation. An experiment by the author, described in Chapter 11, was intended to allow a precise specification of this relationship.

3.5 Conclusions

The aim of specifying the origins of the concept of conservation has not been achieved. Perhaps the concept is simply an elaboration of the concept of qualitative identity, as Bruner suggests. This is not, however, a helpful suggestion in the absence of a clear account of the process of elaboration. We have no clear idea why qualitative identity should even be psychologically necessary for conservation, although the evidence is consistent with the view that it is necessary.

Whether or not qualitative identity plays a role in conservation acquisition, it is likely that the child's discovery of various facts removes impediments to conservation acquisition. Possibly the child discovers the criteria 'If some is added, then there is more' and 'If some is subtracted, then there is less' and, through using these, eventually develops the NAS criterion. This is Smedslund's view. The evidence reviewed in this chapter suggests that children do use the criteria 'If some is added, then there is more' and 'If some is subtracted, then there is less' before they use the NAS criterion, although some tasks involving addition and subtraction may be more difficult than conservation tasks. Further evidence relevant to Smedslund's theory is discussed in Chapter 5, which is concerned with the mechanism of conservation acquisition.

Whether or not qualitative identity plays a role in conservation acquisition, it is likely that the child's discovery of various facts removes impediments to conservation acquisition. Possibly the child discovers the criteria 'If some is added then there is more' and 'If some is subtracted then there is less', and through using there eventually develops the NAS criterion. This is Smedslund's view. The evidence reviewed in this chapter suggests that children do use the criteria 'If some is added then there is more' and 'If some is subtracted then there is less' before they use the NAS criterion, although some tasks involving addition and subtraction may be more difficult than conservation. Further evidence relevant to Smedslund's theory is discussed in Chapter 5, which is concerned with the mechanism of conservation acquisition.

Observation of the effects of addition and subtraction on appearance could have a more direct influence on development of the concept of conservation. The experience necessary for development of the criteria 'If some is added then there is more' and 'If some is subtracted then there is less' may itself help the child towards conservation acquisition. There is some evidence to suggest that nonconservers cannot distinguish between addition/subtraction and deformation in terms of their effects on appearance. Some nonconservers think, for example, that the change in appearance resulting from subtraction and deformation can be cancelled out by deformation alone. Such ignorance is likely to be an impediment to conservation acquisition. If a child judges amount on the basis of appearance alone, he may come to see the transformation performed as a relevant cue only once he recognizes the constraints between transformations and changes in appearance.

A further impediment to conservation acquisition could be ignorance of the uniqueness of reversibility. The child may think that a given short fat sausage can be rolled to look just like a particular long thin sausage, and also like one which is equally thin but different in length. Discovery that this is not the case may help him to acquire conservation.

This knowledge about the effects on appearance of addition, subtraction and deformation could be discovered by the child. A child who judges amount on the basis of appearance alone may have to discover it if he is to invent the NAS criterion. This knowledge is not logically sufficient for development of the NAS criterion, but the child who has made these discoveries may be in a position to invent the NAS criterion once certain changes have taken place in his appearance-based judgments of amount. It is these which will be discussed in the next chapter.

CHAPTER 4

What is the Role of Conservation Acquisition of Changes in Perceptual Criteria?

Summary

Conservation acquisition involves a change in the range of application of perceptual criteria for judging amount; it is also accompanied by changes in the perceptual criteria themselves. This chapter includes a discussion of the perceptual criteria used by nonconservers, and the changes in these criteria as conservation is acquired. Possible roles of such changes in conservation acquisition are considered: they might be irrelevant, they might be responsible for the child's ceasing to make perceptually-based judgments of pre- compared with post-deformation amount, or they might be responsible for the development of the conservation concept itself.

4.1 Introduction

On occasions when a conserver judges in accordance with the criterion 'If nothing is added or subtracted, amount remains the same', a nonconserver seems to judge amount on the basis of appearance; he can be described as using a perceptual criterion. Of course, in many situations both conservers and nonconservers base their amount judgments on appearance, for example at the beginning of a standard conservation test when the equality of two amounts is being established.

It seems, though, that nonconservers can be considered to use perceptual criteria in a wider range of situations than conservers. If so, conservation acquisition involves a narrowing of the range of application of perceptual criteria. There also appear to be changes in the perceptual criteria themselves, that is, in the particular aspects of appearance upon which amount judgments are based. These changes might be mere accompaniments to conservation acquisition, or consequences of it, or they might play an important role in its development. In this chapter, the evidence relevant to each of these possibilities will be discussed.

First will be a consideration of how to describe the perceptual criterion or criteria the child is using, and then a discussion of developmental changes in these criteria, outlining the roles these changes might play in conservation acquisition.

4.2 Identification of the child's perceptual criteria

Suppose we present the child with a series of pairs of plasticine sausages of various widths and lengths, and ask him to judge the relative amounts within each pair. If he always judges that the longer sausage has more, whatever the widths, then we could describe him as using the perceptual criterion 'If longer, then more'. If however we simply present the child with a single pair of sausages, a long thin one and a short fat one, and he judges there to be more in the longer sausage, we cannot assume his judgment was based only on length. He may have considered the greater width of the fat sausage insufficient to compensate for the greater length of the thin one. We would have a similar difficulty in deciding on the child's criteria if, in a series of tasks, the child sometimes judged the longer sausage to be more, and sometimes the fatter one. Was the child simply centring on one or other dimension for each judgment, or did he consider both dimensions each time?

When the child's judgment alone does not give a clear indication of his perceptual criteria, his reasons might be taken into account. If the child says 'This one's more because it's longer and not very thin; the other one's shorter and not very fat' then we may be fairly sure he was taking into account both dimensions. If, on the other hand, he simply says 'This one's more because it's longer' we still cannot be sure he was ignoring the widths. On this evidence alone, then, we often cannot be sure how to describe the child's perceptual criteria.

If, however, we find developmental trends in the judgments and reasons given, trends which do not simply reflect the learning of new words, then we can be more confident in interpreting the responses given by particular children. Suppose when making a perceptual comparison of a long thin sausage with a short fat one (no rolling having been seen), nonconservers most commonly say 'There's more in the long one' whereas conservers are more likely to judge 'There's less in this one because it's thinner and not very long' or even 'There's the same in both, because one's long and thin, and the other one is short and fat'. We could describe such a developmental change by saying that nonconservers generally centre on length, whereas conservers more commonly take into account both dimensions. Evidence for developmental changes of this kind will be considered in the next section.

4.3 Perceptual criteria used by nonconservers and developmental changes in these

In discussing the perceptual criteria used to judge amount, those of very young children (three to four years old) will be ignored, since the interest here is in children who are getting close to conserving amount.

The evidence to be presented supports the view that conservers centre on a single aspect of appearance, usually the length of a plasticine sausage rather than the width, and usually the height of liquid rather than the width of the glass. Intermediate and full conservers are less prone to do this. The evidence comes from two kinds of source: judgments and reasons given within the conservation test itself, and those given in other similar situations.

(a) Responses in conservation tests

Three experiments will be summarized.

(i) Lovell and Ogilvie (1960) provide some evidence about the perceptual criteria used in conservation tests involving plasticine. On the basis of responses given to repeated questioning in a single task involving the rolling of one of two equal plasticine balls into a sausage, children were classified as nonconservers, transitional conservers and conservers. Of the fifty-four nonconservers, forty justified their judgments by referring to a single dimension, e.g. 'It's more because it's longer'. Thirty-four of the fifty-seven transitional children also gave such reasons. (The conservers were not included in this analysis.) These children's judgments and reasons suggest that they were using one-dimensional criteria. Other children may also have used such criteria; Lovell and Ogilvie do not report how many children spontaneously justified nonconserving judgments by referring to both length and width.

(ii) An experiment by the author (Experiment B) allows a similar analysis to be made. Children were given three conservation tasks, each involving the rolling of one of two equal short fat plasticine sausages into a long thin one. After making his amount judgment in a particular task, the child was given a countersuggestion: a nonconserving judgment was suggested to a child who had said the amounts were equal, and a conserving judgment was suggested to a child who had said the amounts were not equal. The amount question was then repeated to see if the child had accepted the suggested judgment. Hence each child made two amount judgments following the rolling in each task. On the basis of their judgments in the three tasks, children were classified as nonconservers (no conserving judgments), intermediate conservers (at least one conserving judgment) and conservers (all conserving judgments).

None of the twelve nonconservers referred to both dimensions when justifying their amount judgments, although eight of the twenty-eight intermediate conservers did so. All but one of the nonconservers gave the same judgment in all three tasks, usually 'More in the long one', whereas six of the intermediate conservers gave judgments of both 'More in the fat sausage' and 'More in the long one' in different tasks. These results support the view that nonconservers use one-dimensional perceptual criteria, and, moreover, tend to centre consistently on a particular dimension, usually length; in contrast intermediate conservers centre less on a single dimension both between judgments and within any one judgment.

Only four of the eighteen conservers gave perceptual reasons for their judgments, and all of the four also gave other reasons such as 'It was the same at first'. Three of the four referred to a single dimension, usually the width, and one referred to both length and width. Such a tiny number of reasons gives no real indication of the perceptual criteria used by conservers; further evidence on this point is given below (section 4.3b).

(iii) More direct evidence of the child's attention while making quantity judgments is provided by O'Bryan and Boersma (1971). They recorded eye movements of children as they made length, area and amount judgments in conservation tests. Children were classified as conservers, intermediate conservers and nonconservers. With improved conservation level, there was decreasing centration, as measured by the number of shifts of fixation during a given time, both within one object and between the standard and comparison objects. That is, increased shifting of gaze was associated with improved conservation performance.

(b) Responses in other situations

Again, three experiments will be given.

(i) In an experiment by the author (Experiment C), each of forty children aged from four to eight years was given three conservation tasks. These were preceded by three corresponding 'perceptual' tasks. Only two of the conservation and perceptual tasks are relevant here. Between the two kinds of task, the child was given others, but again these are not relevant here. In each of the two conservation and perceptual tasks in which we are interested, the child was asked to make an amount judgment of a long thin sausage compared with a short fat one which was in fact about equal in amount. The comparisons in the perceptual tasks were identical to those in the subsequent conservation tasks, except that there was no rolling, so the child could use only perceptual criteria. On the basis of their performance in all *three* conservation tasks, the children were classified into four groups.

Group 1: conservers—all three tasks completely correct, resisting the non-conservation countersuggestions.

Group 2: completely correct in one or two tasks.

Group 3: no task completely correct, but at least one conserving judgment given (e.g. acceptance of the conservation countersuggestion).

Group 4: nonconservers—all tasks wrong, resisting the conservation counter-suggestion on all occasions.

These four groups differed in their judgments in the perceptual tasks: the proportion of children who gave the same inequality judgment in both perceptual tasks decreased with improved conservation performance.

100% of the eight Group 4 children gave the same inequality judgment in both perceptual tasks, as did:

62·5% of the eight Group 3 children,

56% of the sixteen Group 2 children, and

37·5% of the eight Group 1 children.

Using an S-test (Ferguson, 1965) this trend was found to be significant at the 0·02 level (two-tail test).

These results suggest that with improved conservation performance children become less likely to centre on the same dimension over a series of perceptual judgments. Children who gave the same inequality judgment in both perceptual tasks most commonly judged there was more in the longer sausage; this was particularly true of the children in Groups 3 and 4. In all, twenty children judged 'More in the longer one' in both perceptual tasks, compared with five who both times judged 'More in the fatter one'. Four of these five were in Groups 1 and 2.

Equality amount judgments, which presumably were made on the basis of co-ordination of dimensions, became more common at higher conservation level, although there was not a clear trend.

0% of the Group 4 children gave equality judgments in the perceptual tasks,
12·5% of the Group 3 children did so, as did
32% of the Group 2 children, and
25% of the Group 1 children.

These results suggest that at least some intermediate and full conservers coordinate dimensions when making perceptual judgments of amount, but from this experiment we cannot tell whether *all* of them accepted that a long thin sausage could look the same amount as a short fat one.

(ii) Miller (1973) studied children's direction of attention in conservation test settings in which they were not explicitly asked to make amount judgments. The subjects were kindergarten and third-grade children who were classified into conservers and nonconservers on the basis of their performance in a test of liquid amount conservation. Conservers were those who gave correct judgments in all the four tasks, and gave at least one acceptable reason. The children were divided into three groups: kindergarten nonconservers (mean age six years), kindergarten conservers (mean age six years one month) and third-grade conservers (mean age nine years).

In the attention tasks, the child was presented with three beakers of liquid and he was asked to select two that were the same in some way. The task was such that he could base his selection on the width of the beaker, the height of the liquid, or the quantity of liquid. For example, on one task, the child was shown three identical beakers, all filled to the same level with 'Kool-aid'. The contents of these beakers were then poured into three other beakers, one of which already had some liquid in it. Hence only a pair of this second set of beakers had the same quantity of liquid. In addition, a second pair from the three beakers were the same width, and the third pair contained liquid to the same level.

The child was asked 'Which two glasses of Kool-aid are the same?' and to give a reason. He was then asked to choose another pair that were the same in some way. Finally, the experimenter identified each of the three pairs, asking the child in which way they were the same and in which ways they were different. There were two tasks like this, and two in which the child was simply asked to choose a pair that were the same, without being given the opportunity to identify further similarities and differences. The test of conservation followed the attention tasks, so that the child would not be 'set' towards amount in the attention tasks.

The results were analysed in terms of differences between the three groups of children. In their first choice of a similarity, about seventy per cent of the nonconservers chose height of liquid in all the tasks, and about eight per cent always chose the width of the beaker. None of the nonconservers selected amount every time, although a few of them did select it at least once. Since the group of nonconservers probably included children who gave conserving judgments in one, two or three of the conservation tasks, their choosing amount in the attention task is not surprising. The kindergarten conservers' choices were largely similar to those of the nonconservers; these two groups did not differ significantly in the extent to which they chose height. In contrast, forty-eight per cent of the older conservers chose amount in all four tasks.

When asked to choose another pair of beakers that were the same in some way, most of those in the kindergarten groups could not do so. Only three of the twenty-one kindergarten conservers chose amount. A difference between the two kindergarten groups appeared, however, when the children were asked directly about each pair of beakers; the nonconservers gave significantly more height than width responses, but both conserving groups gave as many height as width responses. Presumably the conservers selected both height and width at this stage in the procedure. Selection of amount was still rare among the nonconservers: it was chosen only twice out of a possible two hundred and sixteen times. Amount responses were more common among the conservers—out of a maximum possible of six, the younger conservers gave a mean of 0·76, and the older conservers gave a mean of 3·96. Nevertheless, many of the kindergarten conservers who had selected both height and width failed to select amount.

At first sight, the results of Miller's experiment do not really support the view that conservers are less likely than nonconservers to centre on a single dimension, since a difference in this respect between the young conservers and the nonconservers appeared only in the final stages of questioning. The results may, however, be better interpreted move appropriately in a slightly different way.

In the attention tasks, children who used the concept of conservation to select equal amounts, i.e. the older conservers, also avoided centration on a single dimension. In their first choice of a similarity, only about nine per cent of the older conservers always chose height, and thirteen per cent always chose width. In contrast, children who generally failed to use the concept of conservation in the attention task, i.e. the nonconservers and the young conservers, did tend to centre on a single dimension. The young conservers, however, were able to select both height and width when questioned persistently, even though they often still failed to select amount. These results suggest that in any particular task, use of the conservation concept may be accompanied by avoidance of centration on a single dimension, while a decrease in such centration may be developmentally prior to use of the conservation concept.

(iii) More direct evidence of an association between decentration and conservation acquisition is provided by Lumsden and Kling (1969). Their study followed one by Lumsden and Poteat (1968), who found that when making perceptual judgments of area of rectangles ('Which is bigger?'), five- to six-years-olds tended to make their judgments on the basis of the vertical dimension only, ignoring the horizontal. The children judged the rectangle with the greatest vertical extent to be bigger, even when the comparison rectangle was four times as great in area. Lumsden and Kling trained children to use a multidimensional concept of 'bigger', and this apparently improved their performance in a test of size conservation.

The subjects were aged between five and a half and seven and a half years. The twenty children in the experimental group were presented with a series of tasks, in each of which they had to select the bigger block from a pair of blocks. The bigger block was sometimes the taller one, and sometimes the shorter. Correct answers were rewarded with a penny, and incorrect ones were punished with loss of a penny. After being trained to criterion on such tasks, pairs of blocks equal in volume were introduced, in which one block was both taller and thinner than the other; the child was taught to say that such blocks were the same size. When a child failed to give an equality judgment, the dimensions were pointed out to him. During this time, the control group were presented with objects of different shape, and were asked to judge whether a comparison object was the same or different in shape from the standard.

Both groups were then given a single size conservation task, in which one of two identical cubes of clay was deformed into a taller, thinner block. In order to be classified as a conserver, the child was required not only to give an equality size judgment, but also to give a reason other than 'It's taller but thinner', i.e. he had to give a reason such as 'You didn't add any on or take any away'. Among children aged five and a half to six and a half, there was no difference in conservation performance between the experimental and the control groups, but in the six and a half to seven and a half age group, the experimental group performed significantly better.

Despite the inadequacies of this experiment, there was no pre-testing of the children, and there was only a single task in the post-test, the results provide weak evidence that attention to more than one dimension is relevant in some way to the acquisition of conservation.

(c) Summary and conclusions

The experiments reported in this section found that:

(i) Over a series of tasks, each involving a comparison between a long thin sausage and a short fat one, nonconservers generally gave the same inequality judgment in each, suggesting that they centred on one particular dimension. In nearly all cases, the judgment was 'More in the longer sausage'. In contrast, intermediate and full conservers were less likely to give the same inequality judgment each time, suggesting that they centred less on a single dimension.

(ii) In any one task, the reasons given by nonconservers usually referred to only a single dimension; intermediate conservers sometimes referred to two dimensions when justifying a nonconserving judgment.

(iii) When comparing a long thin sausage with a short fat one in a perceptual task, equality amount judgments appeared only among intermediate and full conservers. Presumably they were based on a coordination of dimensions. More evidence concerning such equality amount judgments is given in section 4.5.

(iv) Training children to attend to both height and width of blocks when judging size seemed in some cases to improve their performance in a test of conservation of size.

(v) Recordings of eye movements of children making amount judgments in tests of conservation showed that improved conservation performance was accompanied by increased shifting of gaze.

(vi) When asked to identify similarities and differences between glasses of liquid, those who used the concept of conservation to select equal amounts were much more likely than those who did not to attend to both height and width rather than to just one of these.

From these results, it seems that nonconservers can be described as using a single one-dimensional perceptual criterion, and intermediate and full conservers are more likely to use more than one such criterion or even a two-dimensional criterion. It also seems that children who attend to only one dimension are much more likely to select length rather than width in the case of plasticine sausages, and to select height rather than width in the case of liquid in glasses. Why should this be? When plasticine is rolled, the change in length is much greater than the change in width; length may therefore be a more salient cue for the child. In the case of liquid, the child might more commonly see changes of height than changes of width; it is the level that changes when liquid is added or subtracted from a glass. A point made by Berko and Brown (1960) may also be relevant here: the child may be taught the meaning of quantity words when liquid is in identical glasses, or only in one glass. Under these circumstances, only liquid level changes; the width is irrelevant. The child may then make an inappropriate generalization to other situations in which there are width differences. Whatever the reasons for the child's selection of height or length rather than width, they are not really relevant here; what is of interest is that the nonconserver focuses on one dimension only, and that intermediate and full conservers do this far less.

Are these changes in perceptual criteria mere accompaniments to conservation acquisition, or consequences of it, or do they play a role in the development of the concept of conservation? If changes in perceptual criteria are irrelevant to conservation acquisition (i.e. if they are accompaniments to or consequences of it), then this implies that a child *could* change directly from using a one-dimensional perceptual criterion to using the NAS criterion. From judging 'There's more because it's longer' he could switch to judging 'It's the same because you didn't add any on or take any off'.

If this is the case, then it is necessary to explain why the child abandons what is to him a perfectly satisfactory basis for amount judgments: the length of the sausage. Why should he decide that a quite different basis is preferable? This problem is avoided if it is assumed that developments take place within the child's perceptual criteria themselves, developments which lead him to grow dissatisfied with appearance-based judgments of pre- compared with post-deformation amount. Unless we can account for the child's abandonment of perceptual criteria for comparing pre- with post-deformation amount, we cannot explain conservation acquisition. The possibility that changes in the perceptual criteria themselves are responsible seems well worth considering. Of course these changes required explanation. Perhaps an account in terms of increasing information-processing capacity would be appropriate; that is, perhaps the changes are symptoms of a very general cognitive development. This is supported by the fact that the results of Miller's attention test are consistent with the results of experiments in which the child was explicitly asked to judge amount. This question will not be considered further here.

That changes in perceptual judgments are not necessary for conservation acquisition seems implicit in Bruner's (1966c) account. Bruner's child can conserve by ignoring the post-deformation appearance, although having acquired the concept of conservation he may justify the appearance by saying 'The sausage is longer but thinner than the ball'. Bruner's account implies that the child does not *necessarily* justify the appearance in this way if he is to conserve in the standard Piagetian test. Sonstroem (1966), one of Bruner's coworkers, suggests that any description of the appearance could be sufficient as long as it forces the child to think of the clay in many different ways.

The assumption that changes in perceptual criteria are not necessary for conservation acquisition seems also to be implicit in Smedslund's theory: Smedslund (1961a) writes of the child's becoming increasingly resistant to perceptual disturbance. It seems that the problem for Smedslund's child is to ignore the appearance and to concentrate instead on the fact that nothing was added or subtracted.

In the rest of this chapter, the view will be presented that changes in perceptual criteria do play a role in the acquisition of conservation, and possible roles will be outlined.

4.4 Awareness of contradictory judgments

(a) Awareness of contradictory judgments of one object's amount

As he centres less on one aspect of the display, the child may become aware that contradictory perceptual judgments are possible. For example, in the case of a ball of plasticine rolled into a sausage, the child could judge 'More in the sausage because it's longer' or 'More in the ball because it was fatter'. Similar contradictory judgments could occur in many cases of deformation: when liquid is poured into a narrower container, the level rises higher; when plasticine is broken into several small pieces, each is smaller than the original piece. In the case of some deformations, though, it is difficult to specify such dimensions, for example, when a sausage is changed into a ring. In such a case, to describe the child's judgment in terms of particular perceptual criteria may be inappropriate; the child may simply make a global judgment. However, the child could still become unsure of his perceptual judgment of pre- compared with post-deformation amount as a result of considering the comparison more carefully. He would then be in a position similar to that arising from awareness of contradictory judgments based on one-dimensional criteria.

In cases in which dimensions can be specified, such as the ball of plasticine rolled into a sausage, it is possible that the child ceases to make perceptually based judgments of pre- compared with post-deformation amount°because he becomes aware of contradictory perceptual judgments. Having abandoned his perceptual criteria, the child is then free to use some other basis to judge amount. He may already have available the criterion 'If nothing is added or subtracted, amount remains the same'. If so, he could now begin to use it.

In Chapter 6, predictions will be derived from this suggested route to conservation acquisition, and experiments to test the predictions will be described in Chapters 7–10.

(b) Bryant's theory of conservation acquisition

Bryant (1972) states that the problem for the child is to learn which quantity cues are reliable (e.g. one-to-one correspondence in the case of number) and which are unreliable (e.g. length of row in the case of number). Although Bryant applies his theory to number conservation in particular, it can also be applied to conservation of amount.

Suppose the child is presented with two objects, A and B, then B is deformed to B'. Bryant argues that the child knows that B = B' (conservation), but he makes contradictory judgments of A compared with B', and A compared with B. Before deformation, he may judge that A = B, while after deformation, judge that A ≠ B'. He has no basis for choosing between these judgments, and selects the more recent, hence making a nonconserving judgment. This theory predicts that if the child did not make a confident perceptual judgment of A compared with B', then there would be no conflict, and he would give a conserving judgment.

Bryant tested this prediction for number judgments. He constructed three kinds of display, each consisting of a pair of rows of counters, and the child had to choose which row had more. In the first kind of display (A), the children seemed to use one-to-one correspondence, and they consistently gave correct judgments. In the second kind (B), children apparently used a length cue, and consistently gave incorrect judgments. In the third kind of display (C), children responded at about chance level. Although this could have been due to within-child consistency but between-child inconsistency, it appears from the data given that each child did change his judgment over trials, and hence it is possible, as Bryant assumes, that children were not confident in their number judgments of the C displays.

Bryant's theory predicts that if the pre-deformation display were of the A or the B type, and the post-deformation display of the C type, young children should demonstrate their possession of conservation by repeating the A or the B judgment after the deformation, since they could make no confident contradictory post-deformation judgment.

Bryant's results supported the prediction. When the C displays were shown on their own, children responded at chance level; if A was deformed to C, they responded above chance; and if B was deformed to C, they responded below chance. On the other hand, if A was deformed to B, or B to A, so that the children made confident and contradictory judgments of pre- and post-deformation number, they judged as they did when B or A (respectively) were presented alone—they seemed to select the more recent of their confident judgments.

But are these results surprising? At best they show that if the child is unsure of his perceptually based judgment of the post-deformation quantity, he repeats his pre-deformation judgment. This would be quite consistent with Piaget's statements about the young child's expectancy of conservation (see Chapter 2, section 2.2f). Yet Bryant assumes his results provide evidence against Piaget's views on conservation.

A strange aspect of Bryant's results, moreover, is that there was no significant improvement in performance with age. The children were aged from three to six years, and since number conservation is normally acquired at about six years, better performance in the A–B tasks would be expected among the older children.

Bryant provides the results of a conservation training experiment as further support for his theory. He argues that if children were shown which of their number criteria were unreliable, they would no longer make inconsistent judgments of pre- and post-deformation number, and hence would conserve. He attempted to show children that the length criterion was an unreliable one for number judgments: he performed repeated deformations of pairs of rows and after each deformation the child judged which row had more. The deformations were such that a child using the length criterion would change his judgment after each deformation; he would make inconsistent judgments of number. Bryant also showed the children that one-to-one correspondence was reliable, by presenting repeated deformations which the child would judge on that basis, and which would lead to consistent judgments over deformations. The children were given pre- and post-tests using $A-B$ and $B-A$ deformations. The experimental group, trained in the way just described, were compared with a control group who experienced only deformations which led to consistent judgments, although arrays were shown which were expected to be judged on the basis of length as well as one-to-one correspondence.

The experimental group performed significantly better than the controls in the post-test, but only in the $A-B$ trials. This is as expected, since the children already performed about chance in the $B-A$ trials in the pre-test, simply because they made correct perceptually based judgments of the A displays. Hence the results of the training experiment support Bryant's theory.

There are problems both with Bryant's theory and with his evidence. His criterion for conservation is weak and idiosyncratic, a response indicating that the child's pre-deformation judgment influenced his post-deformation judgment is considered sufficient evidence of conservation.

A major difficulty is that the theory refers to equivalence rather than to identity tests of conservation, although Bryant does not make this explicit. If only one object were used (as in an identity test of conservation) and the child had to judge after deformation 'Is there as much now as there was at first?' then from Bryant's point of view, the child should make no contradictory amount judgments, and all children should conserve. According to Bryant, a problem arises only when a comparison object is used, as in an equivalence test of conservation. Yet the evidence suggests that although identity tests of conservation may be a little easier than equivalence tests, children do indeed fail to conserve in identity tests. For example, Hooper (1969) found that only six out of twelve six-year-old children conserved in his identity tests. Hence Bryant's theory appears not to provide a sufficient explanation of conservation acquisition.

(c) Summary and conclusions

Bryant's theory does not provide a sufficient explanation of conservation acquisition, since it applies only to judgments in an equivalence test of conservation and implies that the child has no difficulty with identity tests.

It is quite possible, however, that awareness of contradictory judgments of one object before and after deformation is necessary for conservation acquisition. In the case of a ball of plasticine rolled into a sausage, the child could judge there was more in the ball because it was fatter, or more in the sausage because it is longer. Awareness of these contradictory judgments could lead the child to abandon perceptual criteria for judgments of pre- compared with post-deformation amount, and to use instead an already developed NAS criterion; the development of the NAS criterion is not explained. Evidence relevant to this view will be described in Chapters 7–10.

Awareness of contradictory perceptual judgments of pre- compared with post-deformation amount may, however, be necessary for the development of the NAS criterion. Piaget's view of how this could happen is discussed in the next section.

4.5 Compensation

(a) Piaget's theory and his evidence

Piaget sees awareness of contradictory perceptual judgments as leading not only to the child's ceasing to make perceptually based judgments of pre- compared with post-deformation amount, but also to the development of the conservation concept. For Piaget, an essential component of the concept of conservation is the child's interpretation of the increase in one dimension during deformation as exactly compensated by the decrease in the other dimension. The dimensions may be length and width in the case of a plasticine sausage rolled longer, or size and number of small pieces into which a large ball has been broken, or length of row and density of elements in a number conservation task. Piaget elaborates this idea for the case of amount conservation with clay or plasticine: a ball is rolled into a sausage.

Piaget (1957) describes a sequence of 'strategies', or criteria, the child is supposed to use at various stages in conservation acquisition. At first, he centres on one dimension (e.g. length), but as he develops he begins to change his centration, judging sometimes on the basis of length and sometimes on the basis of width. He begins to switch more easily, first of all in successive judgments, but eventually while making a single judgment he becomes aware of both the length increase and the width decrease. Finally, he becomes capable of handling both dimensions at once, and he concludes that the changes are compensatory. Compensation, along with the operations of identity and reversibility, characterizes the conserver. More details of Piaget's sequence of strategies are given in Chapter 5.

Evidence for use of the early strategies, centration on a single dimension followed by an increasing tendency to take into account the second dimension, was given in section 4.3. Oscillation between dimensions may be illustrated by an example from 'The Child's Conception of Number' (Piaget, 1952; French edition, 1941). The child was given two containers, equal in height but one wider than the other. The wider glass contained liquid, and the child was asked to pour liquid into the narrower glass so that both glasses contained same amount to drink. It is reported that the nonconservers poured liquid to the same level, ignoring the width difference, but intermediate conservers showed evidence of alternating attention to height and width. For example Lac, aged five and a half, first filled his glass to a higher level, but judged he had more, so he poured some out until the levels were equal. Then he judged that the wider glass had more, and he added some to his narrow glass, judged that he had more, and so on (p. 15). Unfortunately there is no numerical data, so we cannot tell how common such responses were among intermediate conservers. A similar test was used to investigate compensation; this is described below.

Piaget argues that at the intermediate stages of conservation acquisition, the child is unable to coordinate the dimensions completely; but even if he could, this would not be sufficient for the child to conclude that the amount remained the same:

> 'It is obvious, however, that even if the operation of logical multiplication of relations were carried through by the child of this stage (intermediate) it would not suffice for the construction of conservation of the whole quantity unless the height and width were simply permutated. A column of liquid whose height increases and whose width diminishes with respect to another column may be greater, equal or less in volume than the other. . . . there must be partition of some kind to supplement the co-ordination.' (Reproduced with permission from J. Piaget, *The Child's Conception of Number*, Routledge and Kegan Paul, London; New York: Humanities Press Inc., 1952, p. 16)

> 'In a word, logical multiplication of relationships is the necessary intermediary between gross, uni-dimensional quantity and extensive quantification . . .' (Piaget, *op. cit.,* p. 20)

> 'Our contention is that at a given moment the child grasps that the differences compensate one another, and this is the beginning of extensive quantification, because then two heterogeneous qualitative relationships (increase in level and decrease in width) are seen to be equal, though still preserving their value of asymmetrical difference.' (Piaget, *ibid.,* p. 22–23)

('Extensive quantification' has developed when the child has the concept of conservation of quantity: quantity is 'structurized as a sum susceptible of division into units' (p. 23) and is 'no longer viewed as a qualitative totality whose value changes with each change of shape' (p. 23).) Piaget's view seems to be that when the child becomes capable of coordinating dimensions, he also concludes that the changes in dimensions are compensatory, i.e. he accepts the possibility that 'longer × thinner = the same amount' (Piaget, 1968a, p. 18).

Piaget (1957) describes how the child comes to make such a compensation interpretation. Such an interpretation does not involve simply attending to the length increase and the width decrease as rolling takes place, since a child might understand that rolling modifies both the length and the width, without judging that the two changes exactly balance each other. Fully operational compensation involves conceiving of each tiny increase in length during rolling as having an associated tiny decrease in width. Doing this, according to Piaget, is equivalent to reasoning about the rolling itself, rather than about a series of static length and width values:

> '. . . l'enfant considère dorénavant, en plus des caractères A et B (i.e. the length and the width), les actions mêmes transformant un couple $A_n B_n$ en un autre $A_{n+1} B_{n+1}$.' (Piaget, 1957, p. 69)

This account suggests that although Piaget defines compensation as 'longer × thinner = the same amount', he thinks that a compensation interpretation is made only if the child believes that *at each point* in the rolling, an increase in length is balanced by a decrease in width.

In 'Mental Imagery in the Child', Piaget and Inhelder (1971, French edition, 1966) provide evidence to support their view of the relationship between compensation and conservation, i.e. that compensation is a psychological component of the conservation concept. Two experiments on compensation and related abilities are described, one involving liquid and the other clay.

(i) Using liquid, there were four tests, only three of which are relevant here.
1. The child was asked to predict the level of liquid to be poured into a glass of different width (a test of covariation).
2. The child was asked to pour liquid into a glass until it contained the same amount as that in a given glass of different width (a test of compensation).
3. The child was given a standard test of conservation of amount.

Sets of four glasses were used throughout: two identical ones (a standard and a comparison), a wider one and a narrower one. Both the wider one and the narrower one were used in each test.

Test 1 assessed knowledge of 'covariation', i.e. knowledge of a physical law such as 'Liquid goes higher in thinner glasses'. Such a law can easily be discovered by the child. Test 1 has mistakenly been used as a test of compensation by non-Piagetians, as we shall see in section 4.5d. In order to pass the test of compensation, Test 3, the child had to know that for quantities to be equal, the level must be higher in a thinner glass and lower in a wider glass. The most common error was to pour liquid until it reached the same level in both glasses.

Although many of the data are not given, Piaget and Inhelder state that the sixty-eight children, who were aged from four to eight years, fell into three categories.
I. Predict equal levels in Test 1; construct equal levels in Test 2; fail to conserve in Test 3.
II. Predict correct levels; construct equal levels; fail to conserve.
III. Predict correct levels; construct correct levels; conserve.

That is, compensation and conservation were acquired together, but covariation could be acquired much earlier than both of them. Piaget and Inhelder conclude that '. . . the correct image of the liquid level does not itself incorporate a compensation scheme . . . such a scheme depends on the operations' (p. 266).

In a second experiment, a greater variety of wide and narrow glasses were used, but a smaller sample of children, only twenty-three of them, aged five years to seven years, five months. The results of the first experiment were replicated; only one child failed compensation but passed conservation, and he had acquired conservation during the experiment. None passed compensation but failed conservation. There was no difference in difficulty between the wide and the narrow glasses. There are hints, however, that introducing glasses of different heights as well as widths produced less clear-cut results in the test of covariation.

(ii) In the tests with clay the procedure was more complicated. Again, not all the tests are relevant here. The child was told that a ball of clay was to be deformed into a sausage, a pancake, or broken into pieces.

1. He was asked to anticipate the shape and size, by means of a verbal description, a drawing, and by selecting from a set of prepared drawings.
2. He was asked to predict whether the amount would be the same after the deformation.
3. After a deformation had been performed, he was asked to judge the amount (a test of conservation).

In this experiment, Test 1 seems to be considered a test of compensation, as we shall see. The subjects were a hundred and thirty-two children aged between five and eight years.

Tests 2 and 3 were equal in difficulty: only one per cent of the subjects failed Test 2 but passed Test 3, while none passed 2 but failed 3. Therefore, we can consider Test 2 to be a test of conservation. This is useful, because the relationship between Tests 1 and 3 is not given, but that between Tests 1 and 2 is given.

Two different criteria of success were used in Test 1: a weak one, according to which the child passed if he showed awareness of both dimensions but only successively, in different tasks; and a strong one, according to which the child passed only if he showed attention to both dimensions in all three tasks, e.g. if he indicated that the sausage would be longer and thinner than the ball, and that each of the pieces into which the ball was to be broken would be smaller than the ball itself, and so on.

When the weak criterion was used, anticipation of shape (Test 1) was easier than conservation (Test 2):

35·2% of the subjects passed 1 but failed 2, while
9·9% of them passed 2 but failed 1.

When the strong criterion of success was used, however, anticipation of shape was slightly more difficult than conservation:

8·1% of the subjects passed 1 but failed 2, while
21·6% of them passed 2 but failed 1.

From these results, Piaget and Inhelder conclude that the pre-operational child has only an 'imprecise and vague' (p. 274) knowledge of the changes in shape which occur when clay is deformed, but later, 'within a framework for which they themselves are not actually responsible, they come to signify compensation' (p. 276). Again, compensation is considered to be acquired only with operational thinking.

The experiments using liquid and using clay were not quite comparable, since there was no clay equivalent of the liquid amount construction test. Piaget and Inhelder's interpretations suggest that it was assumed that the anticipation of shape test using clay was assessing the same ability as was the liquid amount construction test, i.e. compensation. Yet the anticipation of shape test seems to be equivalent to the level prediction test—in both, the child is asked to predict the appearance of the material after deformation. It appears that Piaget and Inhelder assume that level prediction does not require simultaneous handling of dimensions, whereas shape anticipation does.

From his interpretations of these experiments, it appears quite strongly that

Piaget's view is that conservation and compensation develop together. In other writings, however, it seems that compensation is allowed to precede conservation. In 'The Child's Conception of Number' (1952; French edition, 1941), Piaget states that the amount construction test may be slightly easier than conservation. Similarly, Piaget (1957) writes of intermediate conservers achieving a compensation interpretation of the changes in dimensions, resulting in '. . . une conservation de fait (mais non nécessaire) pour certains cas . . .' (p. 52). Taking these statements into account, it is not quite clear precisely how compensation and conservation are related in Piaget's theory. It seems, though, that if the child *does* make a compensation interpretation just on the basis of appearance before he develops fully operational compensation, then this is a brief, unstable phase, and is certainly not a major stage on the route to conservation acquisition. This point is raised again in section 4.6, where a modification of Piaget's theory is suggested.

(b) The amount construction test used by other experimenters

Other experimenters have used Piaget's amount construction test, and have compared performance in that with performance in conservation tests. Three experiments will be described.

(i) Results quite contradictory to Piaget's were obtained by Cohen (1967). Children aged between four years, two months and five years, nine months were divided into two groups of ten. Members of one group were given three amount construction tests: the child had to pour sweets into a wider glass so that there would be the same number as in a given standard glass; he had to do the same with liquid; and he had to share differently shaped pieces of plasticine into two lots of equal amount. The other group were given three conventional conservation tests using the same materials.

Children were classified as passing or failing each test. To pass the compensation test with liquid or sweets, the child had to pour them to a lower level in the wider glass. In the case of the plasticine, he had to share the pieces as if he assumed that pieces of different shape (a circle and a square) were equal in amount. In the conservation tests, the child passed if he gave a conserving judgment.

There were many more passes in the compensation tests than in the conservation tests: twenty-three, compared with eight. Cohen does not relate her results to Piaget's theory of the relationship between compensation and conservation, but assumes implicitly that the compensation tests were themselves tests of conservation. She suggests that the difference in difficulty might be due to differences in the wording used, words like 'More' and 'Bigger' were replaced in the instructions of the compensation test by 'Fair' and 'Share'. She also points out that in the compensation tasks the children participated and did not simply give verbal judgments. Such procedural variations could have had some effect, but the interesting difference between the two kinds of test is that they assess logically distinct abilities.

Cohen's finding that tests of compensation were much easier than tests of conservation has not been replicated by other experimenters.

(ii) Gelman and Weinberg (1972) investigated the relationship between compensation and conservation, using liquid. Compensation was assessed in two ways: by pouring, as in Piaget's amount construction test (both wider and narrower glasses were used), and by an 'explanation' test. In this, the child was presented with equal quantities of liquid in glasses of different width, and he was told 'We both have the same to drink. Do you think you know why?' Each child was given two compensation tasks of each kind, and two conservation tasks: liquid was poured into a wider glass and into a narrower one.

Gelman and Weinberg compared the relationship between compensation and conservation using various criteria for compensation. Their subjects were eighty children aged from six and a half years to eleven years, nine months.

Of the fifty-nine children who gave a conserving judgment and an adequate reason in at least one of the two conservation tasks, fifty-five showed some sign of compensating by the weakest criterion—they passed at least one of the compensation tasks, or justified a conserving judgment by saying something like 'One is taller and thinner than the other'. On the basis of this weak criterion, four children compensated but failed to give at least one conserving judgment with a reason. Forty-nine of the fifty-nine conservers took the widths of the containers into account in the 'pouring' compensation test, and thirty-two referred to both dimensions in the 'explanation' test. In contrast, three children who failed to conserve passed the 'pouring' compensation test, and one child who failed to conserve passed the 'explanation' compensation test.

These results show that if the weakest criterion for compensation is used, then compensation and conservation were about equal in difficulty; if stronger criteria for compensation are used, then a proportion of children who conserve failed to compensate. Compensation in the absence of conservation was rather rare, whichever criterion for compensation is used. Gelman and Weinberg conclude rather tentatively that their results are inconsistent with Piaget's theory that compensation is necessary for conservation.

(iii) Engelmann (1967) carried out an amount construction test using liquid. This was similar to Piaget's, except that cardboard models were used, with adjustable 'liquid' levels. Out of thirty children, there were five who passed this test but failed a real liquid conservation test, compared with one child who conserved but failed the amount construction test. Only one child passed both, and twenty-three failed both. The numbers of children who passed each test are too small for any firm conclusions to be drawn, but it seems that the amount construction test was a little easier than the conservation test.

There is, then, no consensus as to how amount construction tests and conservation tests compared in difficulty. The comparison may not, however, be a particularly useful one. In conservation tests, the child performs a recognition task; it may be inappropriate to use a construction task to see whether compensation is acquired simultaneously with conservation. One would expect a test of construction to be more difficult than a test of recognition even if both were assessing the same ability. In experiments carried out by the author and reported in Chapters 9 and 10 a recognition test of compensation was used.

(c) Other interpretations of Piaget's compensation

Non-Piagetians have used tests other than amount construction to assess Piaget's compensation, and have used their results to draw conclusions about the validity of Piaget's view of the relationship between conservation and compensation. Whether or not these experimenters have misinterpreted Piaget's compensation is not of major interest; it is, however, valuable to specify the various tasks used and to see how performance in each is related to performance in conservation tests. By doing this we might clarify the relationship between conservation and other abilities and so move towards an understanding of how conservation is acquired. We can distinguish three tasks the child might be asked to perform.

(i) We could ask him to predict the effects of deformation on appearance in a general way, e.g. to predict whether the level of liquid will rise, fall or stay the same when liquid is poured into a narrower glass, or to predict the shape of a ball of plasticine after it has been rolled.

(ii) We could ask him to predict the effects of deformation on appearance in a more precise way, e.g. we could give him a set of glasses, some equal in height but not in width, and others equal in width but not in height; we could show him that one of these glasses exactly fills a given standard glass; we could then ask him to predict whether each of the others will overfill, exactly fill, or underfill the standard glass.

(iii) We could ask him to construct entities which could be equal in amount although different in shape, e.g. to pour liquid into a thin glass until it contains the same amount as that in a given wider glass, or to chop off from a length of thin plasticine an amount equal to that in a given short fat sausage.

In each of these tasks, a child who gives a correct response may be described as using a certain rule.

(i) 'Liquid goes higher in thinner glasses'; 'Rolling plasticine makes it longer and thinner'.

(ii) This requires greater understanding of the constraints between height and width changes, for example '... given that nothing has been added or subtracted, then a change in one dimension must be accompanied by one and only one change in another dimension.' (Halford, 1970a, p. 306)

(iii) 'If A is thinner than B, then to be the same amount, A must be longer/higher.'

As shown in section 4.5a, Piaget assumes that Task (iii) assesses compensation when liquid is used, but Task (i) does when clay is used. Task (i) using liquid is assumed by Piaget to require only understanding of covariation. Task (iii) seems most like a concrete realization of Piaget's definition of compensation: 'Longer × thinner = the same amount': only Task (iii) requires the child to construct equal amounts. It seems that anticipation of shape (Task (i)) when clay is deformed is assumed to require handling of both dimensions at once. According to Piaget's theory, handling of both dimensions at once only occurs when the child also makes a compensation interpretation of the changes in dimensions.

Non-Piagetians have on occasion assumed that level prediction (Task (i)) assessed Piaget's compensation. For example, Larsen and Flavell (1970), on finding that level prediction was under some conditions easier than amount construction (Task (iii)), conclude that '... the suggestion that the terms used to present a cognitive task are a factor in performance on the task is supported ...' (p. 973). That is, they assume that both tasks assessed compensation, just asking for it in different words. Curcio *et al.* (1972) and Bruner (1966c) both assume that level prediction tasks assess Piaget's compensation.

Task (ii) has been used by Halford (1968, 1969, 1970b, 1971) to investigate compensation, which he defines as

'... where quantities are equal, then for each value of one dimension there must be one and only one value of the other dimension; that is, for equal quantities, the dimensions are "uniquely paired".' (Halford, 1970a, p. 310)

Halford fails to distinguish between two abilities: full recognition of the constraints between height and width changes when liquid is transferred between containers; and interpretation of the changes in height and width as balancing each other and therefore resulting in no change in quantity. These are logically distinct; psychologically, they may be acquired together, but this cannot be assumed.

In Chapter 3, it was suggested that Halford's constraint system might be more closely related to Piaget's reversibility than to compensation. The term 'the uniqueness of reversibility' was used to refer to one aspect of Halford's constraint system—the fact that when nothing has been added or subtracted, then a particular change in one dimension must be accompanied by one particular change in another dimension. In the case of plasticine sausages, for example, a given short fat sausage B can be rolled to look like only one of a set of equality thin sausages of different length, B', $B'+$, $B'++$ ... B cannot be rolled to look like both B' and $B'+$.

There is a logical relationship between the uniqueness of reversibility and Piaget's compensation as this was interpreted in section 4.5a. If the child assumes that for each tiny increase in length as B is rolled, there is a tiny decrease in width (compensation), then he must also assume that B cannot be rolled to look like both B' and $B'+$ (uniqueness of reversibility). That is, we could not say the child was making a compensation interpretation of the deformation, without also implying that he understands the uniqueness of reversibility. It is not necessarily the case, however, that the two develop simultaneously. Logically, a child could understand the uniqueness of reversibility without making a compensation interpretation. It could be, though, that in psychological development, knowledge of the uniqueness of reversibility does not occur without compensation.

Having identified each of these interpretations of compensation, those assessed by Tasks (i), (ii) and (iii), we can ask how each is related to conservation.

(i) It is well established that covariation (assessed by a level prediction task) precedes conservation (e.g. Bruner, 1966c; Curcio *et al.*, 1972; Piaget and Inhelder, 1971; French edition, 1966), although Craig, Love and Olim (1973), provide results which suggest that if the comparison container is both higher and narrrower than the standard, a child may appear to be using the rule 'Liquid goes higher in thinner glasses' when in fact he is simply assuming that the liquid will fill both glasses just as full. If, for example, the standard is half full, the child may assume that the comparison, whether wider or narrower, will also be half filled. There is also some suggestion in Piaget and Inhelder (1971; French edition, 1966) that when glasses of different heights were used, the results were less clear-cut than when all the glasses were the same height. Nevertheless, it seems that when glasses are the same height, many nonconservers do demonstrate knowledge of the physical laws 'Liquid goes higher in thinner glasses' and 'Liquid goes lower in wider glasses'.

Piaget and Inhelder (1971; French edition, 1966) suggest that knowledge of covariation may not even be necessary for conservation, although they make contradictory statements on this (p. 264 and p. 266) and their evidence is scanty: they found some children who moved directly from failing level prediction, conservation and amount construction tests with liquid to passing all three, without going through an intermediate stage of passing only the level prediction test. Curcio et al. (1972) found that nonconservers who failed level prediction tasks were less likely to benefit from conservation training than children of the same age who could predict levels correctly. This suggests that level prediction may be relevant in some way to conservation acquisition, although the link may not be a direct one. Children who know about covariation may merely have some other ability which does help them to conserve.

It was argued in Chapter 3 that knowledge of the uniqueness of reversibility is likely to be necessary for conservation acquisition. If it is necessary, then knowledge of covariation is probably necessary too. It seems very unlikely that a child could learn that B can be rolled to look like only once of B', B' +, B' + + ..., without having learned that 'As B is rolled, it gets longer and thinner'; it seems probable that knowledge of the latter (covariation) is psychologically necessary for knowledge of the former (uniqueness of reversibility).

(ii) Halford's experiments (1968, 1969, 1970b, 1971) purport to show that conservers are more likely than nonconservers to recognize the constraints between height and width changes when liquid is transferred between containers, and also that training children in the constraint system helps them to acquire conservation. These can be interpreted as experiments on the uniqueness of reversibility, and they were summarized in Chapter 3. A similar experiment by the author, in which plasticine was used rather than liquid, is described in Chapter 11.

(iii) The evidence concerning the relationship between performance in amount construction and conservation tests was given in sections 4.5a and b. Although the precise relationship between performance in these two tests is not clear, only one study has found amount construction to be substantially easier than conservation, while others have found them to be more equal in difficulty.

There is a problem with the amount construction test which has not yet been mentioned. It is not necessarily the case that a child who passes the amount construction test is making a compensation interpretation of the changes in dimensions at each point in the deformation. That is, the amount construction test could, logically, be passed by a child who did not possess Piaget's operational compensation (as it has been interpreted in this chapter). The child might simply use a perceptual criterion 'If A is thinner than B, then to be the same amount, A must be higher/longer'.

According to Piaget's theory, the child only fully accepts that objects different in shape can be equal in amount when he has acquired operational thought. If we assume, therefore, that Piaget's theory is correct, then the amount construction test is indeed an adequate test of Piaget's compensation. Unfortunately, we are not yet in a position to assume that Piaget's theory is correct. Whether a perceptual criterion like the one mentioned does develop before the child is a true conserver, is investigated in experiments by the author, described in Chapters 9 and 10.

(d) Evidence and arguments against Piaget's theory

(i) The results of Frank's screening experiment, described by Bruner (1966c) may provide evidence against Piaget's theory that compensation is an integral part of the conservation concept. As shown in Chapter 3, there is a possibility that when non-conservers do not see the post-deformation appearance, they give conserving judgments. If it were shown convincingly that under screened conditions non-conservers do use the concept of conservation, this would suggest that the ability to compensate was not necessary for the development of the concept of conservation. According to Piaget's theory, the child should not find it easier to conserve when he is protected from the post-deformation appearance, since he has no ability to conserve until he can interpret the changes in dimensions as compensating each other.

Verification of the screening experiment results would not, however, mean that changes in the child's perceptual criteria are irrelevant to conservation acquisition; it could be that the child must be able to consider changes in two dimensions before he uses the concept of conservation in unscreened situations.

(ii) An argument commonly made against the view that compensation is necessary for conservation is that exact compensation cannot be seen. It is impossible to tell just by looking at a long thin sausage, whether it is exactly the same amount as a short fat one; it is argued that compensation must therefore be a consequence rather than a pre-requisite of conservation acquisition. This view is held by Green and Laxon (1970):

> 'It is curious that this red herring of Piaget's should have lain around so long when it is perfectly obvious that most adults find the task of measuring volume by eye well beyond their capacities.' (Green and Laxon, 1970, p. 27)

If one reads what Piaget has to say about compensation (section 4.5a) it is perfectly obvious that this red herring was not laid by him. The child is considered not simply to be making a perceptually based judgment of compensation, but an interpretation of the effects of the deformation on appearance.

(iii) A further argument against the view that compensation is necessary for conservation is that, under certain conditions, there is no compensatory change in dimensions. Gelman and Weinberg (1972) point out that when a row of elements is changed into a circle, or when plasticine is changed from a ball to a 'square', there is no obvious demonstration of compensation. They make the tentative suggestion that '... in some sense, conservation mediates compensation' (p. 381). It is, however, quite possible that the child comes to accept that pieces different in shape can look equal in amount, even though dimensions cannot be specified.

Elkind (1966) argues more strongly against the view that compensation is necessary for conservation, using visual illusions as an example of a situation in which a certain quality is conserved although it appears to change, and in which there are no compensatory changes in dimensions. Elkind's assumption that understanding of illusions is analogous to understanding conservation of quantity may not be valid: most illusions effect qualities such as shape, and not quantities. Even if Elkind's analogy is valid, it could be that when there are compensating attributes, awareness of these helps the child to conserve. It may not be appropriate to try by means of a single theory to account for understanding of both illusions and quantity conservation.

(e) Summary and conclusions

Piaget's theory of the relationship between compensation, identity and reversibility and conservation will be discussed further in Chapter 5. In this section, the concern has been with Piaget's view of the relationship between compensation and conservation. Several difficulties arose in trying to understand this relationship.

(i) In some of Piaget's writings, it is clear that compensation and conservation are supposed to develop together, but in others it seems that a form of compensation may develop before conservation.

(ii) Piaget defines compensation as 'Longer × thinner = the same amount', but it seems that the child who makes a compensation interpretation assumes that for each tiny increase in length as deformation takes place, there is an associated tiny decrease in width. A child could, logically, judge in accordance with the rule 'Longer × thinner = the same amount' without making such an interpretation of the deformation.

(iii) Piaget uses two logically distinct tests for assessing compensation: a test of amount construction is used for liquids, but a test of anticipation of shape is used for clay. The former test (amount construction) is more closely related to the definition of compensation.

(iv) The child could, logically, pass either of these two tests without making a compensation interpretation of the effects of deformation on appearance. The amount construction test could be passed by applying the perceptual criterion 'If A is thinner than B, then to be the same amount, A must be longer/higher'. The anticipation of shape task could be passed simply by applying the rule 'When plasticine is rolled longer, it gets thinner'.

The evidence is rather inconclusive concerning the relationship between performance in the amount construction test and in the conservation test. It was suggested that it may be inappropriate to compare performance in a test of construction with that in a test of recognition (the conservation test), since even if they were assessing the *same* ability, the test of construction would be expected to be more difficult.

Liquid level prediction (covariation) has consistently been found to be easier than conservation. Piaget's anticipation of shape test with clay, which seems to be

assessing covariation rather than compensation, was found to be a little more difficult than conversation, but only when a very strict criterion was used for passing the
shape anticipation test.

Knowledge of the uniqueness of reversibility is a logically necessary prerequisite
of Piaget's compensation, if this has been correctly interpreted by the author, and it
appears on the basis of Halford's evidence to be more common among conservers
than nonconservers, although its precise relationship to conservation and to compensation cannot yet be specified.

There is no conclusive evidence against Piaget's theory. However, if it were
shown convincingly that nonconservers do conserve when they are screened from
the post-deformation appearance, would suggest that conservation and compensation are not acquired together.

The argument that there are some situations to which conservation is applied but
in which there are not compensatory changes in dimensions, e.g. illusions, need not
be damaging to Piaget's theory if it purports to explain only the application of the
concept of quantity conservation to the more common situations in which there are
compensatory changes in dimensions, or at least changes of shape which can be interpreted as balancing each other.

4.6 Conclusions

It is clear that changes in the child's perceptual criteria do accompany the acquisition of conservation, but it is not clear what their role may be. The assumption that
they are irrelevant raises the problem of explaining why the child ceases to make
what is to him a perfectly satisfactory judgment of 'More in the longer sausage', and
begins instead to use the NAS criterion. This problem is avoided if we can account
for the child's becoming increasingly aware of more than one dimension, such that
he eventually becomes dissatisfied with appearance-based judgments of pre- compared with post-deformation amount. His route to conservation acquisition could
then be as follows.

(i) The child's becoming aware of contradictory judgments of pre- compared
with post-deformation amount could lead him to abandon perceptual criteria in
favour of an already developed NAS criterion. No account of the development of
the NAS criterion is provided by this suggestion.

(ii) Piaget's theory is that the child resolves the conflict between alternative one-
dimensional judgments of pre-compared with post-deformation amount by making
a compensation interpretation of the effects of deformation on appearance
simultaneously with developing the operations of identity and reversibility.

(iii) What seems to be a simpler way of resolving the conflict is to develop a
perceptual criterion on the basis of which dimensions are coordinated, such that it is
accepted that a long thin sausage can *look* equal in amount to a short fat one. Use of
such a perceptual criterion could eventually lead to the development of the NAS
criterion. This possibility will be mentioned again in Chapter 5, in which
mechanisms of conservation acquisition are discussed.

CHAPTER 5

What is the Mechanism by which Conservation is Acquired?

Summary

Four theories of conservation acquisition are discussed: Piaget's, Smedslund's two theories, and Bruner's. They all specify a conflict mechanism of development, but the particular conflict supposed to be responsible for conservation acquisition is different in each case. Both Bruner's theory and Smedslund's addition–subtraction theory are unacceptable as they stand, because their accounts of conservation acquisition are incomplete, and also because the evidence is against rather than in favour of them. Smedslund's social conflict theory draws attention to what could be an important stimulus to cognitive development, but it does not provide a sufficient account of conservation acquisition. Piaget's theory is more difficult to evaluate, because of the problems of interpreting the concepts involved, and because direct tests of the theory are rare. However, Piaget's theory seems to be potentially the most promising of the four. A modification of Piaget's theory is suggested, which is more plausible in that it allows the child to resolve in a simpler way the conflict between alternative judgments of pre-compared with post-deformation amount.

5.1 Introduction

In Chapter 1 it was argued that the child could not discover that amount is conserved by interacting with the physical world. Even among conservations which could in principle be discovered (e.g. number and weight), discovery seems not to be sufficient for their acquisition. A theory in terms of direct or indirect social learning could not alone account for the facts of conservation acquisition. A maturation theory was also ruled out as insufficient to explain conservation acquisition. It is important to remember, however, that the argument is merely that these factors are not *sufficient* to explain all cases of conservation acquisition; there is no suggestion that they are not necessary. Furthermore, there is no wish to rule out the possibility that conservation of amount can be directly taught to the child. The interest here, however, is in those who invent the concept themselves.

One aim of a theory of conservation acquisition is to specify which discoveries are relevant, how far towards conservation the child can get by discovery alone, and how the discoveries are used in the invention process. In Chapters 3 and 4 some discoveries the child can make about transformations were suggested. When a ball of plasticine B is rolled into a sausage B′, he can discover:

Covariation—As B is rolled, it gets longer but thinner.

Empirical return—If B′ is rolled back, it will look the same as at first, and will be the same amount.

If some material were added or subtracted during rolling, rolling the sausage back will not make it look the same as at first.

Uniqueness of reversibility—B cannot be rolled to look like a sausage of the same width at B′ but different in length (B′ + or B′ −); B′ + and B′ − cannot be rolled up to look just like B.

Each of these discoveries may help the child towards conservation acquisition, but none of them is logically sufficient for conservation.

In this chapter, the child will be viewed as an inventor who constructs internal representations of the world to enable him to deal with it more effectively. Conservation is seen as a construction which is more adaptive than nonconservation; more adaptive in that an assumption of conservation does not lead to contradictions, whereas an assumption of nonconservation can lead to contradictions. The nonconserver is seen as becoming aware of some inconsistency in his thinking, the resolution of which leads him to construct the concept of conservation. The mechanism of development can therefore be described as one of cognitive conflict. What is the contradiction that leads the child to conserve?

Halford (1971) argues that the giving of nonconserving judgments is intrinsically unsatisfactory to the child. Since the child judges pre- and post-deformation amounts to be unequal,

'. . . for the non-conservation S the identity of the material (i.e., the fact that it is the same material on all . . . occasions) does not provide a criterion for quantity, so that uncertainty and inconsistent judgments of quantity result.' (Halford, 1971, p. 151)

But Halford is unwittingly describing the situation from the adult point of view. From the point of view of the young child, there is probably no inconsistency: attributes such as length, shape, etc., are independent of qualitative identity, so why should not amount also be independent?

Nonconservation need not be intrinsically unsatisfactory. A child who always judged liquid amount on the basis of level only need never come across a contradiction. A more plausible view is that at some point in his development, the child has available two (or more) criteria for judging amount, criteria which can lead to contradictory judgments. Assuming that the child already knows that an amount cannot *simultaneously* be more and less than, or equal and unequal to, another amount, then he could become aware of a contradiction in either of two ways.

(i) He could become aware of a contradiction through encounters with new events. The child might have two criteria for judging amount, which are normally applied in different situations. With wider experience, he could come across situations to which both criteria are applicable but lead to conflicting judgments. It would be supposed that the more the child encountered these conflict situations, the less could he ignore the contradiction, and eventually he would be forced to reorganize his thinking. The newly constructed criterion would be applicable to a wider range of situations without leading to contradictions. This is similar to Smedslund's suggestion, to be described in section 5.3; the child is supposed to come across situations in which both the addition–subtraction schema and the deformation schema are activated and lead to contradictory judgments.

(ii) A second possibility is that the child becomes aware of more aspects of situations. Whereas originally the child used only one criterion for a particular comparison, he might begin to realize that a second criterion is equally applicable. Contradiction between judgments based on two criteria could lead him to reorganize his thinking. Both Piaget and Bruner account in this way for the development of conservation. Piaget's child becomes aware of a conflict between judgments based on alternative one-dimensional perceptual criteria: a sausage could be more than a ball because it is longer, but also less because it is thinner. Bruner's child becomes aware of a conflict between a symbolically represented conserving judgment and an ikonically represented nonconserving one.

Aspects of each of these theories, Piaget's, Smedslund's and Bruner's, have already been discussed, but little has been said about the mechanisms by which they suggest that conservation is acquired. The theories will now be considered from that point of view.

5.2 Piaget's theory: conflict between alternative perceptual judgments of amount

Piaget accepts that maturation and experience of the physical and social world are important factors in cognitive development, but he considers that these alone cannot provide a full explanation of it. Something must determine the coordination of these three factors, and produce the sequence of intellectual development. That is Piaget's justification for introducing a fourth factor, equilibration, or self-regulation. Equilibration is the process by which the child develops better and better adapted structures to deal with the world; he attains better and better levels of equilibrium:

'Such transformations arise, in effect, only in the presence of problems, gaps, conflicts, i.e. states of disequilibrium. The operational solution consists in reacting to restore equilibrium. . . . the equilibrium of intelligence is not a state of rest but a "mobile equilibrium". This means that a subject faced with external disturbances tends to compensate these by transformations oriented in the opposite direction.' (Reproduced with permission from J. Piaget and B. Inhelder in *Experimental Psychology: Intelligence* (Oleron, Piaget, Inhelder and Greco, Eds.) London: Routledge and Kegan Paul, New York: Basic Books Inc., 1969)

Piaget elaborates and makes clearer the meaning of such statements through a discussion of conservation acquisition. His most detailed account occurs in 'Logique et Équilibre dans les Comportements du Sujet' (1957), and it is this account which will be concentrated upon here. Piaget first describes the sequence of stages in conservation acquisition, and then consideres how equilibration can account for this sequence.

When a ball of plasticine is rolled into a sausage, two dimensions or characteristics change, the length and the width. The 'strategies' used by the child to judge amount are described in terms of the attention paid to these two dimensions, which can be labelled A and B.

1. The most primitive strategy consists of paying attention to only one dimension, A, and ignoring the other. This leads to a judgment of nonconservation. (A might be either the length or the width; the important point is that it is only one of them.)

2. The second strategy consists of centring on the other dimension, B. There are three phases through which this strategy might run.

    (i) At first the child changes from A to B only when his attention is drawn to B by the experimenter.

    (ii) The child changes his focus of attention from A to B when the deformation is very quick or extreme, e.g. when the sausage is rolled extra thin.

    (iii) The child changes spontaneously to B without such external aids.

In none of these cases does the child coordinate A and B. As soon as he changes to B, he ignores A, and vice versa. His amount judgment is a nonconserving one.

3. In the third strategy there is the beginning of coordination between A and B. This is shown in a variety of ways.

    (i) The child oscillates between A and B in successive judgments and then begins to hesitate before making a judgment. This is referred to as oscillation between strategies 1 and 2 which becomes quicker and quicker.

    (ii) The child is aware of both dimensions at the beginning, but for any particular judgment he chooses the one which seems predominant to him.

    (iii) The child explicitly refers to both dimensions but is unable to choose between them.

    (iv) The child makes equality amount judgments, but for small modifications only.

    (v) The child attempts to put the material back to its original form without concluding that the amount in the sausage was the same as that in the ball.

Each of these shows some decentration. It is not clear whether Piaget considers that they form a sequence through which all children move, or whether any one child could show only one of them. They represent intermediate stages between complete nonconservation (strategies 1 and 2) and perfect conservation (strategy 4).

4. The child considers conservation to be necessary, and gives reasons referring to identity, reversibility or compensation: 'You didn't add any on or take any away', 'If you rolled it back it would be the same', or 'The sausage is longer than the ball but it's thinner'.

Assuming for the moment that the strategies described actually occur, Piaget must explain why the child begins by using strategy 1, why he proceeds through the sequence described, and why he stops at strategy 4.

To explain this, Piaget first analyses the objective (i.e. from the adult's point of view) psychological costs and gains of each strategy. The costs increase from strategy 1, which requires only a single centration, through to strategy 4, which requires attention to the rolling itself. Attention to the rolling is supposed to require a set of retroactions and anticipations (i.e. remembering the change in A while centring on B, and also anticipating the change in B while centring on A). This involves more cognitive effort than does attention to the static characteristics (i.e. a particular value of A or B at some point in the rolling). Although requiring increasing costs, the strategies also show increasing gains. Strategy 1 is insecure, since it rests on an arbitrary choice and ignores other aspects of the field. The fourth strategy, in contrast, takes into account the relationship between A and B and the rolling; because there is now assumed to be complete compensation between the changes in A and B and between the rolling and its reverse (rolling back), there is redundancy, security and predictability.

Piaget admits that the child cannot be seen as working out these relative costs and gains, because that would presuppose that the nonconserver already had the ability to consider the final conserving strategy. He thinks, however, that the child can be seen as comparing successive couples: 1 and 2, 2 and 3, 3 and 4. Although the child would not be able to make the change from strategy 1 to strategy 4 in a single move, he can approach strategy 4 by successive small steps.

Piaget uses a probabilistic language to explain this path: he considers the probability of a given event as a function of all possible events, and he considers as possible all those which have been realized by the final stage, that is, consideration of A or B, of A and B together, and of the rolling itself.

According to Piaget, attention to a single dimension, A or B, has the highest probability at first because the child thinks that A and B change independently, and so the simplest solution is to pay attention to only one of them. This strategy cannot be completely satisfactory, because the child cannot continue to ignore what is really there. (This seems to be an assumption of equilibration theory.) The longer the child centres on A, the more likely he becomes to change to B. This second strategy, though, is just as unsatisfactory as the first.

Gradually, the child begins to oscillate between the two strategies, and begins to remember about A as he changes to B. He begins to learn the relationship between the changes in A and B, so that while he is centring on one, he can anticipate what is happening to the other. Piaget argues that understanding the relationship between A and B cannot be explained simply in terms of association, since this would not account for the late appearance of strategy 3. Rather, it is necessary to see the child as building up a set of anticipations and retroactions as a result of the oscillation between strategies 1 and 2.

The complete learning of the relationship, attention to the original A and B, and to the sequence of changes leading to the final A and B, is equivalent to paying attention to the rolling itself. Thus, as the child begins to coordinate A and B, the probability of paying attention to the rolling itself increases until in strategy 4 this is so strongly established that the child thinks conservation is necessary. At this point, the changes in A and B are interpreted as cancelling each other out at each point in the rolling (compensation) and the rolling is interpreted as being completely reversible (reversibility).

A characteristic of the equilibration account of conservation acquisition is that development is seen in terms of successive stages which approach a state of equilibrium. Equilibrium is achieved when the child

'. . . finally (arrives) at meanings satisfying to the mind and at the same time compatible with experience.' (Beth and Piaget, 1966, p. 197; French edition, 1961)

The child takes into account all aspects of the situation and interprets them in the simplest way. An interpretation or strategy which was highly improbable at the outset becomes increasingly probable during development. According to Piaget

'Equilibration has explanatory value because it is founded on a process with increasing sequential probabilities.' (Piaget, 1970, p. 725)

The equilibration account of conservation acquisition implies that the child could not acquire conservation in a way other than he does, because he has to incorporate new events gradually, and once having reached the stage of hesitation between A and B, to interpret the changes as compensatory is the simplest solution.

Piaget accepts that the equilibration account does not specify simple causal connections. Rather, invoking equilibration is similar to invoking the principle of 'least action': the path of an object is described as that which corresponds to the least action from the starting point to the finishing point. (In English this corresponds to the principle of least effort.)

Piaget's account of conservation acquisition is not explanatory in the usual sense, but we might accept his argument that to try and specify causal connections using the factors of maturation, physical and social experience would be to ignore the complexity of intellectual development. However, three specific criticisms will be made.

(i) The account of the transfer of attention from static configurations to the rolling itself is perhaps the least satisfactory part of the account, since it is not clear how it could be applied to materials which cannot be deformed gradually as can plasticine or clay. In the case of liquid, the child could not see the pouring in terms of compensatory changes in dimensions, since the changes are observable only when the deformation is complete.

(ii) A further problem is that there is no specification of what discoveries are necessary. It seems that during use of strategy 3, the child is discovering physical laws such as 'As the sausage gets longer, it gets thinner' and 'If we roll it back it will be the same as at first', but this is not made explicit.

(iii) In his descriptions of the fully developed conservation concept, Piaget emphasizes that three operations, identity, reversibility and compensation, are all necessary. Yet in this, his most detailed account of the development of conservation, no mention is made of identity. Defined as 'Nothing added, nothing subtracted = the same amount', identity is the only one of the three operations which is of itself logically sufficient for conservation. We would therefore most like to know how this develops.

Evidence relevant to Piaget's theory has already been considered in Chapter 3, where reversibility was discussed, and in Chapter 4, where perceptually based judgments in general were considered, and compensation in particular. Evidence for the occurrence of the first strategy is strong; there is also evidence that the child is less likely to centre on a single dimension as he approaches conservation acquisition. However, strategy 3 has little empirical support apart from examples of particular children given in 'The Child's Conception of Number' (1952; French edition, 1941) and 'Le Developpment des Quantités Physiques chez l'Enfant' (1941). Strategy 3(iv) states that the child gives conserving judgments for small modifications only. Hooper (1969) compared the number of amount conservation responses given in tests in which the deformation (pouring seeds into a different container) was either moderate or extreme, i.e. the second container was only a little narrower than the comparison, or was much thinner. He found no difference in difficulty between the two conditions. However, Hooper had no category of intermediate conservers, and it could be the case that children show their first signs of conserving in tests involving moderate deformations.

Several experiments by the author, described in Chapters 7–10, were designed to test aspects of Piaget's theory, in particular the relationships between conservation, compensation and reversibility.

5.3 Smedslund's earlier theory: conflict between addition–subtraction and deformation schemata

The conflict envisaged by Smedslund to lead to conservation acquisition is that between the addition—subtraction schema and the deformation schema. These schemata were introduced in Chapter 3. It seems that when fully developed the addition–subtraction schema is sufficient for adult conserving behaviour. The deformation schema appears to be responsible for judgments that amount changes with rolling, pouring, etc.

The child becomes aware of conflict between the two schemata by coming across situations in which both are activated in equal strength. For example, if a ball of plasticine is rolled into a sausage, and a piece taken off, then the conflicting judgments might be 'More in the sausage because it's longer' (deformation schema) and 'Less in the sausage because some was taken off' (addition–subtraction schema). The addition–subtraction schema begins to dominate because it has 'greater clarity, simplicity and consistency', whereas the deformation schema will eventually disappear completely because it 'has a high degree of ambiguity, complexity and internal contradiction' (Smedslund, 1961d, p. 157).

Smedslund uses Piaget's term 'equilibration' to describe this process, but his use of the term is very different from Piaget's. For Piaget, the process of equilibration results in the child's taking into account more and more aspects of the situation and relating them to each other. Smedslund, in contrast, emphasizes the increasing domination of the deformation schema by the addition–subtraction schema; the two do not become integrated. It seems that when conservation is fully developed,

Smedslund's child ignores the change in appearance. This would not be a state of equilibrium in Piaget's terminology.

In order to test his theory, Smedslund (1961d) attempted to invoke conflict in nonconservers to help them to acquire conservation. He tried to train thirteen non-conservers, aged from five and a half to six and a half years, to conserve amount of plasticine. The children were given a series of training tasks; in each of these two objects were used. In each task there was a deformation and an addition or subtraction, and the children was then asked for an amount judgment. After this, either the deformation or the addition/subtraction was reversed, and the child was again asked for an amount judgment. For example, in one task two equal balls were used, and one of these was deformed into a snake and a piece was added to the other ball, then the snake was deformed back into a ball. The intention was that the addition–subtraction and the deformation schemata would come into conflict, i.e. that the child would want to judge 'More in the snake because it's longer' but also 'More in the ball because a piece was added'.

Unfortunately, Smedslund found little evidence of conflict (in the form of hesitation, etc.) being aroused by these tasks, and the nonconservers nearly always responded consistently on the basis of addition/subtraction or on the basis of appearance. None of the eight children who responded on the basis of appearance during training gave conserving responses in the post-test; four of the five who responded on the basis of addition–subtraction during training did give conserving responses in the post-test. None of the children had shown any sign of conserving in the pre-test.

Smedslund sees the finding that some children did acquire conservation as important, because they had not been told what the accepted answer was:

'The belief in conservation of substance did not seem to be acquired by observations of an empirical law, or by reinforcement from the experimenter, but as a solution of a conflict between the incompatible schemata of addition/subtraction and deformation, or some other kind of conflict.' (Smedslund, 1961d, p. 159)

In a second experiment (1961a) the children were presented during training with tasks each comprising a sequence of deformation, addition and subtraction. The child was asked after each of these transformations to give an amount judgment. Whereas in the previous experiment both a deformation and an addition or subtraction were performed before the child made his judgment, in this one the effects of the two kinds of transformation were judged separately. One might expect this to make the child *less* likely to become aware of conflict between the addition–subtraction and the deformation schemata. Indeed, the results were not spectacular. Among children trained using plasticine, four out of fifteen showed signs of conserving in the post-test of amount conservation using plasticine. Children trained in discontinuous quantity (linoleum squares) responded little better to their training: six out of fifteen showed signs of conserving in the post-test using linoleum squares. One out of the fourteen control children improved in each of these post-tests.

Gruen (1965) found that a method of number conservation training similar to that used in Smedslund's second training experiment (1961a) was not very effective. During training, the children gave an amount judgment after the elements had been deformed, and then the experimenter added or subtracted elements until the child changed his judgment. The post-test consisted of six number conservation tasks. Only five of the fifteen children gave three or more conserving responses, compared with two of the fifteen controls.

Wohlwill and Lowe (1962) attempted to train children in number conservation using a procedure similar to Smedslund's first one (1961d). An element was added or subtracted before the row of elements was lengthened or shortened. Trials of this kind were interspersed with trails in which there was only deformation. Only two of the eighteen children conserved in the standard number conservation post-test, as did two of the eighteen controls. Overbeck and Schwartz (1970) and Smith (1968) also found this kind of training to be totally unsuccessful.

Quite apart from the lack of supporting evidence for Smedslund's theory, it is not clear why the child should resolve the conflict between the deformation and the addition–subtraction schemata in the way he is supposed to. Smedslund does not make explicit what are the 'ambiguities' and 'contradictions' inherent in the deformation schema which lead to its disappearance. It has already been argued in section 5.1 that nonconserving judgments need not be unsatisfactory.

The evidence relevant to Smedslund's theory which was reviewed in Chapter 3 was largely consistent with the view that the child uses the criteria 'If some is added then there is more' and 'If some is subtracted then there is less' by the time he uses the NAS criterion. The evidence reviewed in this chapter, however, provides hardly any support for the view that through using these criteria, the child becomes aware of conflict which leads him to develop the NAS criterion. This directs us back to the suggestion made in Chapter 3, that the experience necessary for the child to develop the addition and subtraction criteria itself has a direct influence on the acquisition of conservation, and not an indirect influence via use of these criteria. This view accommodates the developmental relationship between the three transformational criteria without predicting that Smedslund's conflict training technique would be successful.

5.4 Smedslund's later theory: social conflict

Smedslund's more recent suggestions about the mechanisms of cognitive development (1966) emphasize social factors. He argues that nonsocial situations are of little interest to the young child, and that the conflict situations which he had previously thought led to conservation acquisition would rarely be found in the everyday lives of children. The mechanism of development is still seen to be one of conflict, but now the conflict is between what one child thinks and what another says, so forcing the first child to see another point of view.

Although Smedslund does not elaborate this idea to account for conservation acquisition, perhaps it can be applied in the following way. One child might judge that, when a ball of plasticine is deformed into a sausage, there is more in the sausage because it is longer. Another child might judge on the basis of width, that there was more in the ball. Two children at the same stage of development could come to contradictory judgments in this way, and each might see that the other's judgment was possible. Hence each child might become aware that judgments on the basis of a single dimension are unsatisfactory. This is quite different from a situation in which an older child gives a conserving response, also contradictory to the young one's judgment. If the young child failed to understand the reasoning leading to the conserving judgment, he might ignore it.

There seem to be no experiments which test directly the role of peer interaction in conservation acquisition. Brison (1966) and Rothenburg and Orost (1969) both used more advanced children to help nonconservers in their conservation training experiments, but in neither experiment was it possible to evaluate the role of other children apart from the training procedure itself.

While awareness of contradictory judgments made by peers may be an important stimulus to cognitive development, it could not be sufficient for conservation acquisition; other factors must account for the resolution of the conflict in a particular way. Simply becoming aware that a judgment on the basis of width is as possible as a length-based judgment is not sufficient to lead the child to conclude that amount is conserved when only the shape is changed.

5.5 Bruner's theory: conflict between ikonic and symbolic representations

Bruner (1966a–d) considers awareness of conflict between different representations of the situation, enactive, ikonic and symbolic, to be necessary for conservation acquisition. These three forms of representation and the developmental changes in their occurrence were outlined in Chapter 1. Knowledge represented in the form of actions is the first to develop; representation in the form of images is next to be acquired, and symbolic representation is the last. The major part of Bruner's discussion of conservation acquisition is concerned with the conflict between ikonic and symbolic representation, although we shall see later in this section that enactive representation may support the symbolic form in its fight against ikonic representation.

The preferred mode of representation of the nonconserver is ikonic, but if he can be forced to use symbolic representation, he may demonstrate that he really can conserve. Bruner (1964) states that

'It is plain that if a child is to succeed in the conservation task, he must have some internalized verbal formula that shields him from the overpowering appearance of the visual displays . . .' (Bruner, 1964, p. 7)

This is illustrated by Frank's screening experiment (referred to by Bruner, 1966c), one aspect of which was considered in Chapter 3. The hypothesis discussed then was that when protected from seeing the change in appearance after liquid was poured into a thinner or wider glass the nonconserver would represent the situation symbolically and give a conserving judgment. It was concluded that the evidence supporting that hypothesis was meagre. Now the second hypothesis will be considered; this is that when the screen is removed, the child becomes aware of conflict between his conserving judgment (made when the screen was in place) and the appearance of nonconservation (when the screen is removed), and resolves this conflict by justifying the appearance in symbolic terms: 'The level is higher but the glass is thinner'. It seems from Bruner's account (and that of his coworker Sonstroem, 1966) that such a justification is not necessarily made, but that is not entirely clear.

If the first hypothesis is incorrect, then the second one must be too; unless the child does conserve when the screen is in place, he cannot become aware of conflict when it is removed. However, we can evaluate the evidence relevant to the second hypothesis independently of that relevant to the first.

In Frank's experiment, many children who failed to conserve in the pre-test did judge that the amount remained the same when the liquid was poured behind the screen. However, when the screen was removed, all but one of the youngest children (four years) reverted to nonconserving judgments. In contrast, all but two of the five-, six- and seven-year-olds maintained their equality amount judgments. They were also more likely to conserve in the post-test than they had been in the pre-test. It appears that for these children the screening procedure acted as a conservation training situation. Bruner's theory seems to be supported.

Of course, Piaget (1967) does not accept this interpretation. He maintains that conservation was not really induced, and that this would have been detected had the pre- and post-testing been more thorough. Other experimenters, some using pre- and post-testing just as brief as Frank's have failed to support Frank's results.

Fleischmann, Gilmore and Ginsburg (1966) used an opaque covering on a glass, which enabled the liquid level to be seen through a slit when the glass was vertical but not when it was horizontal. The deformation was simply tilting the glass from vertical to horizontal. They found that this was not an effective training method: none of the fifteen children gave more than two conserving responses in the four-task post-test.

Feigenbaum and Sulkin (1964) blindfolded their subjects, asked them to put beads in two jars by one-to-one correspondence, and then to pour the contents of one of the jars into a differently shaped jar. Fourteen of the thirty children gave conserving judgments in the one-task post-test, but neither pre- nor post-testing was at all thorough; many of the children may have been intermediate conservers before training.

A third experiment which also fails to provide support for Bruner's theory is by Strauss and Langer (1970). In their experiment, which was much more thorough than the two just described, there were four training conditions. The first (screening and conflict, SC) was like the third part of Frank's experiment: liquid was poured into a different glass behind a screen; the child was asked to make amount and level judgments; the screen was removed; and the child was again asked to make an amount judgment. The second training condition was more like the second part of Frank's experiment (no screening and conflict, SC): the child was asked to predict the amount and level before liquid was poured into a different container; after pouring, he was asked for an amount judgment. In the third and fourth conditions, there was no conflict. The third condition, $S\bar{C}$, was like the first except that the screen was never removed. The fourth, $\bar{S}C$, was like the second, except that the liquid was never poured.

Strauss and Langer argue that if Bruner's theory is correct, then only the conflict-inducing conditions should be effective in training the child to conserve. In fact, however, there was no difference between the four conditions, although the trained children as a whole did perform significantly better than the controls in the post-test. Many of the children in the training and control groups had given at least one conserving judgment in the pre-test; even those classified by Strauss and Langer as 'pre-operational' may have shown signs of conserving in the pre-test. It is not clear, therefore, whether any children who showed no sign at all of conserving in the pre-test, improved as a result of the training.

All the screening experiments described so far have used liquid or discontinuous material in glasses. Sonstroem (1966), one of Bruner's coworkers, describes a screening experiment using plasticine. This was a little difficult to design because by allowing the child to see the deformation, the experimenter is also allowing him to see the final appearance. In Sonstroem's experiment, the child was simply protected from seeing the comparison and deformed objects simultaneously—while one of the two equal balls was being deformed, the comparison ball was hidden, then the deformed ball was also hidden. It is not surprising that this procedure was ineffective in inducing conservation responses in the post-test, since the child would easily be able to make his preferred perceptually based judgment during screening by remembering how each piece of plasticine looked. Sonstroem does not report whether conserving responses were given during screening; she was simply concerned with the effectiveness of screening as a training procedure.

Sonstroem (1966) also discusses a different kind of training experiment to test Bruner's theory. In this, the child was encouraged to use language to describe the changes in appearance as plasticine was deformed. For example, a child might deform one of two equal balls into a sausage. He was then asked by the experimenter which (the ball or the sausage) was longest, and which was fattest, and then he was asked to judge the relative amounts. The appearance descriptions were corrected, but the amount judgments were not. Finally, the child rolled the sausage back into a ball, and he was made aware that it was now just as long and just as fat as the comparison ball. Sonstroem sees this experience as providing the child with verbal labels for compensating attributes.

While labelling did help the child to conserve in the post-test, it was effective only if the child did the manipulating himself. If the experimenter performed the rolling, then labelling was ineffective as a training method. The trained groups were compared with a control group who had neither manipulation nor labelling experience, but simply watched the experimenter do the rolling. All the children were about seven years old. While sixteen of the twenty-one children in the 'labelling and manipulation' group conserved in the one post-test task, only eight out of twenty in the 'labelling' group conserved, as did six of twenty in the 'manipulation' group and five out of twenty in the control group.

Sonstroem's interpretation of the results is that the manipulation encouraged the child to use enactive representation, which would support symbolic representation and conflict with ikonic representation:

'An enactive message, "It *feels* the same" ... pitted against a most compelling "But it *looks* different", may have a poor chance of survival in the ikonic child. The same thing is perhaps true with respect to a verbal message by itself. But when both enactive and verbal messages are saying "same" and perception alone is signalling a difference, the two win out over the one. ... It is when the child is both saying and doing that he learns not to believe fully what he is seeing. Except for the interaction among different modes of representation, learning could not occur.' (Sonstroem, 1966, p. 244)

It is not clear why the verbal message is signalling 'same', since the child has merely described the sausage as longer but thinner than the ball. Neither is it clear why the enactive message is signalling 'same'. Presumably this refers to qualitative identity, 'It feels the same piece of plasticine'. There is no reason why this should lead to an equality amount judgment; the child could equally well say 'It feels different' in the same way that he says 'It looks different'. If, therefore, the training was successful, then it is not clear why it should be. Since the pre- and post-testing were far from thorough, we cannot be confident that any of the children moved from nonconservation to conservation as a result of training. Some of them could have been intermediate conservers before training began.

Further evidence that this kind of description of post-deformation appearance is insufficient for conservation is provided by Sinclair (1967) (also reported in Sinclair, 1969, and in Inhelder and Sinclair, 1969). Sinclair compared descriptions given by conservers, intermediate conservers and nonconservers, of stimuli such as a long thin crayon and a short fat one. The children were aged between five years four months and six and a half years. Sinclair found that conservers were more likely than nonconservers to use comparatives rather than absolute terms ('More' rather than 'Big'), to use differentiated terms for dimensions rather than global ones ('Long' and 'Thin' rather than 'Big'), and to give coordinated descriptions of the dimensions rather than separate sentences, i.e. to use a bipartite rather than a quadripartite structure ('This crayon is long but thin; the other is short but fat' rather than 'This crayon is long, the other is short; this crayon is thin, the other is fat'). In describing the differences between a long thin crayon and a short fat one, differentiated terms were used by a hundred per cent of conservers, thirty-seven per cent of intermediate conservers, and by twenty-seven per cent of nonconservers. A bipartite structure was used by eighty-two per cent of conservers, thirty-one per cent of intermediate conservers, and by sixteen per cent of nonconservers. In a simple comprehension task using such utterances, there was no difference between conservers, intermediate conservers and nonconservers; they all understood perfectly well.

Sinclair then tried to teach nonconservers to use the descriptive language of conservers, to see if this would help them to conserve. The bipartite structure and the comparatives were difficult to teach, and those who did succeed in learning the language rarely became conservers. Only three out of thirty-one children changed from nonconservation to conservation, and eighteen of the children made no progress at all. Nine of these eighteen nonprogressing children used the language they had been taught, but they did so in justification of nonconserving judgments.

From the results of the training, it appeared that the descriptive language taught was insufficient for conservation acquisition, although Sinclair suggests that language may help to direct the child's attention to the relevant attributes. This is plausible: a child who describes a sausage as 'Big' compared with the ball from which it was made is perhaps less likely to notice that alternative perceptual judgments are possible, than one who describes it as 'Longer but thinner'. If awareness of both dimensions is necessary for conservation acquisition, then a child who uses only global descriptive language may be at a disadvantage.

There is, then, little reason to accept Bruner's theory of conservation acquisition. The predicted training effect of screening has failed to occur in several experiments, and, as we saw in Chapter 3, it is not even clear that the child does conserve when the screen is in place.

Apart from the lack of supporting evidence for the theory, the theory itself is incomplete. Although Bruner accepts that use of language to describe a situation does not necessarily imply that symbolic representation is being used (his theory is that it is through using language that symbolic representation is acquired) it is not at all clear how the change from ikonic to symbolic representation might occur. There is, for example, no specification of the 'internalized verbal formula' which supposedly is necessary if the child is to conserve. Use of the criterion 'If nothing is added or subtracted, amount remains the same' is sufficient for adult performance in conventional conservation tests. But it is a large move from defining behaviour in accordance with this rule as the minimum requirement for labelling a child a 'conserver', to saying that the child actually uses this rule in conservation tests. Bruner does not say that the child does this, and his theory leaves open the rather crucial problem of specifying the language used by the child when he conserves.

Sonstroem (1966) discusses this problem, but does not solve it:

'The verbal labels must in effect be giving the child a "conservation" message in the symbolic medium. But the form this message takes is not nearly so obvious to us as the ikonic message, "It looks different", or even the enactive message, "It feels the same", . . . it is difficult to determine by what process the "message" gets to its destination. As we have seen, the process does *not* seem to be a matter of activating the logical operation of compensation, which is then used to deduce conservation. . . . Perhaps the process is simply a matter of providing the child with many different words with which to describe the same clay, thus forcing him to think of the clay in many different ways.' (Sonstroem, 1966, p. 224)

A second hole in Bruner's theory concerns the changes which must take place in thinking before language can intervene to refine it, to organize it symbolically. In Chapter 3 Bruner's statement was given, that before the child's use of language can help him to conserve, there must develop '. . . the sort of hierarchical structures that

permit him to organize a series of experiences into variants of a base form ...'
(p. 205). Bruner makes a similar point when writing about cognitive development
in general, rather than conservation acquisition in particular:

'. . . there is some need for the preparation of experience and mental operations
before language can be used. Once language *is* applied, then it is possible, by
using language as an instrument, to scale to higher levels.' (Bruner, 1966d,
p. 51)

Bruner's theory remains incomplete until it specifies the changes in thinking which
occur *before* language intervenes. These changes seem to result in some elaboration
of the concept of qualitative identity to form the concept of conservation. Unless
this elaboration is explained, Bruner's theory can only account for why the child
begins to use the concept of conservation in standard Piagetian tests; it completely
fails to explain how the concept of conservation originates.

5.6 Conclusions, and another possible route to conservation

Both Bruner's theory and Smedslund's addition—subtraction theory are unacceptable as they stand, because the accounts they provide of conservation acquisition
are incomplete, and also because the evidence is against rather than in favour of
them. There is, as far as the author knows, no evidence directly relevant to
Smedslund's social conflict theory, but in any case this does not provide a sufficient
account of conservation acquisition.

Piaget's theory is more difficult to evaluate. One reason for this is the obscurity of
concepts such as 'reversibility' and 'compensation'. In Chapters 3 and 4, attempts
were made to interpret these, but the interpretations might be unacceptable to
Piaget. Difficulty in evaluating Piaget's theory also arises because of the lack of
direct tests of it. Although in section 5.2 several specific criticisms were made of
Piaget's theory, these were not entirely damaging. It seems possible that Piaget's
theory could be developed into a complete account of conservation acquisition. It is
potentially more complete than either Smedslund's addition—subtraction or
Bruner's theory, because it attempts to account for both the child's ceasing to make
perceptually based judgments of pre- compared with post-deformation amount, and
for the invention of the concept of conservation. Bruner's theory seems at best to
tackle only the former problem, while Smedslund's focuses more on the latter.
Further, both Smedslund and to a lesser extent Bruner seem content to leave the
child ignoring the change in appearance; Piaget's argument that the child necessarily re-interprets this in a way consistent with the NAS criterion is more attractive.

However, a modification of Piaget's theory is more plausible. According to
Piaget, the child resolves the conflict between judgments based on alternative one-
dimensional perceptual criteria by developing operational compensation. A simpler
way of resolving the conflict could be to develop a more complex perceptual
criterion, on the basis of which dimensions are coordinated so that the child accepts
that, for example, a long thin sausage can *look* the same amount as a short fat one.
Use of this perceptual criterion could be an intermediate stage on the route to inven-

tion of the NAS criterion. The child would accept the *possibility* of conservation of amount; while he used only one-dimensional perceptual criteria, the child considered conservation of amount to be impossible. Piaget's child seems to move from considering conservation impossible, to considering it necessary; although he first considers it necessary only under certain circumstances and in an unstable way. (A hint that this may be a misrepresentation of Piaget's theory occurs in his 1957 paper, where he writes of the intermediate child's giving a conservation judgment for small modifications only: '. . . une conservation de fait (mais non nécessaire) pour certains cas, mais pas pour tous.' (p. 52) This problem has already been discussed in Chapter 4.)

Piaget's view (even taking into account the problem just mentioned) contrasts with the alternative suggested above, according to which the child goes through a definite stage of making perceptually based judgments that amount can remain the same despite a change of shape; only later does he consider conservation to be necessary. This idea will be developed further in Chapter 6.

Four Models of Conservation Acquisition

Summary

Four models are presented, each of which specifies a different route from the use of single one-dimensional perceptual criteria to the use of the NAS criterion. Two of the models are consistent with existing theories: those of Piaget and Bruner. Several predictions are derived from the four models; these relate in particular to the stage in conservation acquisition at which certain changes occur in the child's perceptual judgments of amount, e.g. at what stage does the child realize that perceptually based judgments of pre-compared with post-deformation amount are unreliable; at what stage does he accept that a long thin sausage can look equal in amount to a short fat one? These predictions are tested in experiments to be described in Chapters 7–11, and in this chapter a methodological introduction to the experiments is presented.

6.1 The four models

In Chapters 3, 4 and 5, various possible routes to conservation have been outlined. These will now be formalized into four models of conservation acquisition, each of which specifies a different route to conservation, and ascribes a different role to changes in perceptual criteria. Predictions derived from the models will be tested in experiments to be described in later chapters, with the aim of discovering which, if any, of the models might be elaborated to explain conservation acquisition.

An assumption underlying all four models is that an early stage on the route to conservation involves judging consistently with a single one-dimensional perceptual criterion, such as 'If it is longer, then there is more'. Even if the child at this stage has more than one such criterion available, he is unaware of conflict between judgments based on alternative criteria. Evidence for the existence of such a stage was presented in Chapter 4. The models differ in the proposed route taken by the child from this stage, until he judges consistently with the NAS criterion in the standard conservation test. The models are applied to the case of amount judgments when a short fat plasticine sausage is rolled longer. Their applicability to other cases will be considered in Chapter 11. The four routes are illustrated in Figure 6.1.

Model 1 describes the most direct route. According to this model, the child simply switches from judging on the basis of single one-dimensional perceptual criteria, to judging on the basis of the NAS criterion. This need not imply that the change is sudden; there could be an intermediate stage during which the child sometimes uses a one-dimensional perceptual criterion and sometimes the NAS criterion. According to this model, however, changes in perceptual judgments of amount are irrelevant to conservation acquisition, although they may follow it. To this extent, Model 1 is consistent with Bruner's theory (see Chapter 4, section 4.3c and Chapter 5, section 5.5).

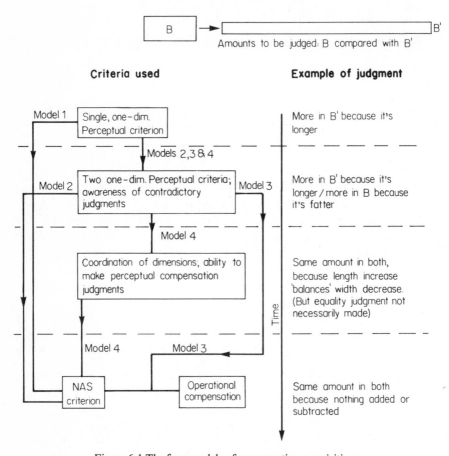

Figure 6.1. The four models of conservation acquisition

According to Models 2, 3 and 4, the transition from use of single one-dimensional perceptual criteria to use of the NAS criterion is indirect. They assume that the child's perceptual criteria develop so that for any particular judgment he has at least two one-dimensional criteria available, e.g. 'If it is longer, then there is more' and 'If it is fatter, then there is more'. Such criteria can lead to contradictory judgments. For example, when comparing the amount in a short fat sausage, A, with that in a long thin one, B' (an A versus B' comparison—AvB'), the criteria lead to the contradictory judgments 'More in B' because it's longer' and 'More in A because it's fatter'. A comparison of pre- with post-deformation amount is always of this kind, it is always an AvB' comparison. Models 2, 3 and 4 propose that the child does become aware of such contradictory judgments of pre- compared with post-deformation amount, but they differ in the way in which the conflict is resolved.

Model 2 assumes that the NAS criterion has already developed independently of changes in the child's perceptual judgments and is ready to replace perceptual criteria when these become unsatisfactory. That is, awareness of contradictory perceptual judgments of pre- compared with post-deformation amount is not necessary for the creation of the NAS criterion, but is a necessary condition for its use in the standard conservation test.

According to *Model 3*, however, the NAS criterion is created only when the child becomes aware of contradictory judgments based on alternative one-dimensional perceptual criteria. The child resolves the contradiction by interpreting the changes in dimensions as compensating each other at each point in the deformation, this interpretation being accompanied by creation of the NAS criterion. This model is consistent with Piaget's theory as interpreted earlier (see Chapter 4, section 4.5, and Chapter 5, section 5.2).

A third way of resolving the contradiction between alternative judgments of pre- compared with post-deformation amount is by coordination of dimensions. When comparing a long thin sausage with a short fat one, the child might decide that the increase in length 'balances' the decrease in width, and therefore make an equality amount judgment. Alternatively, he may decide that the differences in dimensions do not balance each other, and make an inequality amount judgment. The child now accepts that two amounts *can* be equal even though the compared entities are different in shape; previously his perceptual criteria did not allow him to make such judgments. An equality amount judgment of an AvB' comparison, made by a coordination of dimensions rather than on the basis of the NAS criterion, will be called a *perceptual compensation judgment*. An adult conserver may make a perceptual compensation judgment if he is not given any deformational information, but it is also possible that children who do not use the NAS criterion make perceptual compensation judgments.

If such children exist, they may judge on the basis of perceptual compensation that pre- and post-deformation amounts are equal, that is, they may on occasion judge consistently with the NAS criterion. What might lead a child at this stage to develop the NAS criterion?

If it is assumed that the child tries to organize his judgments into a consistent system, then learning about the uniqueness of reversibility could play an important role. If the child makes perceptual compensation judgments, then he will be in a position to judge that sometimes deformation changes amount, but sometimes it does not. If he knows that as sausages are rolled, they get longer and thinner, he is likely to assume that if a particular short fat sausage, A, looks the same amount as a long thin one, X, then A can be rolled to look just like X (A → X). That is, the child may assume that if A = X, then A → X. While he is ignorant of the uniqueness of reversibility, however, he will also assume that A can be rolled to look like other sausages, X+ and X−, just as thin as X but different in length, while judging that these are not the same amount as A. When he has learned about the uniqueness of reversibility, he will know that A can be rolled to look like only of the thin sausages X−, X and X+. He may then decide that sausages which are equal in amount cannot necessarily be rolled to look alike (A = X but A $\neq$ X) or that *only* amounts which are equal can be rolled to look alike (A = X and A → X only, not X− or X+). That he should take the second decision seems more likely, since it allows knowledge about amounts and knowledge about deformation to be integrated into a consistent system, whereas the first decision requires a reorganization of knowledge about amounts. A child who judges that only amounts which are equal can be deformed to look alike, can be described as using the NAS criterion: through learning about the uniqueness of reversibility the child has developed from accepting the possibility of conservation, to acquiring a belief in its necessity.

Model 4, then, proposes the following route to conservation: from using single one-dimensional perceptual criteria, the child becomes aware of contradictory judgments of AvB' comparisons, judgments based on alternative one-dimensional criteria. He resolves the contradiction by coordinating dimensions; he now accepts the possibility of perceptual compensation. The child then develops the NAS criterion. While it seems that learning about the uniqueness of reversibility could play an important role in the last stages of this development, *how* the child develops along the route to conservation is not the present concern; this will not be considered until it has been established which, if any, of the four routes is followed by the child.

6.2 Summary of the models and the relationship between them

Two of the four models are consistent with existing theories: Model 1 is consistent with Bruner's theory, and Model 3 with Piaget's. That is, the routes are as proposed by these theorists, although the models do not prescribe how development along the routes occurs.

All four models assume that one of the early stages on the route to conservation involves use of a single one-dimensional perceptual criterion for any one amount judgment. They differ, however, in the role assigned to changes in perceptual judgments.

Model 1 proposes that such changes are irrelevant, and that the child moves directly from this early stage to using the NAS criterion. The other models assume that awareness of a contradiction between judgments based on alternative one-dimensional perceptual criteria is necessary, so that when comparing pre- with post-deformation amount, the child no longer makes a confident perceptual judgment. Models 2, 3 and 4 differ in the way this conflict is resolved.

Model 2 assumes that the NAS criterion has already developed independently of changes in perceptual judgments, and is used once the child becomes dissatisfied with perceptual judgments of pre- compared with post-deformation amount.

Model 3 proposes that the child makes a creative leap, in that he interprets the changes in dimensions as compensating each other at each point in the deformation, and at the same time develops the NAS criterion.

According to Model 4, the child resolves the contradiction between alternative perceptual judgments of pre- compared with post-deformation amount by coordinating dimensions. He then accepts that entities different in shape can be equal in amount. At this stage he accepts the possibility of conservation; finally he develops the NAS criterion.

6.3 Predictions from the models

The predictions are presented in general terms here; the particular situations used and the detailed predictions will be given in the experimental reports in Chapters 7–11.

The models predict different answers to the following questions.

(i) *At what stage in conservation acquisition does the child become unsure of AvB′ perceptual judgments?* An adult knows that he cannot judge reliably whether a long thin sausage is the same amount as a short fat one, unless the differences in dimensions are extreme, in which case he may be able to make a confident inequality judgment. For example, if one of two sausages were very much longer, but only a tiny bit thinner, than the other, then a confident inequality judgment could be made. In general, however, an adult would consider an AvB′ perceptual judgment to be unreliable, to be corrected if necessary after seeing the fat sausage rolled just as thin as the other. An adult would consider his perceptual judgment to be reliable if it was not the case that one entity was greater in one dimension but less in the other dimension: if, for example, the two sausages were just as thin, or if one was both fatter and longer than the other. Such comparisons will be called AvB comparisons. (In a standard conservation test in which one of two identical short fat sausages is rolled longer, the initial judgment is an AvB one, and after rolling an AvB′ judgment is required.)

Model 1 states that the child moves directly from use of single one-dimensional perceptual criteria to use of the NAS criterion. Therefore, when he first begins to use the NAS criterion in the standard conservation test, he cannot consider AvB′ perceptual judgments to be unsatisfactory—the distinction between AvB and AvB′ perceptual judgments cannot be made on the basis of a single one-dimensional perceptual criterion. If the child is judging amount on the basis of length alone, he will be just as confident in his judgment when comparing a long thin sausage with a short fat one, as in his judgment when comparing two sausages equal in width. So in a conservation test in which a short fat sausage is rolled into a long thin one, a child using such a criterion must make a confident perceptual judgment of the post-deformation amount. Furthermore, his perceptual judgment cannot be consistent with a judgment based on the NAS criterion, he cannot make a perceptually-based equality amount judgment. If, then, the child does apply the NAS criterion, he must be ignoring the post-deformation, AvB′, appearance. Model 1 predicts, therefore, that when the child first begins to apply the NAS criterion in standard conservation tests, he must be ignoring the post-deformation appearance. After the NAS criterion has begun to be used, however, the child may take into account changes in both dimensions, and decide that AvB' perceptual judgments are unreliable.

In contrast, Models 2 and 3 state that prior to the child's using the NAS criterion in the standard conservation test, he must become aware of contradictory judgments of an AvB' comparison, judgments based on alternative one-dimensional perceptual criteria. When the child first begins to use the NAS criterion, he is already aware that AvB' perceptual judgments are unsatisfactory. Like Models 2 and 3, Model 4 states that the child becomes aware of contradictory perceptual judgments of an AvB' comparison, but Model 4's child resolves the conflict by coordinating dimensions. Hence it might be predicted that by the time he applies the NAS criterion in the standard conservation test, he is again confident of AvB' perceptual judgments. It seems likely, though, that even a child who coordinates dimensions is not so confident in an AvB' perceptual judgment as he is in an AvB one, and that when the two judgments are contradictory, it is the AvB' judgment which is accommodated to the AvB one. That is, in a standard conservation test in which the pre-deformation comparison is an AvB one and the post-deformation judgment an AvB' one, it is likely that if Model 4's child applies the NAS criterion he does not ignore the AvB' appearance, but interprets it in a way consistent with the AvB appearance.

Hence Models 2, 3 and 4 predict that when the child first applies the NAS criterion in the standard conservation test, he is less confident in the post-deformation, AvB', judgment than in the pre-deformation, AvB, judgment; he accepts that the AvB' perceptual judgment is unreliable. Model 1, however, predicts that when the child first applies the NAS criterion in the standard conservation test, he is equally confident in the AvB and the AvB' perceptual judgments; these always conflict, and he can only apply the NAS criterion by ignoring one of them. The procedure normally used in the standard conservation test results in him being considered to have used the NAS criterion only if he ignores the post-deformation, AvB' appearance and repeats his pre-deformation judgment.

These predictions were tested in the experiment to be described in Chapter 7, 'Reverse conservation'.

(ii) *Which situations make it easier for the child to use the NAS criterion?* According to Models 1 and 2, changes in the child's perceptual judgments of amount are irrelevant to the creation of the NAS criterion, which could be latent while the child continued to make perceptual judgments of pre- compared with post-deformation amount. Model 1 states that the child continues to use one-dimensional perceptual criteria until for some reason the NAS criterion dominates. Presumably, the NAS criterion must be present in a weak form among some or all children who fail to use it in the standard conservation test. Model 2 holds that the NAS criterion is used in the standard conservation test only when the child becomes dissatisfied with his perceptual judgments of pre- compared with post-deformation amount. Again, some or all children who do not use the NAS criterion in the standard test must be able to demonstrate their possession of it in certain situations if Model 2 is to be tenable. These would be situations in which the potential conflict between judgments based on perceptual and NAS criteria was removed or reduced, so that the child was not tempted to ignore the NAS-based judgment in favour of a conflicting perceptually based judgment.

Models 3 and 4, in contrast, predict that reducing this potential conflict should not make it easier for the child to apply the NAS criterion, since they state that if the child possesses the NAS criterion then he also accepts on the basis of appearance that amounts before and after deformation can be equal. Hence there is no real conflict between perceptual and NAS-based judgments. Furthermore, these two models predict that it may even be more difficult for the child to apply the NAS criterion when he is prevented from making a perceptually based judgment, but this point is considered in (iii) below.

In Chapter 8, performance in two reduced conflict situations was compared with performance in the standard conservation test, to see whether Models 1 and 2, or Models 3 and 4 provide more appropriate accounts of conservation acquisition.

(iii) *At what stage in conservation acquisition are deformational and perceptual information each sufficient for the child to make an equality amount judgment?* In the standard conservation test, the child sees the change in appearance from pre- to post-deformation (perceptual information) and he also sees that nothing was added or subtracted, that the material was only deformed (deformational information). Logically, the knowledge that nothing was added or subtracted is sufficient for him to give a conserving judgment, and as shown in (ii) above, Models 1 and 2 state that it is also psychologically sufficient from the early stages of conservation acquisition; if given only deformational information, these models predict, all children who use the NAS criterion in the standard conservation test, as well as some who do not, should give conserving judgments. On the other hand, these two models state that it is only as a result of using the NAS criterion that the child comes to accept that two entities different in shape can *look* the same amount, that a long thin sausage can look the same amount as a short fat one. When the comparison objects are different in shape, Models 1 and 2 predict that perceptual information is not sufficient for the child to give an equality amount judgment before he uses the NAS criterion in the standard conservation test.

According to Model 3, the child develops the operation of compensation at the same time as he develops the NAS criterion. In the standard conservation test, he uses both deformational and perceptual information when making a conserving judgment. It might be expected that he would find it more difficult to use each kind of information separately: children who apply the NAS criterion in the standard conservation test may fail to do so when they do not see the change from pre- to post-deformation appearance, and they may also fail to accept that a long thin sausage can look the same amount as a short fat one when not given deformational information. A stronger prediction from Model 3 is that it should be equally difficult for the child to use each type of information alone, since compensation and the NAS criterion develop together.

Model 4, like Model 3, states that seeing the change in appearance from pre- to post-deformation does not make it any more difficult for the child to apply the NAS criterion, but unlike Model 3, Model 4 states that the child must already accept the possibility of perceptual compensation if he is to develop the NAS criterion. Hence this model predicts that some children who accept that a long thin sausage can look the same amount as a short fat one, will be unable to apply the NAS criterion when they do not see the change in appearance. It also predicts, like Model 3, that applying the NAS criterion when given deformational information alone, may be more difficult than applying it in the standard conservation test.

The models differ then in the predicted relative difficulty of using deformational and perceptual information alone, and in the predicted stage of conservation acquisition at which the child can use each of these two kinds of information. These predictions were tested in the experiment to be described in Chapter 9, 'Compensation and screening'.

(iv) *Does the child make perceptual compensation judgments which are always consistent with his judgments about the effects of deformation on appearance?* According to Models 1, 2 and 3, the child first accepts that entities different in shape can be equal in amount when he uses the NAS criterion. If, then, he judges that a long thin sausage is the same amount as a short fat one, even if he is interpreting the differences in dimensions as compensatory, he must reason in a way consistent with the NAS criterion. For example, if the short fat sausage were rolled until it was just as thin as the other, and the two sausages were not then equal in length, the child should accept that his initial equality amount judgment had been incorrect.

Model 4, in contrast, holds that the ability to make perceptual compensation judgments is necessary for the development of the NAS criterion, and that the child may make perceptual compensation judgments without using the NAS criterion. If Model 4 is appropriate, then it should be possible to find children who do not correct their perceptual compensation judgments after seeing the fat sausage rolled just as thin as the other one.

In general terms, Models 1, 2 and 3 predict that among children who accept that a long thin sausage can look the same amount as a short fat one, there must be consistency between judgments of amount and judgments about the possibility of making the sausages look identical by deformation. Model 4, on the other hand, allows the child to make inconsistent amount and deformation judgments. These predictions were tested in the experiment to be described in Chapter 10, 'Compensation and the NAS criterion'.

(v) *Does the child make perceptual compensation judgments only if he knows about the uniqueness of reversibility?* This question relates to a difference between Model 3 and Models 1, 2 and 4. Model 3 states that the child resolves the contradiction between judgments based on alternative one-dimensional perceptual criteria by interpreting the changes in dimensions as exactly compensating each other at each point in the deformation. Such an interpretation of the effects of deformation on appearance logically requires knowledge of one aspect of the uniqueness of reversibility. This relationship between operational compensation and the uniqueness of reversibility was examined in Chapter 4, and knowledge of the uniqueness of reversibility was defined in Chapter 3. This includes the knowledge that a given short fat sausage can be rolled to look like only one of a set of thin sausages, equal in width but different in length, and it is knowledge of this aspect which is logically necessary if the child is to make a compensation interpretation in the way outlined above.

Model 3, therefore, predicts that any child who is willing to select a long thin sausage which he thinks is equal in amount to a given short fat one, must also think that the fat sausage can be rolled to look like that thin sausage only, and not like any which are equally thin but different in length. Models 1, 2 and 4, however, allow the child to select one of the thin sausages as being the same amount as the short fat one, while being ignorant of the uniqueness of reversibility. Nevertheless, Models 1 and 2 do require that the child reasons consistently with the NAS criterion (as shown in (iv) above), so if he thinks that the fat sausage can be rolled to look like several of the thin sausages, then he should also want to judge that these, in addition to the one he has already selected, are the same amount as the fat sausage. The child may well become aware of the contradiction in judging several unequal thin sausages to be the same amount as the short fat sausage. Model 4, however, does not require that the child reasons consistently with the NAS criterion, since a child may judge that the fat sausage can be rolled to look like several of the thin sausages while considering that only one of these is the same amount as the fat one. These predictions were tested in the experiment to be described in Chapter 10, 'Compensation and the NAS criterion'.

(vi) *At what stage in conservation acquisition does the child learn about the uniqueness of reversibility?* This question relates to a suggestion about how the child might move through the last stage of the route proposed by Model 4. Detailed predictions arose from the interpretation of the results of the experiment on 'Compensation and the NAS criterion (Chapter 10), so they will not be presented yet. An experiment designed to test those predictions is presented in Chapter 11, 'Conservation and knowledge of the uniqueness of reversibility.'

6.4. Methodological introduction to the experiments

(a) Interpretation of responses in the conservation test

Several of the predictions listed in the preceding section refer to the behaviour of children who are just beginning to use the NAS criterion in the standard conservation test. It is important therefore to be able to identity such children. That is, we must not only be able to distinguish those who do from those who do not use the NAS criterion, but also be able to distinguish from among those who do use it, children who are only just beginning to do so.

The working assumption was that a child used the NAS criterion if he seemed not to be judging solely on the basis of appearance, but did seem to be taking into account deformational information. Children who did this at least once but not on all occasions were considered to have a 'weak' NAS criterion, i.e. to be those who were just beginning to apply it in conservation tests. In Chapter 2, several ways were suggested to differentiate between children in terms of the 'strength' of their NAS criterion, and some of these were used in the experiments to be described in Chapter 7–10.

(i) If the child gave a deformational reason for a conserving judgment, then he was considered to have a 'stronger' NAS criterion than a child who gave no such reason. Reasons classified as deformational were: references to lack of addition and/or subtraction; references to the initial, pre-deformation amount ('They were the same at first'); references to empirical return ('If you rolled it back it would be the same'); references to equivalent action ('If I rolled mine it would be the same'). Each of these reasons indicated that the child was taking into account deformational information, and not just the appearance.

(ii) If the child gave a conserving judgment, then he was given a nonconservation countersuggestion, e.g. 'Somebody else said I've got more, because mine's longer. Do you think that was right or wrong?' A child who resisted this countersuggestion, repeating his conserving judgment, was considered to have a 'stronger' NAS criterion than a child who accepted it. Justifications for using countersuggestion were given in Chapter 2.

(iii) Similarly, if the child gave a nonconserving judgment, he was given a conservation countersuggestion, e.g. 'Somebody else said we've both got the same to eat still, because I just rolled mine, I didn't add any on or take any away. Do you think that was right or wrong'? A child who accepted this was considered to have a stronger NAS criterion than one who rejected it.

(iv) Each child was given more than one conservation task. The greater the proportion of occasions on which the child gave conserving judgments, the stronger his NAS criterion was considered to be.

Various attempts were made to avoid assuming that conserving judgments were necessarily based on the NAS criterion, since if Model 4 is correct, the child could give a conserving judgment just be coordinating dimensions. One solution to this problem would be to classify a child as using the NAS criterion only if he gave a deformational reason for his judgment, but this is unsatisfactory since it cannot be assumed that a child who is just beginning to apply the NAS criterion verbalizes his reasoning. A second possible solution is to test the child on both the standard test of conservation of equality and on inequality tasks in which the pre-deformation AvB comparison is of amounts which are unequal. For example, two equally fat sausages might be used, one noticeably longer than the other, and then the shorter one could be rolled much longer and thinner. A child judging on the basis of length would change his judgment from pre- to post-deformation, but a conserver would not. A child judging on the basis of perceptual compensation would be unlikely to give the correct judgment in both equality and inequality tests; if the child manages to do this, then he is probably using the NAS criterion. This method was used in one of the experiments to be described (see Chapter 10), where it was found that there was no difference in difficulty between the two kinds of conservation test. This method has the disadvantage, however, that the experimenter may not be sure whether the child used the NAS criterion for any particular judgment.

In another experiment (see Chapter 7) an alternative method was used. Each child was given a pre-test in which his perceptual judgments of the AvB' comparisons used in the conservation tasks were investigated. Any child who gave a correct AvB' judgment in the perceptual pre-test was excluded from the analysis unless in the corresponding conservation task he gave a deformational reason for a correct judgment. With this procedure, it was possible to be fairly confident that correct judgments in the conservation tasks were based on the NAS criterion rather than on perceptual criteria.

(b) General procedural features

A cross-sectional method was used to test the predictions, i.e. children of different ages were tested on the assumption that all children acquire conservation in the same way, and therefore that each child can be placed at some point on the route to conservation acquisition. A consequence of this assumption was that no attempt was made to control such variables as socio-economic class or intelligence.

The children came from six schools in London and two in Southampton. Five of the schools were local authority run, and three were independent. Children from a wide range of social classes were included. They were always tested individually, in a room alone with the experimenter, and the sessions were tape-recorded.

In all the tests plasticine was used. At the beginning of his first task, the child was encouraged to pretend that the plasticine was toffee, and the standard amount question, used in all the experiments, was 'Have we both got the same to eat, or have you got more, or have I got more? Why?'. Justification for using this question can be found in Chapter 2. The deformations were performed by the experimenter, since in some tests it was essential that a particular post-deformation appearance should result. The exception was at the beginning of any test in which it was necessary to establish that two amounts were equal. In these cases, the child was allowed to make any necessary adjustments unless he preferred the experimenter to make them.

Some of the experimental details are omitted from Chapters 7–10 but appear in Appendix I. Complete reports of most of the experiments presented in Chapters 7, 8 and 10 are given in Peill (1972).

CHAPTER 7

Uncertainty in Perceptual Judgments of Amount

7.1 Introduction

The experiment described in this chapter was intended to test whether Model 1 or Models 2–4 provide more appropriate accounts of conservation acquisition. Does the child move directly from using single one-dimensional perceptual criteria to using the NAS criterion (Model 1), or must he go through an intermediate stage of uncertainty in some perceptual judgments of amount (Models 2–4)? The experiment investigated the stage in conservation acquisition at which the child becomes unsure of AvB′ perceptual judgments. If Model 1 is correct, this happens only when the NAS criterion is firmly established and is used in standard conservation tasks; according to Models 2, 3 and 4, however, uncertainty in AvB′ perceptual judgments is a necessary prerequisite of use of the NAS criterion in standard conservation tests.

7.2 Reverse conservation

In order to test the predictions, a 'reverse conservation test' was used. In this test, the subject was first presented with a short fat sausage A and a long thin one B′, which was in fact slightly less in amount. The fat sausage was rolled until it was just as thin as B′, and it was then noticeably longer than B′. The pre-deformation judgment was one which an adult could not make confidently on a perceptual basis; it was of an AvB′ comparison. An adult would correct his initial judgment if necessary after seeing the deformation to an AvB comparison.

A child who acquired conservation in the way specified by Model 1 would, when he first began to use the NAS criterion in the standard conservation test, respond incorrectly in the reverse test: he would make a confident AvB′ perceptual judgment, sticking to this after the deformation, and ignoring the AvB appearance. Models 2–4, in contrast, predict that if a child uses the NAS criterion in the standard conservation test, he should use it appropriately in the reverse test, correcting if necessary his initial AvB′ judgment after seeing the AvB appearance.

The difference between Model 1's prediction and that of Models 2–4 may be made clearer in the following way. When one of two amounts is deformed, the NAS criterion can be applied using either of two strategies:

(i) by ignoring the post-deformation appearance, and *sticking* to the pre-deformation judgment, or

(ii) by *correcting* if necessary the pre-deformation judgment after seeing the post-deformation appearance.

In the standard conservation test, the initial judgment is an AvB one, it can be made reliably using perceptual criteria. Strategy (i), the sticking strategy, is the appropriate one. An adult would stick to his AvB amount judgment and ignore the post-deformation appearance, knowing that an AvB′ perceptual judgment was unreliable. In the reverse conservation test, however, an adult would use the correcting strategy. Suppose, for example, that the initial AvB′ comparison was between a long thin sausage and a short fat one, and then the fat sausage was rolled until it was just as thin as the other. An adult might at first judge that the two sausages were equal in amount, but after the rolling, judge on the basis of a length difference that one was more than the other. He would then correct his pre-deformation amount judgment, arguing that the amounts cannot have been equal at first.

A child who uses the appropriate strategy in both the standard and reverse conservation tests must be able to distinguish between reliable (AvB) and unreliable (AvB′) perceptual judgments. Model 1, then, predicts that when a child first begins to apply the NAS criterion in the standard test, using the sticking strategy, he will also apply that strategy in the reverse test, since he will be unable to distinguish between AvB and AvB′ perceptual judgments. Models 2–4 predict that such errors should not occur, that no child who applies the sticking strategy in the standard test should apply it, inappropriately, in the reverse test. As indicated in Chapter 6, to derive this prediction from Model 4 requires the assumption to be made that children who coordinate dimensions but who have not yet fully developed the NAS criterion, choose to accommodate an AvB′ perceptual judgment to an AvB one when accommodation is necessary. It is likely that a child who coordinates dimensions would more readily accept an alternative AvB′ judgment than an alternative AvB one.

A further, weak, prediction from both Models 1 and 2 is that the correcting strategy is easier to apply than the sticking strategy. When applying the correcting strategy, the child can accommodate his NAS-based judgment to one based on immediate appearance. If the child were given the opportunity to correct his pre-deformation judgment after seeing the post-deformation appearance, he might find this an easier way of applying the NAS criterion than ignoring the post-deformation appearance and sticking to his pre-deformation judgment. If the correcting strategy were indeed easier to apply than the sticking strategy, this would support Models 1 and 2 and would provide evidence against Models 3 and 4, since it would suggest that the child has a tendency to conserve which is obscured while he is misled by the post-deformation appearance. Models 3 and 4 hold that the child has no tendency to conserve before he becomes aware that AvB′ perceptual judgments are unsatisfactory.

Procedure

Each child was given four tests in a single session. It is the fourth test which is of interest here—it was composed of three conservation tasks, one of which was a reverse conservation task—but the other three tests will be outlined briefly. The first test was a perceptual test in which the child was presented with the same comparisons as in the conservation tasks, but there was no deformation. An extra piece of plasticine was used in each of the three tasks, identical as far as possible to the post-deformation appearance in each of the three conservation tasks. The main reason for giving this perceptual test was to investigate the child's uncertainty in his AvB′ perceptual judgments; are there children who are aware of the alternative judgments 'More in the longer sausage' and 'More in the fatter sausage'? Since the perceptual tests did not provide clear-cut results on this, details are not given although the test is mentioned again in Chapter 12. A second reason for giving the perceptual test was that it would be possible to see whether the child's AvB′ judgements in that test were those expected on the basis of the NAS criterion. If any were, then the child's 'correct' judgment in the corresponding conversation task might have been based on a perceptual criterion, not on the NAS criterion. The child might be classified inappropriately as a conserver or an intermediate conserver. It will be shown below how the results were analysed to try to ensure that correct judgments in the conservation tasks were based on the NAS criterion.

The second test of the four was a 'reduced conflict' situation similar to those described in Chapter 8, and the third involved subtraction as well as deformation. This latter test was mentioned in Chapter 3, where the study was referred to an Experiment C.

The procedure in the fourth test, the conservation test, will now be described. The materials used are shown in Figure 7.1. Two of the tasks, 1 and 3, were standard in that the pre-deformation amount judgment could be made reliably using perceptual criteria, it was of an AvB comparison. (But these tasks were not exactly like the standard Piagetian ones since the entities A and B were not equal in amount, see below.) The third, task 2, was a reverse conservation test: the pre-deformation amount judgment was of an AvB′ comparison. In all three tasks, the AvB judgment was an obvious one of inequality, because for reasons not relevant here, that made the perceptual test more reliable. Task 3, in which there were no clear dimensions in B′, was included for reasons particularly relevant to the perceptual test, although the data from this task are presented below.

The three conservation tasks (and the corresponding perceptual tasks) were given to the child in one of the following orders: 1, 2, 3; 2, 3, 1; 3, 1, 2. The first child was given the tasks in the first order, the next the second, and so on. Hence approximately equal numbers of children were given each task in first, second and third positions.

In each of the conservation tasks, the procedure was as follows.

(i) Pre-deformation amount judgment. The standard amount question was asked: 'Have we both got the same to eat, or have you got more, or have I got more? Why?.' In tasks 1 and 3, in which the pre-deformation judgment was an AvB one, all the children answered correctly.

Task 1

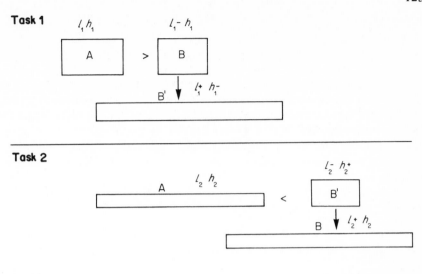

Task 2

Task 3

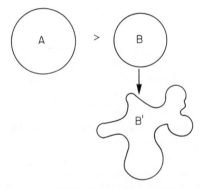

Figure 7.1 Materials used in the experiment on 'Reverse Conservation'
Note: l and h refer to the lengths and widths of the sausages. $l-$ is less than l; $l+$ is more;
similarly for $h-$ and $h+$.

(ii) Deformation and post-deformation amount judgment. The experimenter rolled her piece of plasticine, and the standard amount question was repeated.

(iii) Countersuggestion. If the child gave the same amount judgment for both the pre- and the post-deformation comparisons, he could have been using the NAS criterion, and he was given a nonconservation countersuggestion, e.g. 'Somebody else said I've got more because mine's longer. Do you think that was right or wrong?' Unless it was clear what the child now thought the amount was, the standard amount question was repeated.

(iv) Pre-deformation amount judgment repeated or corrected. The child was given the opportunity of applying the correcting strategy: he was asked 'Did we both have the same to eat before I rolled/squashed mine just now, or did you have more, or did I have more?'

(v) Empirical return. The child was asked 'What if I roll mine back again, will we both have the same to eat, or will you have more, or will I have more?'

(vi) Countersuggestion. Finally, unless the child had been given a nonconservation countersuggestion at stage (iii), or had applied the correcting strategy at stage (iv), he was given a conservation countersuggestion, e.g. 'Somebody else said I've still got more to eat now, because I just squashed mine, I didn't add any on or take any off. Do you think that was right or wrong?' Unless it was clear what the child now thought the post-deformation amount was, the standard amount question was repeated.

Subjects

There were 23 boys and 24 girls, aged from four to eight years, but seven children were excluded (see below), leaving 20 boys and 20 girls.

Treatment of results

Before being given the conservation test, the children had been given the perceptual test in which they judged AvB and AvB' in each of the three displays without seeing any deformation. It was possible, therefore, to tell for each of the conservation tasks, whether his perceptual judgment of AvB' had been correct. Children who gave correct AvB' judgments in the perceptual test, but did not give deformational reasons for these judgments in the conservation test, were excluded from the analysis on the grounds that it was not clear whether the child was given the right answer for the right reason: his correct judgment in the conservation test might have been based on the NAS criterion, but it might equally have been based on a perceptual criterion. Four children were excluded on these grounds; two of them judged all three AvB' comparisons correctly in the perceptual test, and two of them made two correct AvB' judgments. Possibly their correct judgments had been based on width rather than length criteria. Seven other children gave correct AvB' perceptual judgments but were not excluded from the analysis because in the conservation test they justified their correct judgments by deformational reasons. Threee other children were not included in the analysis because they did not pay attention during testing.

After these exclusions, 40 children remained. Their responses in the conservation test were analysed to see whether, in each task, they had used a sticking or a correcting strategy. Since the predictions refer to children who are just beginning to use the NAS criterion in the standard conservation test, it was necessary to analyse the responses of children who accepted the countersuggestions to see whether they implied use of sticking or correcting strategies. Table 7.1 shows an analysis of possible ways of answering the questions in any one conservation task. Not all possible responses are included; some consistency across question has been assumed. The Table includes all responses which did actually occur, as well as some plausible ones which did not in fact occur.

Table 7.1. Responses in the conservation tasks

(ii) Post- def. judgmt.	(iii) Nonconservation c. suggn.	(iv), (v) Correct, emp.retn.	(vi) Conservation c. suggn.	Response type
Different from pre- def. judgt.	—	Don't correct	Reject Reject then correct Accept	1 noncons, 2 partial correct 3 partial stick
		Correct emp. retn. only	Reject Reject then correct Accept	4 partial correct 5 partial correct 6 ?
		Correct both (iv) and (v)	—	7 correct
Stock to pre-def. judgt.	Reject Accept	Don't correct Don't correct Correct emp. retn. Correct both	— — — —	8 stick 9 partial stick 10 ? 11 ?

Response type 7 is the *correcting strategy*, appropriate in the reverse conservation test. For example, the child's pre-deformation judgment might be that he has more to eat, his post-deformation judgment that the experimenter has more, and he might then judge that the experimenter had more at first and would have more if her sausage were rolled back again.

Response types 2, 4 and 5 are partial correcting strategies. For example, in response type 2, the child does not, when given the opportunity in part (iv), correct his pre-deformation judgment to be consistent with his post-deformation judgment. Neither does he make a consistent empirical return judgment. So in the example given above, the child would answer in parts (iv) and (v) that he had more at first, and that he would have more if the experimenter's sausage were rolled back again. The child does, however, reject the conservation countersuggestion, and decides that his pre-deformation and empirical return judgments were incorrect. It seems that in this case, the child is reminded about the NAS criterion by the counter-suggestion, but he does not accept the way the experimenter has applied it, i.e. by the sticking strategy, and the child then applies the correcting strategy. In response types 4 and 5, also classified as partial correcting strategies, the child makes an empirical return judgment which is consistent with his post-deformation judgment. In response type 5, he also corrects his pre-deformation judgment after rejecting the conservation countersuggestion.

Response type 8 is the *sticking strategy*, appropriate in the standard conservation test. For example, the child might make a pre-deformation judgment that he has more to eat, repeat this judgment after the deformation, reject the nonconservation countersuggestion, repeat his pre-deformation judgment in part (iv), and estimate that he would have more if the experimenter's sausage were rolled back again.

Response types 3 and 9 are partial sticking strategies: in type 3, the child accepts the countersuggestion that he should stick to his pre-deformation judgment; in type 9, he sticks to his pre-deformation judgment in part (ii) but accepts the nonconservation countersuggestion.

Response types 6, 10 and 11 cannot be classified as either sticking or correcting strategies, since they show aspects of both.

Response type 1 is a *nonconserving response*: the child makes no attempt to apply the NAS criterion, but insists that pre- and post-deformation amounts are different.

Results and discussion

Table 7.2 shows the number of children who responded in each way in each of the three conservation tasks.

Table 7.2. Numbers of children giving each response type in each conservation task

Strategy: response type	Stick 8	Partial stick 3 9	Correct 7	Partial correct 2 4 5	? 6, 10, 11	Non-cons. 1	Total
Standard conservation	Task 1	17	4 0	0	0 1 0	0	18	40
	Task 3	18	4 3	0	0 0 0	0	12	40
Reverse conservation	Task 2	0	1 0	16	4 4 0	0	15	40

Model 1 predicts that there should be children who apply sticking or partial sticking strategies in the reverse conservation test. Models 2–4, however, predict that there should be no such children, since when they first begin to apply the NAS criterion in conservation tests, they know that AvB' perceptual judgments are unreliable.

Table 7.2 shows that only one child applied a partial sticking strategy in the reverse conservation test. This child was a nonconserver in task 3 and gave response type 3 in task 1. All the children who used the sticking and correcting strategies (rather than partial forms of these) applied them appropriately. Response type 7 was never given in tasks 1 or 3, and response type 8 was never given in task 2. Even children who applied partial sticking or correcting strategies nearly always applied them correctly, although one exception was mentioned above, of the child who applied a partial sticking strategy in the reverse conservation test; another child used a partial sticking strategy in task 1, a standard conservation test. This child was a nonconserver in both the other tasks.

Hence on all 51 occasions when the sticking or correcting strategies were used, they were applied appropriately; only two of the 24 applications of partial sticking or correcting strategies were inappropriate. Response types 6, 10 and 11, which showed aspects of both sticking and correcting, never occurred. It appears that if a child applied the NAS criterion, even in the form of one of the 'partial' strategies, then he nearly always knew that AvB' perceptual judgments were unreliable. These results support Models 2, 3 and 4 rather than Model 1.

It had also been predicted from Models 1 and 2 that the correcting strategy might be easier to apply than the sticking strategy, since in the correcting strategy the child can accommodate an NAS-based judgment to one based on immediate appearance. This prediction would have been supported if some children had applied correcting or partial correcting strategies in all three tests, but as shown above this did not occur. It would also be supported if task 2 (to which the correcting strategy is appropriately applied) were easier than task 1 (the comparable standard conservation task).

In order to test whether these two tasks differed in difficulty, each child was given a score between 0 and 3 for each of them. Response types 7 and 8 were given a score of 3; response types 4 and 9 (those in which the NAS criterion seemed to be applied spontaneously rather than in response to countersuggestion, but not as an adult would apply it) were given a score of 2; response types 3 and 2 (in which the NAS criterion was applied in response to countersuggestion) were given a score of 1; response type 1 (nonconservation) was given a score of 0. A Wilcoxon test was used to compare performance in task 1 with that in task 2, and there was found to be no significant differences ($T = 65 \cdot 5$. $p > 0 \cdot 05$). Hence the prediction from Models 1 and 2 that the correcting strategy would be easier to apply than the sticking strategy was not supported. The absence of a difference in difficulty is consistent with Models 3 and 4.

Summary and conclusions

This experiment was primarily intended to test the prediction from Model 1 that when the child first begins to apply the NAS criterion in the standard conservation test, he is unable to distinguish between reliable and unreliable perceptual judgments, and so should perform incorrectly in the reverse conservation test. There was no support for this prediction, since only one child used a partial sticking strategy in the reverse conservation test, compared with eight who used partial correcting strategies. Only two out of 24 applications of partial sticking and correcting strategies were inappropriate, and all 51 applications of sticking and correcting strategies were appropriate. There were no instances of responses which showed aspects of both sticking and correcting. These results strongly support the idea that when the child first begins to apply the NAS criterion in the standard conservation test, he considers AvB' perceptual judgments to be unreliable. These results support Models 2, 3 and 4 rather than Model 1.

A further, weak, prediction from Models 1 and 2 was tested in the present experiment. If the child has a tendency to conserve which is at first obscured because he is misled by the AvB' appearance (Models 1 and 2), then the correcting strategy may be easier to apply than the sticking strategy, since in the correcting strategy the child can accommodate an NAS-based judgment to one based on immediate appearance. There was in this experiment no evidence that the two two strategies differed in difficulty; this is consistent with Models 3 and 4.

CHAPTER 8

Use of the NAS Criterion in Reduced Conflict Situations

8.1 Introduction

The aim of the experiments to be presented in this chapter was to see whether the child has available the NAS criterion before he uses it in the standard conservation test. According to Models 1 and 2 he has; according to Models 3 and 4, he has not. Models 1 and 2 state that the child who has available the NAS criterion may fail to use it because he makes a confident perceptual judgment which is contradictory with the NAS-based judgment. Model 1's child eventually comes to ignore his perceptual judgment, whereas Model 2's child becomes aware of contradictory perceptual judgments based on alternative one-dimensional criteria. If these models are correct, then if the potential conflict between perceptually and NAS-based judgments were reduced or removed, the child should use the NAS criterion.

In the standard conservation test, the child is given three items of information: the pre-deformation appearance (AvB), the deformation itself, and the post-deformation appearance (AvB'). Potential conflict occurs between different perceptually based judgments of AvB and AvB' on the one hand (A = B but A ≠ B'), and on the other, the NAS-based judgment that B and B' are equal in amount, so A must be equal to B'. This potential conflict may be removed or reduced by giving the child less information; he may be screened from the pre-deformation appearance, from the post-deformation appearance, or from the deformation itself. Under these conditions of reduced information, do children who fail to use the NAS criterion in the standard conservation test demonstrate their possession of it? That is the question of interest in the present chapter.

A child screened from the pre-deformation appearance (AvB) may indicate possession of the NAS criterion by making a guess about the pre-deformation amount which is consistent with his perceptually based post-deformation amount judgment (AvB'); on the basis of AvB' appearance he may judge that B' is more than A, and since nothing was added or subtracted, judge that there must have been more in B' at first. Such consistency may arise, however, from lack of imagination that B looked different from B'. To reduce the likelihood of this, in the first experiment to be described below, the child was shown a set of three sausages, one of which was to be his. The three were equally fat, but differed slightly in length. The child did not see which one was chosen for him; it was rolled and shown to him after the rolling. The post-deformation appearance (B') was not sufficient to identify which one of the three (B) had been chosen, but hopefully the child would remember that all of them looked different from B'.

Screening from the post-deformation appearance (AvB') occurred in Frank's experiment (Bruner, 1966c), which was discussed in Chapters 3 and 5. In this situation, the child can make a confident perceptually based judgment of the pre-deformation (AvB) amount, and demonstrate his possession of the NAS criterion by repeating this judgment after the deformation. Here again, the child may assume that B' still looks the same as B, and so may give consistent judgments just on the basis of assumed appearance. He may, however, be able to guess enough about the effects of the deformation on appearance to know that B' can no longer look the same as A; if so, he may not really be in a reduced conflict situation. This particular problem does not arise in the case of screening from pre-deformation appearance, since in that situation even if the child knows that B must have looked different from B', he cannot be sure whether B looked the same amount as A, or more, or less. For this reason, screening from post-deformation appearance seems to be a less satisfactory way of reducing potential conflict than does screening from pre-deformation appearance. Screening from post-deformation appearance was used in the second study described below.

Least satisfactory of all is screening from the deformation itself. In this situation, the child can only directly indicate his possession of the NAS criterion if he makes a perceptually based equality judgment of pre- compared with post-deformation amount. Yet according to Models 1 and 2, the child is unable to do this until he applies the NAS criterion in the standard conservation test. So these models predict that children who possess the NAS criterion, but fail to use it in standard conservation tests, should also fail to apply it in this reduced conflict situation. Hence it seems that this reduced conflict situation must fail in its attempt to show that the NAS criterion is available to children who fail to use it in the standard conservation test, even if such children exist. Only screening from pre- and from post-deformation appearance seem to be suitable for testing the prediction from Models 1 and 2 concerning use of the NAS criterion in reduced conflict situations.

8.2 Screening from the pre-deformation appearance: the 'rolled' situation

In this and the next study (screening from post-deformation appearance) the same experimental situation was used, and the same subjects served.

The child knew that one of three fat sausages (B, B+, B++) was to be his. The three were equal in width, but different in length. The experimenter had one sausage (A), equal in width to the other three, and equal in length (and amount) to B+. These materials are shown in Figure 8.1. The experimenter chose B for the child, rolled it to B', and asked the child to compare the amount in B' with that in A. In the 'rolled' situation, the one to be described here, the child did not see which of the three fat sausages was chosen to be his, but he did see it after it had been rolled. In the 'choice' situation, to be described in the next section, the child saw which of the fat sausages was chosen for him, but he did not see it after it has been rolled. In both cases, the child was asked to compare the amount in B' with that in A.

The only way to be sure of giving the correct AvB' amount judgment was to see which of the fat sausages was chosen; in the 'rolled' situation the child could make only a perceptually based AvB' amount judgment. After he had made his amount judgment, he was asked to guess which of the three fat sausages had been chosen, B, B+ or B++, and he could demonstrate his possession of the NAS criterion by making consistent pre- and post-deformation amount judgments. For example, if he judged on the basis of appearance that B' was more than A (as a nonconserver would be expected to judge), then if he applied the NAS criterion he would guess that B++ (more than A) had been chosen. A child who judged that B' was more than A but then guessed that B or B+ had been chosen, could not be applying the NAS criterion. However, the child might give consistent pre- and post-deformation judgments just because he failed to imagine that B' had looked different before rolling. Since all the children saw the set of three fat sausages from which theirs was to be chosen, it was expected that this would not be common.

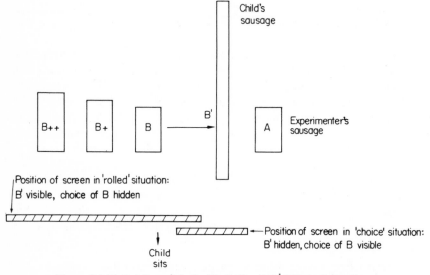

Figure 8.1. Materials used in the 'Rolled' and the 'Choice' situations

If it were found that the NAS criterion were easier to apply in the 'rolled' situation than in the standard conservation test, this would support Models 1 and 2 and would provide evidence against Models 3 and 4.

Procedure

Each child was given two standard conservation tasks. The first involved the deformation of one of two equal balls into a sausage, and in the second task one of two equal balls was broken into four pieces.

In each of the conservation tasks, the standard amount question was used, 'Have we both got the same to eat, or have you got more, or have I got more? Why?', and after he had given his post-deformation amount judgment, the child was given a countersuggestion. A conservation countersuggestion was given if the child had given a nonconserving judgment; this was 'Somebody else said we've both got the same to eat still, because I have rolled mine/broke mine up, I didn't add any on or take any off. Do you think that was right or wrong?'. A nonconservation counter-suggestion was given to a child who had given a conserving judgment; this was 'Somebody else said I've got more because mine's longer/I've got four bits and you've only got one. Do you think that was right or wrong?' Finally, the standard amount question was repeated to see if the child had accepted or rejected the countersuggestion.

The 'rolled' situation was then introduced to the child. The experimenter explained that sausage A was hers, and that she was going to choose one of the other three (B, B+, B++) to be his. He agreed that B+ was the same to eat as A, that B was less, and that B++ was more. The experimenter mimed how she was going to take one of the three for the child, and roll it, and then ask the child for an amount judgment.

The experimenter then placed the screen so that the child could not see which of the three fat sausages was chosen for him. The smallest one was chosen (B), the experimenter rolled it behind the screen until it was much longer than the other sausages, and then she placed it beside A and asked the standard amount question. Then, the child was asked which sausage had been chosen: 'Which sausage did I choose to be yours, the one that was the same to eat as mine, or the big one, or the little one?'. Finally, the standard amount question was repeated to give the child a last opportunity to make his amount and 'which chosen' judgments consistent.

Subjects

The subjects were 34 children who attended three London schools. There were 23 girls and 11 boys, aged between seven and nine years.

Treatment of results

In each conservation task, the child was given a score of 0, 1, 2 or 3. A score of 0 was given if the child gave a nonconserving judgment and rejected the conservation countersuggestion, repeating a nonconserving judgment; a score of 1 was given for a nonconserving judgment with acceptance of the conservation countersuggestion; a score of 2 was given for a conserving judgment with acceptance of the nonconservation countersuggestion; and a score of 3 was given for a conserving judgment with rejection of the nonconservation countersuggestion.

On the basis of their scores in the conservation test, the children were classified into five groups.

Group 1: conservers; score 3 in both tasks.
Group 2: score 3 in one task, and less than 3 in the other.

Group 3: score 2 in at least one task, and less than 3 in the other.

Group 4: score 1 in at least one task, and less than 2 in the other.

Group 5: nonconservers, score 0 in both tasks.

In the 'rolled' situation, the child gave three judgments: the first post-deformation amount judgment (with a reason); the 'which chosen' judgment; and the second post-deformation amount judgment, which could be the same as or different from the first. On the basis of these three answers, the child was scored as consistent (C), inconsistent (I), or inconsistent followed by correction (I–C). A consistent response was one in which the first and second post-deformation amount judgments and the 'which chosen' judgments were consistent, e.g. a judgment that B′ was the same to eat as A, and a guess that B+ (the same amount as A) had been chosen. An inconsistent response was one in which these judgments were not consistent, e.g. a judgment that B′ was more than A, but that B (less than A) had been chosen. An inconsistent response followed by correction was one in which the first post-deformation amount judgment was inconsistent with the 'which chosen' judgment, but the second post-deformation amount judgment was not, e.g. a judgment that B′ was more than A, that B had been chosen, and then a judgment that B′ was less than A.

Results and discussion

Models 1 and 2 predict that the NAS criterion should have been easier to apply in the 'rolled' reduced conflict situation than in the conservation test, whereas Models 3 and 4 predict that it should not have been easier to apply.

The children in conservation groups 1, 2 and 3 all appeared to use the NAS criterion spontaneously (rather than in response to the countersuggestion); those in group 4 seemed to use it only in response to the countersuggestion; and those in group 5 showed no signs of using the NAS criterion in the conservation test. Hence Models 1 and 2 predict that all the children in groups 1, 2 and 3 should have used the NAS criterion in the 'rolled' situation, as well as some children in groups 4 and 5. Models 3 and 4, on the other hand, predict that none of the children in groups 4 and 5 should have used the NAS criterion in the 'rolled' situation, and those in groups 1, 2 and 3 need not have done so.

In the 'rolled' situation, children who used the NAS criterion should have given C or I–C responses, although others may have given such responses without having used the NAS criterion. Ways of deciding whether a C or I–C response was based on the NAS criterion are discussed below.

Table 8.1 shows performance in the 'rolled' situation related to performance in the conservation test. All the children in conservation groups 1 and 2 gave C or I–C responses in the 'rolled' situation, as did 58% of the group 3, 75% of the group 4, and 60% of the group 5 children. If all these children used the NAS criterion, then Models 1 and 2 are clearly supported. Their consistent judgments may, however, have been based on perceptual criteria: they may have assumed that the pre- and post-deformation appearances were the same. All the children saw the three fat sausages from which theirs was chosen, but they may have failed to use this information to help them answer the 'which chosen' question.

Table 8.1. Numbers and percentages of children in each conservation group who gave C, I—C and I responses in the 'rolled' situation

		Conservation level						
		cons. ←			noncons.			
	groups:	1	2	3	4	5	Total	
	I	0	0	3	2	2	7	
Responses in 'rolled' situation	I—C	1	2	2	2	1	8	Numbers of children
	C	8	3	2	4	2	19	
	Total	9	5	7	8	5	34	
	I	0	0	42	25	40		
	I—C	11·5	40	29	25	20		Percentages of children in each of groups 1—5
	C	88·5	60	29	50	40		

The reason a child gave for his post-deformation amount judgment might indicate that he was using the NAS criterion. If, for example, the child said 'I've got more because I think you chose the big one', then he was probably using the NAS criterion. This kind of reason was given only by children in conservation groups 1 and 2, so further analysis is necessary to decide whether or not the C and I—C responses given by those in groups 3, 4 and 5 were based on the NAS criterion.

Table 8.2 shows the relationship between conservation level, consistency and amount judgments. Amount judgments were classified as M, L or S, referring to judgments of 'more', 'less' or 'same' in the child's sausage compared with the experimenter's. All but one of the seven M—C responses were given by group 4 and 5 children, and these children gave no L—C or S—C responses. Children in groups 1—3 who were consistent nearly always gave amount judgments of L or S. It also appears, from Table 8.3, that M—I responses were associated with a higher conservation level than M—C responses. Three out of seven group 3 children gave M—I responses, but none gave M—C responses. If a child gave inconsistent amount and 'which chosen' judgments, then he must have imagined that the pre-deformation appearance differed from the post-deformation appearance. It was assumed, in designing this reduced conflict situation, that a child who had available the NAS criterion would find it easy to accommodate his guess about the pre-deformation appearance to his perceptual post-deformation amount judgment. The post-deformation appearance could quite reasonably be supposed to have resulted from any of the three sausages from which the child's was chosen. If the above assumption was valid, then it is unlikely that children who gave inconsistent responses had available the NAS criterion. Since inconsistent responses were associated with better performance in the conservation test than were M—C responses, then presumably the M—C responses were not NAS-based. The suggestion is, then, that the group 4 and 5 children who gave consistent amount and 'which chosen' judgments were assuming that pre- and post-deformation appearances were the

Table 8.2. Results given in Table 8.1 broken down according to the amount judgment given

Amount	Consistency	cons. 1	2	3	4	noncons. 5	Total
M	I	0	0	3	1	2	6
	I—C	0	0	1	1	0	2
	C	1	0	0	4	2	7
L	I	0	0	0	1	0	1
	I—C	0	1	1	1	1	4
	C	4	2	0	0	0	6
S	I	0	0	0	0	0	0
	I—C	0	1	0	0	0	1
	C	3	1	2	0	0	6
?	I—C	1	0	0	0	0	1
Total		9	5	7	8	5	34

(Column header group: Conservation level)

Amount judgments; M: more in long thin sausage; L: more in short, fat sausage; S: same in both; ?: don't know; In the case of I—C judgments, the first amount judgment is given

Table 8.3. Summary of Table 8.2 demonstrating relationship between conservation level (groups 1—5) and performance in the 'rolled' situation

	Amount Consistency	cons. 1	2	3	4	noncons. 5	Total	
	M C	1	0	0	4	2	7	
Performance	L,M I	0	0	3	2	2	7	
in 'rolled'	?,L,M,S I—C	1	2	2	2	1	8	Number of children
situation	L,S C	7	3	2	0	0	12	
	Total	9	5	7	8	5	34	
	M C	11·5	0	0	50	40		
	L,M I	0	0	42	25	40		Percentage of children in each conservation group
	?.L,M,S I—C	11·5	40	29	25	20		
	L,S C	77	60	29	0	0		

(Column header group: Conservation level)

same, and judged amount on the basis of appearance; they were not using the NAS criterion. However, three out of the 13 group 4 and 5 children did give I–C responses. But since three children in group 3, who did seem spontaneously to use the NAS criterion in the conservation test, nevertheless gave inconsistent responses in the 'rolled' situation, the performance of the three in groups 4 and 5 cannot be taken as support for Models 1 and 2.

Summary and conclusions

The aim of this experiment was to see whether the NAS criterion is easier to apply when the child is screened from the pre-deformation appearance. Models 1 and 2 predict that it is; Models 3 and 4 predict that it is not. At first sight the results provided clear support from Models 1 and 2, since many of those who failed to conserve spontaneously in the conservation test did give consistent pre- and post-deformation amount judgments in the 'rolled' situation. However, their consistent judgments appeared to be different from those given by children who did conserve spontaneously in the conservation test, and it was argued that they were not based on the NAS criterion. Nevertheless, three children who failed to conserve spontaneously in the conservation test did give I–C (inconsistent followed by correction) responses in the 'rolled' situation; they were probably based on the NAS criterion. Since three children who did conserve spontaneously in the conservation test gave inconsistent responses in the 'rolled' situation (indicating failure to use the NAS criterion), that result does not demonstrate that the NAS criterion was easier to apply in the reduced conflict situation than in the conservation test. Hence the results fail to support Models 1 and 2, but are consistent with Models 3 and 4.

8.3 Screening from the post-deformation appearance: the 'choice' situation

Procedure

The same subjects and the same materials served in the 'choice' situation as in the 'rolled' situation, and the order in which the two situations were presented was varied. In the 'choice' situation, the child saw the experimenter choose the smallest sausage, B, to be his. B was then taken behind the screen and rolled to B', and it remained hidden from the child. The experimenter said 'Now I've rolled yours, here's yours behind here' (indicating behind the screen). It was made clear which sausage was the experimenter's, and the child was asked the standard amount question: he was asked to compare the amount in A with that in B'. He was then asked which sausage had been chosen for him, as in the 'rolled' situation, but this time all children were expected to give the correct answer. Next, the child was asked 'How long do you think your sausage is (pointing): is it just as long as mine, or is yours longer, or is mine longer?' (pointing). Finally, the standard amount question was repeated.

Treatment of results

As shown in section 8.2, the children were classified into five groups on the basis of their performance in the two conservation tasks which had preceded the 'choice' situation. Children in group 1 were considered to be conservers, they answered perfectly in both tasks; children in group 5 were considered to be nonconservers, they showed no signs of using the NAS criterion in either task. The children in groups 2 and 3, as well as those in group 1, did seem to use the NAS criterion spontaneously, but those in group 4 used it only in response to the countersuggestion.

In the 'choice' situation, all the children answered the 'which chosen' question correctly, as expected. They did, however, differ in three other respects: the first post-deformation amount judgment (and the reason given); the estimated length of their sausage compared with that of the experimenter's; and the second post-deformation amount judgment, which could be the same as or different from the first one.

Results and discussion

The predictions are just the same as in section 8.2: Models 1 and 2 predict that the NAS criterion should have been easier to apply in the 'choice' reduced conflict situation than in the conservation test, whereas Models 3 and 4 predict that it should not have been easier to apply.

A child who used the NAS criterion in the 'choice' situation should answer that he had less to eat than the experimenter because she chose B (which was less than A) to be his. It is possible, though, that a child could give the correct amount judgment just because he assumed that B' still looked the same as B, or at least that it was still shorter than A. Table 8.4 shows the first post-deformation amount judgments given in the 'choice' situation. Six of the children did not answer at all; presumably they felt they must see the post-deformation appearance in order to make their amount

Table 8.4. First post-deformation amount judgments given in the 'choice' situation, related to conservation level

| | | cons. | | | noncons. | | |
	groups:	1	2	3	4	5	Total
Amount Judgment	M	0	0	2	1	2	5
in 'choice' situation	L	9	5	3	1	2	20
	S	0	0	0	3	0	3
	?	0	0	2	3	1	6
	Total	9	5	7	8	5	34

M: more in hidden, longer sausage; L: more in experimenter's fatter sausage; S: same in both; ?: don't know; Correct judgment: L judgment. These children were all in groups 3, 4 and 5. All the children in groups 1 and 2 gave the correct judgment, as did six of those in groups 3, 4 and 5.

Table 8.5 shows the length judgments given, and their relationship to amount judgments. These responses were classified into five kinds, with the aim of deciding which children may have used the NAS criterion.

Table 8.5. Numbers of children in each conservation group who gave each amount and length judgment in the 'choice' situation

		Conservation level					
		cons.	←————		noncons.		
Amount	Length	1	2	3	4	5	Total
X–X	=,>	0	0	2	4	2	8
?–X	=,>	0	0	2	2	0	4
√–X	=,>	0	2	1	0	2	5
?–√	<	0	0	0	1	1	2
√–√	<	0	0	2	1	0	3
√–√	=,>,?	9	3	0	0	0	12
Total		9	5	7	8	5	34

Amount: (in hidden sausage)
X: more in hidden sausage; same in both.
√ : less in hidden sausage; correct judgment.
?: don't know.
First symbol refers to initial post-deformation judgment; second symbol refers to judgment given after length judgment.

Length: (of hidden sausage)
=: same length as experimenter's sausage.
>: longer than experimenter's sausage.
<: shorter than experimenter's sausage.
?: don't know.

The top row of Table 8.5 gives the children whose amount judgments were incorrect, and seemed to be based on guessed length of the hidden sausage. The child might, for example, judge that there was more to eat in his hidden sausage than in the experimenter's, and also that his sausage was longer. Often the reasons showed that the child had worked out the length of his hidden sausage—'I've got more, because I think the smaller one has got longer because you've rolled it now' or 'I've got more 'cos you rolled it longer'. Responses of this type were given by eight out of the 20 children in groups 3–5.

The second row of the table gives responses apparently based on similar reasoning. At first the child was unable to give an amount judgment, but when he was asked the length question he guessed that the hidden sausage was the same length as, or longer than, the experimenter's. He then made an amount judgment consistent with his length guess. Four out of the 15 children in groups 3 and 4 responded in this way.

Children in the third row first gave correct amount judgments, but changed these to be consistent with their length guesses. For example, a child who guessed that his sausage was longer than the experimenter's, changed his judgment to 'more' in his sausage. The initial, correct amount judgment may have been based on the NAS criterion, which was not strong enough to withstand the length judgment. Alternatively, the correct judgment may have been based on assumption of unchanged appearance, which was abandoned when the child was asked the length question and was reminded about the effects of rolling. The two nonconservers (group 5) in this category seemed to base their correct judgments on appearance:

> Janet: Post-deformation amount judgment—'You have (more), 'cos it's long' (the child assumes the experimenter's sausage is longer). Amount judgment following length question—'I have (more) 'cos you rolled it'.
>
> Henry: Post-deformation amount judgment—'You've got more, yours is a bit too long'.
> Amount judgment following length question—'I have (more), mine's rolled up long'.

The one child in group 3 who fell into this category may, however, have used the NAS criterion for the correct amount judgment:

> Joanna: Post-deformation amount judgment—'You got more, 'cos you took the smallest one'.
> Amount judgment following length question, having judged both sausages were equal in length—'We've got the same'.

Two children in group 2 reasoned in a similar way. They gave correct post-deformation amount judgments, and gave as their reason, the experimenter's choice of the smallest sausage. When asked the length question, both guessed that their hidden sausage was longer than the experimenter's, and then changed to equality amount judgments:

> Gulsen: Post-deformation amount judgment—'You've got more, I've got less, 'cos you took the smallest one'.
> Amount judgment following guess that hidden sausage was longer—'Same, mine's long and it's big, yours is fat'.
> Amount judgment after reminder that his was the smallest sausage —'Same'.

Children in the fourth and fifth rows guessed that the hidden sausage was still shorter than the experimenter's. Since the two children in the fourth row were unable to judge the amount until they had guessed the length, they were probably using perceptual criteria for their correct amount judgments. Children in the fifth row gave correct amount judgments before guessing that the hidden sausage was shorter than the experimenter's. The group 4 child apparently based her correct amount judgment on a guess that her sausage was thinner:

> Karen: Post-deformation amount judgment—'No, you (have more), you made it skinnier (i.e. her)'.

The two other children in the fifth row, both in group 3, may have based their correct amount judgments on the NAS criterion and then accommodated their length judgments to be consistent:

> Shelley: Post-deformation amount judgment—'You have (more), you chose the little one'.
> Length guess—'Shorter'.
> Amount judgment—'You have (more)'.

The bottom row of the table contains children who gave correct amount judgments and stuck to these while admitting that the hidden sausage was not shorter than the experimenter's. All the conservers (group 1) and three out of the five group 2 children fell into this category. Even these children, however, were sometimes concerned about the appearance of the hidden sausage.

> Lucie: Post-deformation amount judgment—'You've got more, yours is longer . . . well I think they're both the same length . . . you've got more'.
> Soraya: Post-deformation amount judgment—'You've got more, 'cos mine's smaller than your one . . . mine's high (long) but yours is fat, wider'.

The results suggest, then, that three children in group 3 may have used the NAS criterion in the 'choice' situation, as did all the children in groups 1 and 2. All these children spontaneously gave correct judgments in at least one of the conservation tasks. There was no evidence to suggest that group 4 and 5 children used the NAS criterion in the 'choice' situation. The prediction from Models 1 and 2 was not supported, but the results are consistent with Models 3 and 4.

Summary and conclusions

The 'choice' situation was used to test the same predictions as the 'rolled' situation; according to Models 1 and 2, the NAS criterion should be easier to apply when the child is screened from the post-deformation appearance, than when he is presented with the standard conservation test. According to Models 3 and 4, it should not be. The results of this study showed that three of the children who failed to conserve spontaneously in the conservation test did give consistent pre- and post-deformation amount judgments in the 'choice' situation, but their reasons for these judgments suggested that they were based on appearance rather than on the NAS criterion. The results therefore support Models 3 and 4 rather than Models 1 and 2, and are consistent with those obtained in the 'rolled' situation.

CHAPTER 9

Compensation and Conservation: I

9.1 Introduction

The experiments to be presented in this chapter and the next one are both concerned with the relationship between perceptual compensation judgments and the NAS criterion. A perceptual compensation judgment is one in which entities different in shape are judged to be equal in amount (e.g. a long thin sausage and a short fat one) on the basis of a coordination of dimensions, not on the basis of the NAS criterion. According to Models 1, 2 and 3, the ability to make perceptual compensation judgments appears only when there is also use of the NAS criterion in the standard conservation test; according to Model 4, this ability is necessary for its use. The experiments described in this chapter and the next were intended to investigate different aspects of this general question of the developmental relationship between compensation and conservation.

In Chapter 4, it was shown that the existing evidence does not provide a clear indication of the relative difficulty of compensation and conservation, and it was argued that in any case the procedures used were unsatisfactory. In the standard conservation test, the child has to recognize equal amounts if he is to be considered a conserver; the compensation tests used have been tests of construction, which would be expected to be more difficult even if compensation and conservation were in fact equal in difficulty. In the experiments to be presented in this chapter and the next, a recognition test of compensation was used, rather than a construction test.

9.2 Compensation and screening

It was shown in Chapter 6 how the four models make different predictions about the child's use of the two kinds of information given in the standard conservation test: perceptual information (the pre- and post-deformation appearances) and deformational information (the fact that nothing was added or subtracted). According to Models 1 and 2, the presence of perceptual information makes it more difficult for the child to use the deformational information to give a conserving judgment. These models predict that if presented with only deformational information, conserving judgments should be made by all those who give them in the standard test, as well as by some of those who do not do so.

In contrast, Models 3 and 4 state that perceptual information does not make it more difficult for the child to conserve; if anything, it makes it easier. Model 3's child acquires the operation of compensation along with the NAS criterion, and in the standard conservation test he uses both perceptual and deformational information. He might find it more difficult to give a conserving judgment if presented only with deformational information. Model 4's child acquires the ability to make perceptual compensation judgments before he develops the NAS criterion, and it is through making perceptual compensation judgments that the child acquires the NAS criterion. Like Model 3, Model 4 predicts that being given deformational information alone could make it more difficult for the child to conserve.

If he is presented with perceptual information only, and not deformational information, then the child cannot be expected always to give correct amount judgments when the pieces to be compared are different in shape. However, the four models make different predictions about the stage in conservation acquisition at which the child is prepared to make perceptual compensation judgments, to judge on the basis of appearance alone that a long thin sausage is or could be the same amount as a short fat one. According to Models 1 and 2, the child comes to accept the possibility of perceptual compensation only as a result of using the NAS criterion; children who use the NAS criterion in the standard conservation test may fail to make perceptual compensation judgments. According to Model 3, perceptual compensation judgments are based on the operation of compensation, which involves making an interpretation of the effects of deformation on appearance. For this reason, the child may find it more difficult to accept that entities different in shape can be equal in amount when he is given only deformational information. Models 1, 2 and 3, then, predict that only strong conservers should make perceptual compensation judgments. Model 4, however, requires that all children who use the NAS criterion in the standard conservation test can make perceptual compensation judgments, and some who fail to use the NAS criterion may do so too.

Whereas Model 4's child finds it relatively difficult to use deformational information alone to make an equality amount judgment, he finds it relatively easy to use perceptual information alone when the entities to be compared are different in shape. According to Model 3, it is equally difficult to use deformational information alone and to use perceptual information alone. Models 1 and 2 state that it is easier to use only deformational information than it is to use only perceptual information.

In this experiment, the investigation of the child's use of deformational information alone involved the use of a screening situation rather like one of those described in Chapter 8: 'screening from the post-deformation amount'. There, the intention was to see whether the NAS criterion was easier to use in the reduced conflict situation than in the standard conservation test. The same comparison can be made in the present experiment, but the major aim here is to compare performance in the screening situation with performance in a test of perceptual compensation.

Procedure

There were three parts: firstly, the child was given a 'compensation and screening' test (CS); next, he was given a conservation test composed of three tasks; finally he was given a second CS test.

Different materials were used for the first and second CS test, but they differed only in the colours and sizes of the sausages. Each of the two sets comprised two identical short fat plasticine sausages, A and B, and a set of thin ones all the same width but different in length, sausages 1–5. Sausage 1 was the same length as A and B but thinner, and sausages 2, 3, 4 and 5 were longer. The relative amounts were $2 < A = 3 < 4, 5$.

The procedure in both the CS tests was identical. The child was presented with sausages A and B, he was asked whether they were both the same to eat, and any necessary adjustments were made until he agreed that they were. Then the experimenter took B behind a screen and rolled it, saying 'Now I'm going to take the green sausage behind here and roll it'. The experimenter's arm movements were visible, and the rolling action was audible to the child. This rolled sausage, B', remained behind the screen, hidden from the child. The experimenter then took the other fat sausage, A, and placed it in front of her saying 'Now this is my sausage, I'm having this one. See if you can choose one so you've got *just* the same to eat as me. There's all these (indicating sausages 1–5) and this one behind here (B') to choose from. See if you can choose one so you've got just the same to eat as me.' The child was allowed to move the thin sausage and A to make his judgment, but he was not allowed to peep behind the screen.

If the child made a choice, the procedure differed slightly depending on whether he first chose B', or one of the visible thin sausages.

(i) If he first chose one of the thin sausages 1–5, then the chosen sausage was placed before the child and he was asked 'If this one's yours, and this one's mine (A), have we both got the same to eat, or have you got more, or have I got more? Why?' If he now denied that the two were equal, the thin one was replaced among the others and the child was asked to make another choice, unless he decided that the thin one was a tiny bit too long, in which case he was allowed to cut a piece off. If the child confirmed that his thin sausage was the same amount as A, he was asked whether any of the other sausages were also the same amount as A. If he still failed to select B', he was asked directly whether B' was the same to eat as A, and to give a reason for his judgment.

(ii) If B' was the child's first choice of a sausage, he was asked to give a reason. Care was taken to try and discover whether he was simply assuming that B' still looked the same as A: the child was asked 'What do you think it looks like?' and if necessary 'Is it the same shape as mine?'. The child was also asked whether any of the visible thin sausages were the same to eat as A, and if he selected one, the procedure described in (i) above was followed.

By the end of the testing, then, the child could have chosen both B' and one (or more) of the thin sausages. He could, however, have decided that none of the sausages was the same to eat as A, or he could have chosen only one of them: either B' or one (or more) of the thin sausages. If he chose B' and gave an appropriate reason (see below), he was assumed to have used deformational information alone, and if he chose a thin one which was longer than A, he was assumed to have used perceptual information alone to make a perceptual compensation judgment.

After the first CS test, the child was given three conservation tasks. In each, one of two identical short fat sausages was rolled longer. After he had given his post-deformation amount judgment, the child was given a countersuggestion. In the first two tasks, no reason was given for the suggested judgment: 'Somebody else said we've both got the same to eat still. Why do you think they said that?' or 'Somebody else said I've got more to eat. Why do you think they said that?' The rationale behind this, and the results of this part of the experiment, were presented in Chapter 2 and will not be repeated here. In the third conservation task, a reason was given for the suggested judgment, e.g. 'Somebody else said I've got more because mine's longer. Do you think that was right or wrong?'. Finally, the standard amount question was repeated, to see whether the child had accepted or rejected the counter-suggestion. He was considered to have accepted it if he repeated the suggested judgment; otherwise he was considered to have rejected it.

Finally, the child was given a second CS test. CS tests were given both before and after the conservation test because it was expected that seeing the effects on appearance of rolling in the conservation test might help the child to select B'.

Subjects

The subjects were 50 children aged between five years, eleven months and seven years, nine months, all of whom attended an infants' school near Southampton. One child's results were excluded from the analysis because he did not pay attention during testing.

Predictions

The predictions refer to (i) the relationship between choosing X and choosing B', and (ii) the relationship between these choices and performance in the conservation test.

(i) Models 1 and 2 predict that no child should choose X but not B', although there should be children who choose B' but not X.

Model 3 predicts that there should be no difference in difficulty between choosing X and B'; children who choose only one should be equally likely to choose either, but most children should choose neither or both.

Model 4 predicts that there should be children who choose X but not B', but none who choose B' but not X.

(ii) Models 1 and 2 predict that choosing B' should occur among nonconservers, and all intermediate and full conservers should choose B', while not all of them should choose X.

Model 3 predicts that nonconservers should choose neither X nor B'. It might be expected that choosing either B' or X would be more difficult than conserving in the conservation test, in which full information is given, and so children who conserve in the conservation test may fail to select either B' or X or both.

Model 4 predicts that all intermediate and full conservers should choose X, but choosing B' may be more difficult than conserving in the conservation test.

Treatment of results

In the CS tests, if the child selected one of the sausages 2–5 and confirmed that it was the same to eat as A, then he was considered to have made a compensation judgment, X = A.

If he selected B' and indicated that his judgment was not just based on the assumption that B' still looked the same as A, then he was considered to have made a conservation judgment, B' = A. Indications that the judgment B' = A was not just based on such an assumption were the child's denial that B' was the same shape as A, a statement that he did not know what B' looked like, or the giving of a deformational reason for judging B' = A (e.g. 'You just rolled it'). Deformational reasons were specified in Chapter 6.

Children who selected B' but seemed to base their judgments on an assumption that B' looked the same as A were identified but were classified differently from those described above.

In each of the three conservation tasks, the child was given a score of 0, 1, 2 or 3. A score of 0 was given for a nonconserving judgment with rejection of the conservation countersuggestion; a score of 1 was given for a nonconserving judgment with acceptance of this countersuggestion; a score of 2 was given for a conserving judgment with acceptance of the nonconservation countersuggestion; and a score of 3 was given for a conserving judgment with rejection of this countersuggestion.

On the basis of his overall performance in the conservation test, the child was placed in one of four groups.

Group 1: conservers—score 3 in all three tasks.
Group 2: intermediate conservers—score 3 in one or two tasks.
Group 3: intermediate conservers—score 1 or 2 in at least one task, but never
        scored 3.
Group 4: nonconservers—score 0 in all three tasks.

Results and discussion

Table 9.1 shows the relationship between performance in the first CS test and performance in the conservation test; Table 9.2 shows that between performance in the second CS test and in the conservation test.

(i) The relationship between choosing X and choosing B' will be considered first. Table 9.1 shows that in the first CS test, 10 children chose X but not B', whereas only one child chose B' but not X. Similarly, Table 9.2 shows that in the second CS test, nine children chose X but not B', but only one child (a different one) chose B' but not X.

Models 1 and 2 predicted that no children should choose X but not B', while a number should choose B' but not X; Model 3 predicted that children who chose only one of the two should be equally likely to choose either B' or X; Model 4 predicted that a number of children should choose X but not B', while none should choose B' but not X. Clearly, the results are most in accordance with Model 4.

Table 9.1. Numbers of children in each conservation group who chose X and B' in the first CS test

| CS test | | cons. | | | noncons. | Total |
X	B'	1	2	3	4	
—	—	0	7	5	10	22
√	—	5	2	2	1	10
—	√	0	1	0	0	1
√	√	10	3	2	1	16
Total		15	13	9	12	49

A tick in the X column means that the child chose X; similarly for the B' column.

Table 9.2. Numbers of children in each conservation group who chose X and B' in the second CS test

| CS test | | cons. | | | noncons. | Total |
X	B'	1	2	3	4	
—	—	0	1	2	10	13
√	—	2	3	3	1	9
—	√	0	0	1	0	1
√	√	13	9	3	1	26
Total		15	13	9	12	49

There was quite a change in performance from the first CS test to the second. Table 9.3 shows that it was mainly the intermediate conservers (groups 2 and 3) who changed; all the nonconservers (group 4) and most of the conservers (group 1) performed in the same way in both the CS tests. The changes in performance might merely indicate that the CS tests were rather unreliable. An analysis of the particular changes which occurred, however, suggests that the changes reflected development, however superficial, rather than unreliability. There seems to be a developmental sequence in performance in the CS test, the earliest stage being to choose neither B' nor X, the middle stage being to choose one of them (commonly X) and the final stage to choose both. None of the changes from the first to the second CS test were in a backward direction along this sequence, only four of them were moves from the first to the last stage, while the others (11) were moves from the first to the middle stage, or from the middle to the last stage. That it was the intermediate conservers who changed, and that their changes were orderly, suggests that the tests were not simply unreliable.

Table 9.3. Changes in performance from the first to the second CS test

| CS tests | | | | Conservation level (groups 1—4) | | | | |
| 1st | | 2nd | | cons. | ← | — → | noncons. | Total |
X	B'	X	B'	1	2	3	4	
—	—	√	—	0	3	1	0	4
—	—	—	√	0	0	1	0	1
—	—	√	√	0	3	1	0	4
—	√	√	√	0	1	0	0	1
√	—	√	√	3	2	0	0	5
Total who changed				3	9	3	0	15
Total no change				12	4	6	12	34

There were other changes from the first to the second CS test, changes in the reasons given for choosing B'. In the first CS test, ten children chose B' and said they thought it still looked the same shape as A. They were two children in group 2, three in group 3 and five in group 4 (nonconservers). In the second CS test, the number fell to two, both of whom were group 4 nonconservers. As a result of being given the conservation test, the children do seem to have learned or remembered that rolling changes the shape of sausages.

In the first CS test, four children chose B' and gave as their only reason, that they thought it looked like X; one other child's only stated reason for choosing B' was that he thought it was longer and thinner than A. These four children seem to have been basing their B' amount judgments either partly or wholly on a guess about the appearance of B'. This kind of reason was only given once in the second CS test, and that by a child who also gave another reason, that B' had been the same as A at first.

Children who chose X but not B' also seemed on occasion to be guessing the appearance of B'—five of them said that B' was or might be too long. These results suggest that screening the child from the post-deformation appearance may not allow him to ignore it and to judge the amount on the basis of deformational information alone. Indications of this were also found in the screening experiments reported in Chapter 8.

(ii) Secondly, the relationship between performance in the CS tests and performance in the conservation test will be examined. Because of the changes in performance from the first to the second CS test, the predictions concerning this relationship need to be specified more precisely. In the conservation test, children who failed to conserve spontaneously were given a conservation countersuggestion. In contrast, children who failed to choose B' or X in the CS tests were not given any further help. It seems reasonable, therefore, to compare performance in the first CS test with that prior to countersuggestion in the first conservation task: Models 1 and

2 require that children who spontaneously conserved in their first conservation task (scored 2 and 3) should all have chosen B' in their first CS test, as should some children who scored only 0 or 1. These models require that X should have been chosen only by children who scored 2 or 3, and not necessarily by all of these children. Model 3 predicts that no children who scored 0 or 1 should have chosen B' or X; it allows some who scored 2 or 3 not to have done so. Model 4 requires all who scored 2 or 3 to have selected X, and allows some who scored 0 or 1 to have done so. Model 4 does not, however, permit any child who scored 0 or 1 to have selected B', and it allows some who scored 2 or 3 not to have selected B'. These predictions are summarized in Table 9.4, which also gives the actual results.

Table 9.4. Scores in the first conservation task related to choice of B' and of X in the first CS test

Score in first cons. task	Choice of B'		
	Results obtained	Predicted results	
		Models 1 & 2	Models 3 & 4
0, 1	$\frac{3}{29} = 10 \cdot 3\%$	> 0%	0%
2, 3	$\frac{14}{20} = 70\%$	100%	⩽ 100%
	Choice of X		
	Results obtained	Predicted results	
		Models 1, 2 & 3	Model 4
0, 1	$\frac{8}{29} = 27 \cdot 6\%$	0%	⩾ 0%
2, 3	$\frac{18}{20} = 90\%$	⩽ 100%	100%

Model 4 seems to accommodate the results best; only this model predicts the results to within about 10%; the other models are in error by about 30%. The discrepancies from the predicted results will be discussed further below. Before going into these, performance in the second CS test will be considered.

It is appropriate to compare performance in the second CS test with overall conservation performance. These results were presented in Table 9.2. Models 1 and 2 predicted that B' would be chosen by all the children in groups 1, 2 and 3, as well as by some of the group 4 nonconservers. Models 3 and 4 predicted that none of the group 4 nonconservers would choose B', and that choosing B' would be more difficult than conserving in the conservation test.

In fact, in the second CS test B' was chosen by 87% of the group 1 conservers, 69·2% of the group 2 children, 44·4% of the group 3 children, and by 8·3% of the group 4 nonconservers. These results are more in accordance with Models 3 and 4 than with Models 1 and 2. This is consistent with the conclusions drawn from the results of the first CS test; there too, Models 3 and 4 made the same predictions about choice of B', and the results were most in accordance with these predictions.

The results obtained here are also consistent with those presented in Chapter 8, where it was shown that the NAS criterion was no easier to apply in reduced conflict situations than in the standard conservation test. Why, then, did any of the group 4 nonconservers and group 3 children select B'? The predictions concerning choice of B' were based on an assumption that children would not be prepared to judge B' = A on the basis of the guessed appearance of B'. This assumption seems to have been inappropriate: as mentioned above, reasons for choosing or not choosing B' quite often referred to the guessed appearance of B', particularly in the first CS test.

The predictions about choosing X in the second CS test were as follows: Models 1, 2 and 3 predicted that none of the nonconservers should have chosen X, neither should all of those in groups 1, 2 and 3, choosing X should have been more difficult than conserving in the conservation test. Model 4, in contrast, required all intermediate and full conservers to choose X, and allowed nonconservers to do so.

Table 9.2 shows that X was chosen by all 15 of the group 1 conservers (100%), by all but one of the 13 group 2 children (92.3%), by six of the nine group 3 children (66.7%), and by two of the 12 group 4 nonconservers (16·7%). These results are more in accordance with Model 4 than with Models 1, 2 and 3. Again, this is consistent with the conclusions drawn from the results of the first CS test. In that, two children failed to select X yet scored 3 in their first conservation task; one of these did at first make a perceptual compensation judgment only to reject it, with hesitation, when she was asked to conform her judgment X = A. Four other children failed to select X in their second CS test although they had conserved in the conservation test. The scores of these four in the three conservation tasks were 1, 3, 3; 0, 1, 2; 0, 0, 1; and 0, 0, 2; one of them never spontaneously gave a conserving judgment so need not, according to Model 4, have spontaneously made a perceptual compensation judgment, and another two spontaneously conserved only in their last conservation task. It seems, then, that the ability to make perceptual compensation judgments did appear sufficiently early in conservation acquisition to support Model 4.

Summary and conclusions

The aim of this experiment was to compare the child's use of two kinds of information—using the information that nothing was added or subtracted during deformation to make an equality amount judgment, and using perceptual information to judge a long thin sausage to be equal in amount to a short fat one (a perceptual compensation judgment). Both kinds of information are given in the standard conservation test, and the four models made different predictions about the child's use of them.

It was found that the ability to make perceptual compensation judgments developed prior to the ability to use only deformational information; in the CS tests, nine or ten children chose X (perceptual information) but not B' (deformational information), while only one child chose B' but not X. The ability to make perceptual compensation judgments appeared early in conservation acquisition, but the ability to use only deformational information appeared rather late. The results were interpreted as supporting Model 4 rather than Models 1, 2 and 3.

CHAPTER 10

Compensation and Conservation: II

10.1 Introduction

The aim of the experiment to be described in this chapter was to answer two of the questions raised in Chapter 6: 'Does the child make perceptual compensation judgments which are always consistent with his judgments about the effects of deformation on appearance?' and 'Does the child make perceptual compensation judgments only if he knows about the uniqueness of reversibility?'.

10.2 Compensation and the NAS criterion

According to Models 1 and 2, the ability to make a perceptual compensation judgment arises only as a consequence of applying the NAS criterion in the standard conservation test; Model 3 states that this ability is acquired along with the NAS criterion. In contrast with these three models, Model 4 states that the ability to make a perceptual compensation judgment is a necessary prerequisite for the development of the NAS criterion. Suppose the child selects on the basis of appearance a long thin sausage which he thinks is the same amount as a given short fat one, and then the fat sausage is rolled until it is just as thin as the other. If the two sausages are not then equal in length, Models 1, 2 and 3 require that all children should accept that their initial equality amount judgment was wrong; Model 4 does not require all children to correct their perceptual compensation judgments in this way, a child who can make perceptual compensation judgments need not use the NAS criterion.

In general, as pointed out in Chapter 6, Models 1–3 require that among children who are prepared to make perceptual compensation judgments, there should be consistency between these, and judgments about the possibility of making the two entities look identical by deformation. Model 4, however, allows the child to make inconsistent amount and deformation judgments.

The models also differ in their prediction about the relative difficulty of perceptual compensation and conservation judgments. The concern is not whether the child can make correct perceptual compensation judgments, but simply whether he accepts that entities different in shape can be equal in amount. Model 4 predicts that any child who uses the NAS criterion in conservation tasks must be able to make perceptual compensation judgments. Models 1–3, however, predict that only strong conservers should make perceptual compensation judgments. If the child first accepts that entities different in shape can be equal in amount because nothing was added or subtracted during deformation, as is the case according to Models 1 and 2, then he should find the equality more difficult to accept when he is required to make a perceptual comparison between two amounts without seeing deformation. Model 3 states that perceptual compensation judgments are based on the operation of compensation; since this involves an interpretation of the effects of deformation on appearance, it would presumably be more difficult to make a compensation interpretation of changes in dimensions when no deformation had been seen. These predictions have already been tested in the preceding experiment (Chapter 9).

The relationship between compensation and knowledge of the uniqueness of reversibility was also examined in the present experiment. The models' predictions about this relationship were given in Chapter 6, but they will be presented again here for the sake of convenience since they are a little complicated. According to Model 3, perceptual compensation judgments are based on the operation of compensation, which involves interpreting the changes in dimensions as cancelling each other out at each point in the deformation. As summarized in Chapter 6, such an interpretation logically requires knowledge of one aspect of the uniqueness of reversibility. In the case of a plasticine sausage rolled thinner, for example, the child cannot be considered to have the operation of compensation unless he knows that a given short fat sausage can be rolled to look just like only one of a set of equally thin sausages different in length. It is, however, logically possible that a child could have this knowledge yet be unable to make perceptual compensation judgments or to conserve. Models 1, 2 and 4 do not require such a strict relationship between perceptual compensation and knowledge of the uniqueness of reversibility, although Models 1 and 2 do require any child who makes a perceptual compensation judgment to reason consistently with the NAS criterion. If he thinks, then, that the short fat sausage can be rolled to look like several of the thin sausages, he should want to judge all of these equal in amount to the fat sausage. He may realize the contradiction in judging several unequal thin sausages to be equal in amount to the short fat sausage. In contrast with Models 1, 2 and 3, Model 4 allows the child to judge that the short fat sausage can be rolled to look like several of the thin ones, while judging only one of these thin ones to be the same amount as the short fat one; Model 4's child may make a perceptual compensation judgment while being ignorant of the uniqueness of reversibility and while reasoning inconsistently with the NAS criterion.

Detailed predictions about each of the relationships mentioned above will be specified after the method has been outlined.

Method and predictions

Each child was given a conservation test composed of four tasks and a compensation test. In the compensation test, the child first made a perceptual compensation judgment and was then given the deformational information necessary to correct it. The child was given the opportunity of the following, (i)–(v).

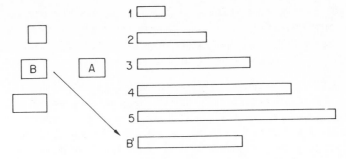

Figure 10.1 Materials used in the compensation test

(i) Choosing from a set of thin sausages, the one (or more) which he thought was equal in amount to a short fat sausage, although longer: X = A (perceptual compensation).

(ii) Judging whether A could be rolled to look just like X, and like other thin sausages not judged equal to A (X+ and X−): A → X, A ∤ X+ or X− (reversibility-before).

(iii) Choosing from a set of fat sausages, the one equal in amount to A: B = A.

(iv) Using the information that B rolled to B′ was unequal to X, to reject the judgment X = A (rejection of compensation judgment).

(v) Again judging whether A could be rolled to look just like X (reversibility-after).

The correct adult performance would be as follows.

(i) Judge X = A.

(ii) Judge that A can be rolled to look like X only, and not like any of the other thin sausages. (A → X only).

(iii) Judge B′ = A.

(iv) Reject the judgment X = A.

(v) Reject the judgment that A can be rolled to look like X.

The models make the following predictions. These predictions are based on the assumption that the child has transitivity, i.e. that he knows if B′ ≠ X, and B′ = A, then X ≠ A. No assumption is made as to whether the child knows about the uniqueness of reversibility, except when this effects the compensation judgments expected by Model 3.

1. Compensation and conservation. The comparison of B′ with A provides a conservation test, although the B′ = A judgment might be based on perceptual compensation. Models 1, 2 and 3 predict that any child who makes a compensation judgment X = A should also judge B′ = A, but that there may be children who judge B′ = A without judging X = A. Model 4 predicts the converse, that any child who judges B′ = A must judge X = A, while a child may judge X = A without judging B′ = A. Underlying this prediction is the assumption that to judge B′ = A on the basis of perceptual compensation would be no easier than to judge X = A.

As indicated above, the models also make general predictions about the relative difficulty of perceptual compensation and conservation in the standard test: according to Models 1, 2 and 3 only strong conservers should be able to compensate, but Model 4 predicts that all intermediate and full conservers can compensate.

2. Compensation and reversibility-before.   According to Model 3 any child who judges X = A must judge that X is the only sausage which A can be rolled to resemble (reversibility-before). Models 1 and 2, while requiring consistency between judgments about amount and judgments about rolling among children who make compensation judgments, allows a weaker relationship than Model 3: if a child judges X = A, then he must judge that, if A can be rolled to look just like a particular thin sausage, then A is equal in amount to that sausage. That is, no child should judge A = X, A ≠ X+, A → X+. Model 4 allows a child to make that sequence of judgments, i.e. a child who makes a compensation judgment need not want his judgments about amount and about rolling to be consistent.

3. Rejection of compensation judgment.   Models 1, 2 and 3 predict that any child who can compensate should subsequently reject his compensation judgment in favour of the conservation judgment B' = A. Model 4 allows a child who judges both X = A and B' = A, to reject B' in favour of X.

4. Compensation and reversibility-after.   Models 1, 2 and 3 predict that any child who has rejected his compensation judgment in favour of B' = A must reject his reversibility-before judgment, A → X, and judge instead that A can be rolled to look like B' only, i.e. he must pass reversibility-after. Model 4 allows a child to reject his compensation judgment but fail reversibility-after: having judged A = X, he may judge A ≠ X, A = B', A → X. He may also pass reversibility-before but fail to reject his compensation judgment.

These predictions are summarized in Table 10.1.

Table 10.1. Summary of the predictions from the four models concerning performance in the compensation test

	Models 1 and 2	Model 3	Model 4
Compensation and conservation	If judge X = A, then judge B' = A	As Models 1 and 2	If judge B' = A, then judge X = A
Compensation and rev.-before	If judge A = X and A → X and X+ or X−, then want to judge A = X+ or X−	If judge A = X, then judge A → X only	May judge A = X and A → X and X+ or X−, without implications for A = X+ or X−
Rejection of compensation	If judge X = A and B' = A, must reject X = A in favour of B' = A	As Models 1 and 2	May prefer X = A to B' = A, or have no basis for choosing
Compensation and rev.-after	If reject X = A, must reject A → X: judge A → B'	As Models 1 and 2	If reject X = A, might not reject A → X

Procedure

The child was given three conservation tasks, followed by the compensation test, and then a fourth conservation task. Two of the conservation tasks involved the deformation of one of two equal amounts, and the other two were inequality conservation tasks. In Chapter 6, it was argued that use of both equality and inequality tasks should provide a more reliable estimate of the child's conservation level than use of equality or inequality tasks alone. According to Model 4, the child might give an equality judgment of pre- compared with post-deformation amount using perceptual compensation rather than the NAS criterion. Similarly, a child might give the correct answer for the wrong reason in an inequality test. However, a child who answers correctly in both equality and inequality tasks is probably using the NAS criterion.

One equality and one inequality task involved the deformation of one of two short fat plasticine sausages into a long thin one; in the other inequality task, the smaller of two balls was broken up into four pieces; in the other equality task, one of two equal balls was squashed into a pancake.

The procedure in each conservation task was the same: first, the pre-deformation amount judgment was agreed upon, then the experimenter performed the deformation and the standard amount question was asked: 'Have we both got the same to eat, or have you got more, or have I got more? Why?'. Next, the child was given a countersuggestion. If he had given a conserving judgment, the countersuggestion was a nonconservation one; if he had given a nonconserving judgment, it was a conservation one. Finally, the standard amount question was repeated to see if the child had accepted or rejected the countersuggestion. The four tasks were given in six different orders, but the fourth task (following the compensation test) was always one of those involving deformation of a plasticine sausage.

The procedure in the compensation test was rather more complicated. The experimenter indicated that sausage A was hers, and the five thin sausages were arranged in no particular order (see Figure 10.1).

1. Compensation judgment. The child was asked 'Is there one of these (pointing to the thin sausages) you can choose so you've got the same to eat as me?'. The child was allowed to reject all the sausages, but if he simply thought none was quite the right length he was allowed to make adjustments. If a child chose one of the thin sausages, this was placed alongside A, and he was asked the standard amount question so that he could confirm his equality judgment. If the child now denied that the amounts were equal, the thin sausage was replaced and he was given another chance to pick one. Any child who confirmed an equality judgment was asked 'Are any of the others the same to eat as mine?', i.e. he could choose more than one of the thin sausages. A child who did so was required to confirm each judgment. If two thin sausages were confirmed to be equal to A, then the child was asked to compare the two thin ones, and the experimenter attempted to discover whether he really thought that both could be equal to A (in which case he presumably did not have the concept of transitivity), or if he simply was not sure which of the two was really equal to A. In the following sections 2 to 4, references to X apply only to children who confirmed compensation judgments in stage 1 of the procedure.

2. *Reversibility-before.*   The child was asked 'If I roll mine (points to A), without adding any on or taking away, if I just roll it, can I make mine look *just* like this one?' (referring to X, or to sausage number 3 if the child had not made a compensation judgment). In a pilot experiment it had been found that children did understand what was meant by 'look just like.' The question was then repeated, referring to any other sausages judged equal to A, and to one of the sausages not judged equal. Sausages 1 and 5 were not referred to unless the child had judged 5 = A (in which case 'X' refers to sausage 5), because he might have learned enough about the effects of rolling on appearance to know that A could not be made to look like these, even though he did not know about the uniqueness of reversibility. Any child who judged that A could be rolled to look like more than one of the thin sausages was asked to confirm this. He was asked 'So if I roll mine, I can make it look *just* like this one (waiting for reply) . . . *and just* like this one?' The child could now make it clear if he knew that A could be rolled to look like only one of the thin sausages, but was unsure which. Children who judged that A could not be rolled to look like a particular thin sausage, were asked for a reason why not. Any child who seemed uncertain at this point was allowed to return to the compensation judgment and make this consistent with his reversibility judgment if he wished.

3. *Rejection of compensation judgment.*   The child was presented with the set of three fat sausages and was asked, using the same question as in section 1, to pick the one, B, which was the same amount as A. The child was allowed to make adjustments to B if necessary. He was then asked to repeat his compensation judgment/judgments (if he had confirmed any). The experimenter rolled B to B' and laid it among the other thin sausages. The child was asked, using the same question as in section 1, to pick any which he thought were the same amount as A. If the child chose B' or X but not both, then he was asked, using the standard amount question, to compare with A the one not chosen (X or B'). A child who judged B' and X equal to A was asked to compare X with B', to help him become aware of the contradiction.

4. *Reversibility-after.*   The uniqueness of reversibility question used in section 2 was repeated, referring successively to B', to X, and to another of the sausages 2–4 which was not judged equal to A.

Subjects

There were 22 boys and 24 girls, aged from seven to nine years. The children attended a junior school in London.

Treatment of results

The child was given a score of 0, 1 or 2 in each of the four conservation tasks. A score of 0 was given for an incorrect judgment with resistance to the NAS counter-suggestion followed by repetition of an incorrect judgment. A score of 1 was given if the child changed his judgment following the perceptual or NAS countersuggestion, repeating the suggested judgment. A score of 2 was given for a correct judgment with resistance to the perceptual countersuggestion and repetition of the correct judgment.

In addition, note was taken of whether a correct judgment was justified by one of the following reasons (deformation reasons): reference to the initial amount; reference to empirical return; reference to equivalent action, e.g. 'If I rolled mine it would be like yours'; or reference to lack of addition and/or subtraction.

On the basis of their judgments and reasons, children were classified into three groups. *Nonconservers* were those who never scored 1 or 2, those who scored 1 or 2 in only one inequality task, or in only two inequality tasks. If, however, the child gave a deformational reason to justify a correct judgment, he was not classified as a nonconserver. *Conservers* were those who scored 2 on three or four of the tasks, and gave at least one deformational reason. *Intermediate conservers* were all the other children; they scored at least 1 in one of the equality tasks, or gave a deformational reason for a correct judgment in an inequality task.

In the compensation test, each child was scored as passing or failing each of the following five items.

Compensation.   The child passed if he chose and confirmed at least one of the sausages 2–5 to be the same amount as A.

Reversibility-before.   The child passed if he judged that A could be rolled to look just like only one of the thin sausages.

Conservation.   The child passed if he judged that B′ was equal in amount to A, and gave a deformational reason. All those who judged B′ = A did give such a reason, usually referring to the initial amount.

Rejection of compensation judgment.   The child passed if, having judged B′ = A, he rejected any previously made compensation judgment X = A, as soon as he was asked or without having to be asked to compare X with B′.

Reversibility-after.   The child passed if, having seen B rolled to B′, he judged that A could be rolled to look like B′ only.

Results and discussion

1. Compensation and conservation.   Those who failed compensation (i.e. failed to judge X = A) were 13 nonconservers and 10 intermediate conservers. Compensation was passed by none of the nonconservers, 13 intermediate conservers and by all 10 conservers.

These results do not support Model 4 which predicts that all intermediate and conserving children should pass compensation. On the other hand, more than half the intermediate conservers did compensate, suggesting that compensation appears earlier in conservation acquisition than is predicted by Models 1, 2 and 3.

However, the comparison between compensation and overall conservation performance does not allow an appropriate test of Model 4, since it cannot be assumed that the ability to coordinate length and width is necessarily accompanied by the ability to coordinate diameter and thickness, or number of pieces and size. Table 10.2 shows compensation compared with performance in the equality sausage conservation task which preceded the compensation test. Only 22 children were given this task in the first, second or third positions. Since there was a dramatic improvement in performance in the fourth conservation task (see below), this task was not included in the present comparison.

Table 10.2. Frequency of children gaining each conservation score who passed and failed compensation

Comp.	Cons. score			Total
	0	1	2	
Fail	8	1	0	9
Pass	3	6	4	13
Total	11	7	4	22

The conservation scores are those obtained in the first equality sausage conservation task.

As shown in Table 10.2, the results do support Model 4, and are inconsistent with Models 1, 2 and 3, since there was compensation without conservation, but no conservation without compensation. The one intermediate conserver who failed to compensate did not spontaneously give a conserving judgment, but merely accepted the NAS countersuggestion.

The relationship between judging $B' = A$ and compensation was as follows: of those who failed compensation, 17 also failed to judge $B' = A$, and 6 did judge $B' = A$. Of those who passed compensation, none failed to judge $B' = A$, and 23 did judge $B' = A$.

Since children who could conserve should have judged $B' = A$ (although this judgment could have been made on the basis of perceptual compensation), Models 1, 2 and 3 predict that all children who passed compensation should have judged $B' = A$ (i.e. no compensation without conservation). The results just reported show that this was the case. Model 4, however, predicts that no child who failed compensation should have judged $B' = A$; six children did this. Hence Model 4 is not supported by these results. The conclusion from these results contradicts that drawn from Table 10.2; this problem is discussed below.

2. Compensation and reversibility-before. Of those who failed compensation, 22 failed reversibility-before and 1 passed. Of those who passed compensation, 15 failed reversibility-before and 8 passed.

Model 3 predicts that any child who passes compensation should also pass reversibility-before. This prediction is not supported by these results, since 15 children passed compensation but failed reversibility-before.

While Models 1 and 2 do not require compensation to be accompanied by knowledge of the uniqueness of reversibility, they do require that any child who passes compensation should want judgments about amount to be consistent with judgments about deformation. Three children did change their compensation judgments after answering the reversibility-before question, and did appear to be trying to make the two judgments consistent. There were, however, six children who were confident in their $X = A$ judgments in that they chose only one thin sausage and stuck to this choice throughout the compensation and reversibility-before questioning, but who failed reversibility-before. These six were apparently content to say $A = X$, $A \neq X+$ (or $X-$), but $A \to X$ and $X+$ (or $X-$). In this respect, their compensation judgments were not consistent with the NAS criterion. These results can be accommodated only by Model 4, which alone allows children to make that sequence of judgments.

3. Rejection of compensation judgment.   Models 1, 2 and 3 require any child who passes compensation (i.e. who judges $X= A$) and who also judges $B' = A$, to reject the judgment $X = A$ in favour of $B' = A$. This prediction is based on an assumption that the child agrees that $X \neq B'$. Model 4, however, does not require that the contradiction between the judgments $X = A$; $B' = A$; $X \neq B'$ is resolved in that way. A child may, according to Model 4, reject $B' = A$ in favour of $X = A$.

As mentioned in section 1, all 23 children who passed compensation (i.e. who judged $X = A$) also judged $B' = A$. Of these 23, seven did not spontaneously reject their compensation judgments but went through a stage of judging both B' and X equal to A while admitting that B' was not equal to X. Two of the seven showed no signs of disturbance when making these contradictory judgments; they apparently did not have the concept of transitivity. Their responses cannot therefore be used to test the predictions from the three theories concerning the resolution of the contradiction. Of the five who did show signs of conflict, three finally rejected their compensation judgments in favour of $B' = A$. The two remaining children attempted to argue about the appearance of the sausages, although to the experimenter's eyes, their arguments were inappropriate, e.g. 'This one's (X) a bit longer than that one, so therefore it would make this one (B') fatter than that'. Even when the experimenter rolled the sausages until the children admitted that one was shorter and thinner than the other, they still refused to reject their compensation judgments, e.g. 'It's the same, only it's a bit too long'. The two who behaved in this way provide some support for Model 4, in that they seemed not to know that compensation judgments should be corrected after seeing B'. Although it could be argued that they simply were not prepared to admit that their compensation judgments had been wrong, a child whose compensation judgment was integrated with the NAS criterion should know that there was no loss of face in making an incorrect $X = A$ judgment. The failure to find any child who resolved the contradiction by rejecting $B' = A$ in favour of $X = A$ suggests that the relationship between conservation and compensation was not so loose as is allowed by Model 4, but neither are the results as predicted by Models 1, 2 and 3.

4. Compensation and reversibility-after. Table 10.3 shows that eight children who rejected their compensation judgments failed to reject their judgments that A could be rolled to look just like X. Three of the eight were children who had at first failed to reject their compensation judgments. Models 1, 2 and 3 do not allow children to behave in this way, while Model 4 predicts that some children will do so, i.e. that they will fail to make consistent amount and deformation judgments. Hence these results are as expected by Model 4.

Table 10.3. Relationship between compensation, rejection of compensation judgment and reversibility — after among children who judged B'=A

Comp.	Reject comp.	Rev-after Fail	Pass	Total
Fail		2	4	6
Pass	Fail	3	1	4
Pass	Pass	8	11	19
Total		13	16	29

General discussion and Modification of Model 4

Models 1 and 2, which state that compensation develops as a consequence of conservation, predicted that (i) no child who failed to conserve should compensate; (ii) no child should make the sequence of judgments A = X, A ≠ X+, A → X+; (iii) all children who could compensate should subsequently reject their compensation judgments in favour of B' = A; (iv) all children who rejected their compensation judgments should pass reversibility-after. Although the results supported (i) to some extent, predictions (ii), (iii) and (iv) were not supported. Hence Models 1 and 2 seem not to be tenable.

Model 3 made predictions (i), (ii), (iii) and (iv), and also two further predictions: (v) only full conservers should be able to compensate; (vi) only children with knowledge of the uniqueness of reversibility should be able to compensate. Neither of these further predictions was supported by the results.

Model 4, which states that perceptual compensation is a necessary precondition for conservation, predicted that (vii) all children who could conserve should be able to compensate; (viii) some children should make the sequence of judgments A = X, A ≠ X+, A → X+ and X; (ix) some children should not reject their compensation judgments in favour of B' = A; (x) some children may, having rejected their compensation judgments, fail reversibility-after, i.e. they may make the sequence of judgments A = X, A → X, then A ≠ X, A → X. While predictions (viii), (ix) and (x) were supported, suggesting that children who could not be described as using the NAS criterion did nevertheless accept that although shapes are different, amounts can be equal, some results were not as predicted by Model 4. These were: (a) only three of the compensation judgments were justified by purely perceptual reasons, and the other 15 reasons referred to changing the shape of one of the sausages (action reasons), e.g. 'If I squash mine like that, it will be the same as that.' Children who judged on the basis of perceptual compensation but did not use the NAS criterion were not expected to justify their judgments in this way; (b) no child rejected B′ = A in favour of X = A, although three children did not without prompting reject X in favour of B′, and two did not make the necessary correction of their compensation judgments although they were aware of a contradiction; (c) six children judged B′ = A but failed to judge X = A. Although the B′ = A judgment need not have been based on the NAS criterion and could have been based on perceptual compensation, all the children did give a deformational reason for this judgment. Anyway, it is not obvious why a perceptual compensation judgment should be easier to make in the case of B′ than in the case of X.

In order to accommodate these results, a modification of Model 4 can be made. It was originally assumed that a perceptual compensation judgment involved making a static comparison to decide whether the length difference 'balanced' the width difference. The concept of 'balance', however, implies a dynamic relationship, i.e. it implies that the two lengths would be equal if, by rearrangement, the widths were made equal. It could be, therefore, that when comparing a long thin sausage with a short fat one, the child justifies his judgment of 'balance' or 'imbalance' of length and width differences by either imagining or performing a rearrangement. In doing this, he would be assuming that deformational information is relevant to the amount judgment, and possibly even that it is necessary, although he may still believe that amount *can* be changed by deformation. The knowledge that nothing was added or subtracted would not be sufficient for the child to make an amount judgment, even though when given deformation information he may use his knowledge of empirical return to justify a perceptual judgment of balance, i.e. of equality of amount. The child could be described as using the rule, 'If A = X, then A → X.' This does not, logically, require that he also uses the rule 'If A → X, then A = X′, which is equivalent to the NAS criterion.

If it is assumed that the child goes through a stage of making such dynamic perceptual compensation judgments before using the NAS criterion, then the results which were not expected by the original 'static' theory can be accommodated: (a) compensation judgments could be justified by action reasons. It was noticeable that action reasons commonly referred to folding over the thin sausage, or to cutting it into short lengths which could be laid side by side, rather than to rolling or squashing. The children seemed to avoid terms which implied the possibility of expansion (by squeezing the sausage longer) or contraction (by squashing the sausage). (b) If a compensation judgment were justified by referring to the effects of rearrangement, and if the B′ = A judgment were made on a perceptual compensation basis, then there would be no reason to reject B′ = A in favour of X = A, since only in the case of B′ was the effect of deformation known. A prediction arising from this is that if the deformation from B to B' were performed so as to suggest expansion or contraction (perhaps if B were hammered vigorously), then the child should be less inclined to reject X in favour of B'. This prediction cannot be tested in the present experiment. (c) It is suggested that deformational information is relevant to a perceptual compensation judgment, although it is not sufficient. Hence a child who had only just learned to coordinate dimensions might be helped to do so by seeing deformation. That is, judging B' = A might be expected to be easier than judging X = A. However, if that is the reason why some children judged B' = A but failed compensation, then it would also be expected that some children who failed compensation should have given correct judgments in the equality sausage conservation task which preceded the compensation test. As shown in Table 10.2, this was not the case. A further factor may be involved: as mentioned earlier, there was improvement in the sausage conservation task which followed the compensation test, compared with performance in the tasks preceding it. In the fourth conservation task, 18 out of 46 children scored 2, compared with 7 out of 46 in the preceding sausage tests ($p = 0.004$, 2-tail test). This improvement, along with the B' judgments, suggests that the experience of analysing the thin sausages and comparing them with the short fat one may have had a training effect, i.e. have made the child less content to centre on a single dimension and encouraged him to use a more advanced strategy which he already had available. Further, children who were able to coordinate dimensions may have realized that several of the thin sausages looked equal in amount to A, and that other information, i.e. deformational information, was crucial for making a firm choice. These can be only weak suggestions on the basis of the present experiment.

By modifying Model 4 in the way suggested, then, the results of the present experiment can be accommodated adequately. They suggest that there exist children who make perceptual compensation judgments but who do not yet use the NAS criterion. These children were classified as intermediate conservers on the basis of their performance in the conservation test. In both this experiment and the preceding one ('Compensation and screening'), it was found to be very rare for non-conservers to make perceptual compensation judgments, but common for intermediate conservers to do so. In this experiment, 23 children were classified as intermediate conservers. Only one of these performed perfectly in the compensation test, passing all five items. He did reason consistently with the NAS criterion, and so could be described as using that criterion. Ten others failed compensation and hence did not have the opportunity to reason consistently or inconsistently with the NAS criterion in the rest of the compensation test. (None of the ten had spontaneously conserved in the 'equality sausage' conservation task preceding the compensation test, and only one of them had accepted the conservation countersuggestion in that task.) The remaining children did reason inconsistently with the NAS criterion in the compensation test, i.e. they made judgments such as 'A = X; A ≠ X+; A → X; A → X+' or 'A = B', A ≠ X; A → B'; A → X'. These results suggest that it may not be appropriate to describe intermediate conservers (i.e. those who give conserving judgments in the standard test on some occasions only) as using the NAS criterion: they appear to be using this criterion in conservation tasks, but when their judgments are examined more closely as in the compensation test, they are shown to reason inconsistently with it. They may be more appropriately described as making dynamic perceptual compensation judgments in the way suggested above; deformational information is relevant to their amount judgments, but is not sufficient.

This suggestion has implications for the way conservation acquisition is conceptualized. A commonsense view of intermediate conservers might be that they have a weak conservation concept which is still likely to be dominated by perceptual criteria. Indeed, in Chapter 6 various precautions were outlined which were intended to ensure that children just beginning to use the NAS criterion were accurately identified. The results of this experiment suggest that it may be misleading to assume that intermediate conservers simply have a weak conservation concept. Their conserving judgments appear to be based on reasoning quite different from the reasoning of those who always give conserving judgments. Perhaps only these latter children are appropriately considered to use the NAS criterion, to have the concept of conservation of amount.

In Chapter 6, it was suggested how learning about the uniqueness of reversibility could be sufficient for the child who makes perceptual compensation judgments to develop the NAS criterion. This suggestion is still applicable to the modified Model 4. It seems that the child who makes perceptual compensation judgments can be considered to use the rule 'If $A = X$, then $A \rightarrow X$'. If he has the concept of transitivity, he may also judge that $A \neq X+$ (longer than X but the same width) and $A \neq X-$ (shorter than X but the same width). While he is ignorant of the uniqueness of reversibility, he may still think that $A \rightarrow X+$ and $A \rightarrow X-$. But when he learns about the uniqueness of reversibility, he will know that A can be rolled to look just like only one of the sausages $X-$, X, $X+$. It was suggested in Chapter 6 that the child would be most likely to decide that *only* amounts which are equal can be rolled to look alike ($A \rightarrow X$ only, not $X-$ or $X+$), since this allows knowledge about amounts and knowledge about deformation to be integrated. The alternative solution, to decide that amounts which are equal cannot necessarily be deformed to look alike, requires modification of knowledge about amounts; the child would consider that 'If $A = X$, then A may or may not be capable of being rolled to look just like X'. It is suggested, then, that learning about the uniqueness of reversibility is necessary and sufficient for the intermediate conserver to attain perfect conservation performance in the standard test.

A prediction from modified Model 4 is that intermediate conservers should be ignorant of the uniqueness of reversibility; they should think that a particular short fat sausage can be rolled to look like more than one of a set of thin sausages, equal in width but different in length. This prediction is tested in the experiment to be presented in Chapter 11.

Summary and conclusions

The aim of this experiment was to investigate the reasoning underlying perceptual compensation judgments. As found in the experiment on 'Compensation and screening' (Chapter 9), the ability to make perceptual compensation judgments appeared too early in conservation acquisition to support Models 1, 2 and 3; the relationship between compensation and conservation was more as expected by Model 4. The present experiment, however, allowed a deeper analysis of this relationship to be made. Among children who accepted that entities different in shape could be equal in amount, judgments about equality and inequality of amount were often inconsistent with judgments about the possibility of deforming the compared amounts to look alike. There were, though, indications that the relationship between compensation and conservation was not as loose as is allowed by Model 4.

In order to accommodate the deviant results, a modification of Model 4 was suggested. In this modification, perceptual compensation judgments were considered to be dynamic rather than static, i.e. when coordinating dimensions, the child was supposed to imagine or perform a rearrangement from an AvB' to an AvB comparison. While use of this dynamic coordination strategy involves an assumption of the possibility of conservation, it is not equivalent to use of the NAS criterion. It was suggested that children classified as intermediate conservers in the conservation test (those who conserve on some occasions only) make such perceptual compensation judgments and do not have available the NAS criterion, and that learning about the uniqueness of reversibility is sufficient (and necessary) for the attainment of perfect conserving performance.

CHAPTER 11

Discovery and Invention: Conservation and Knowledge of the Uniqueness of Reversibility

11.1 Introduction

In Chapter 10, a modified Model 4 was proposed, which accommodated better the results of the experiment on 'Compensation and the NAS criterion'. The aim of the experiment to be presented here was to test predictions from this modified Model 4 about the relationship between knowledge of the uniqueness of reversibility (UR) and performance in the standard conservation test.

More generally, the aim was to examine the relationship between the two processes which have been labelled 'invention' and 'discovery'. The child cannot *discover* that a long thin sausage looks the same to eat as a short fat one: the idea of perceptual compensation must be considered an invention on his part. In contrast, UR could, in principle, be discovered by him: experimenting with rolling sausages could lead him to discover that a short fat sausage can be rolled to look like only one of a set of equally thin sausages different in length. In Chapter 7 it was suggested that a first assumption should be to accept a 'discovery' account of development whenever possible, in preference to an 'invention' account; a discovery account is likely to be simpler since there is a less complex transformation of the input to be accounted for. It will be assumed for the moment, then, that knowledge of UR is discovered by the child, rather than invented. According to this view, modified Model 4's child invents the idea that conservation is possible (perceptual compensation), and then discovers that it is necessary.

11.2 Conservation and knowledge of UR

A person with complete knowledge of UR would know the following facts about a set of thin sausages equal in width but different in length (B$'-$, B$'+$, B$'++$, etc.) and a short fat sausage (B): he would know that B can be rolled to look exactly like only one of the thin sausages, and if he were given certain information about the effects of rolling on B's appearance, he would know which particular one (B$'$); he would also know that only one (that same one) of the thin sausages can be rolled up to look just like B. Only the knowledge about rolling B to look like the thin sausages is relevant here; knowledge about rolling the thin sausages up to look like B will be ignored.

Knowledge of UR is logically necessary for conservation. This was argued in Chapter 3; a child who thinks that B can be rolled to look like both B′ and B′+, and who accepts that B′ and B′+ are not themselves equal in amount, believes that rolling can produce two amounts which are not equal. This child cannot be described as having the concept of conservation of amount. Logically, then, a child cannot be called a conserver if he is ignorant of UR. However, this does not necessarily mean that all children who perform perfectly in the standard conservation test know about UR. It could be that the child can attain perfect performance in the standard test while remaining ignorant of UR. Whether or not he does is an empirical matter, to be investigated here.

Although logically necessary for conservation, knowledge of UR is not logically sufficient; it could be that many nonconservers know about UR. However, learning about UR requires the ability to consider both the lengths and widths of sausages. If the child is capable of doing this, then he will probably accept that a long thin sausage can *look* the same amount as a short fat one; he will probably accept the possibility of perceptual compensation. According to modified Model 4, the ability to make perceptual compensation judgments is sufficient for the attainment of intermediate conserving performance: this was argued in Chapter 10. If so, then knowledge of UR should be rare among nonconservers; if the child is capable of learning about UR, he probably accepts the possibility of perceptual compensation and therefore is no longer a nonconserver.

According to modified Model 4, knowledge of UR is not necessary for intermediate conserving performance. Intermediate conservers, it was suggested in Chapter 10, use the rule 'If A = X, then A → X'. They do not use the rule 'If A → X, then A = X', which is equivalent to the NAS criterion. It was shown in Chapter 10 how learning about UR could be sufficient for the acquisition of this second rule, and could lead to a belief in the necessity of conservation.

Modified Model 4 proposes, then, that nonconservers do not accept the possibility of perceptual compensation and are unlikely to know about UR; intermediate conservers are also ignorant of UR but do understand perceptual compensation; conservers know about UR and also understand perceptual compensation.

The other models will be ignored in this experiment: Models 1 and 2 do not make specific predictions about the stage in conservation acquisition at which knowledge of UR is acquired; Model 3 requires that all those who make perceptual compensation judgments do know about UR and it expects perceptual compensation to appear only among strong conservers, but it does not specify whether knowledge of UR may be acquired before the ability to make perceptual compensation judgments. (In this respect, Model 3 does not follow Piaget's theory. The model is intended to specify only Piaget's views on the relationship between compensation and conservation and it ignores his views on the relationship between reversibility and conservation.)

The present experiment is not concerned with perceptual compensation judgments, which were the focus of interest in Chapters 9 and 10, but is designed to test the three predictions from modified Model 4 concerning the relationship between knowledge of UR and conservation level: nonconservers are likely to be ignorant of UR; intermediate conservers are ignorant of UR; conservers know about UR.

Knowledge of UR was examined in part of the compensation test in the experiment on 'Compensation and the NAS criterion' presented in Chapter 10. There, however, children could be scored only as passing or failing the test of UR: either they knew that A could be rolled to look like only one of the long thin sausages, or they did not (reversibility-before); either they knew that A could be rolled to look like B' only, or they did not (reversibility-after). In the test used here, knowledge of UR could be more finely graded to see whether there was a gradual narrowing of the range of thin sausages which the child thought a given short fat sausage could be rolled to look like. Nevertheless, performance in the items reversibility-before and reversibility-after was not inconsistent with the predictions to be tested here: none of the 13 nonconservers in that experiment passed either reversibility-before or reversibility-after; three of the 23 intermediate conservers passed both of them although eight others passed reversibility-after only; six of the ten conservers passed both of them, while the other four failed both. In order to be classified as a conserver in that experiment, the child had to answer perfectly in only three of the four conservation tasks; all the children who answered perfectly in all four tasks did pass both reversibility-before and reversibility-after.

Evidence consistent with the view that conservers are more likely to know about UR than nonconservers is provided by Halford's series of experiments (1968, 1969, 1970b, 1971). These were discussed in Chapter 3. Unfortunately, Halford's crude classification of children into only two groups, conservers and nonconservers, does not allow a clear specification to be made of the relationship between knowledge of UR and conservation level. A more refined technique is needed to test the predictions of interest here.

Method and procedure

Each child was given a pre-test, then a conservation test composed of three tasks, and finally a three-item test of UR.

In the pre-test, two balls of plasticine were used, one obviously bigger than the other. The larger ball was given to the child, and the smaller one to the experimenter, who suggested pretending that they were toffees. The child was asked the standard amount question. It was assumed that in this pre-test an incorrect answer would indicate failure to understand the question. All the children did answer correctly. The child was then asked 'How could you make it so we've both got the same to eat . . . what could you do?' This question was asked with the aim of distinguishing between more and less advanced nonconservers. Such a distinction would be useful when comparing conservation level with performance in the UR tests. A less advanced answer would refer to squashing or rolling, while a more advanced one would refer to adding and/or subtracting. This expectation was based on observations made in earlier experiments. The pre-test, then, was intended to serve the following functions: (i) to familiarize the child with the testing situation before beginning the more important items; (ii) to identify children who failed to understand the standard amount question; (iii) possibly it would allow nonconservers to be subdivided into more and less advanced groups.

Next, each child was given two equivalence conservation tasks, E, and one identity task, I. The distinction between these two forms of conservation test was discussed in Chapter 2. An identity conservation test involves only a single object, B, which is deformed to B', whereas in an equivalence conservation task (the standard conservation test) a comparison object, A, is also used and the child is asked to compare A with B before the deformation, and A with B' afterwards. Although some experimenters have found that identity tasks are easier than equivalence tasks, it was suggested in Chapter 2 that any such differences might be superficial and disappear after countersuggestions. This aspect of the present experiment was discussed in Chapter 2, and it will not be considered further in this chapter, except to mention that no difference in difficulty was found between the I and E tests of conservation.

All three conservation tasks involved the rolling of a short fat plasticine sausage into a long thin one. Knowledge of the same deformation was assessed in the UR test. Only one deformation was used throughout to maximize the chance of obtaining a clear relationship between conservation level and knowledge of UR. The three conservation tasks did, however, involve plasticine of different colours and sausages of different sizes.

In the conservation tasks, the procedure was like that already described in Chapters 8, 9 and 10: after the deformation, the child was asked the standard amount question (which was modified to suit the identity task), then he was given either a conservation or a nonconservation countersuggestion, and finally the standard amount question was repeated.

The *UR test* consisted of three items, which were introduced in the following way: (i) The child was shown sausages B (big), M (middle) and L (little), (see Figure 11.1). He agreed that they were all just as fat, but not equally long. He was then told 'I had three fat sausages just like these . . . (elaborating) and I rolled them. I didn't add any on or take any off, I just rolled them. And here they are . . . (the child was shown B', M' and L', which were arranged beside the fat sausages as shown in Figure 11.1). The child agreed that B', M' and L' were all equally thin, but not equally long. (ii) *Item 1*. The child was asked 'See if you can tell me which of my fat sausages I rolled to make this one (indicating M').' It was assumed that all children would select M, simply by matching the two series of sausages. If a child did not select M, this could indicate failure to understand the test. No child did fail. (iii) In the next part of item 1, the child was asked 'What if we roll this one (B), could we make it look *just* like this one (M')?' and 'If we rolled it (B) so it was just as long as this one (M'), would it be just as thin as this one (M')?' If the child answered 'No' to this last question, he was asked whether it would be fatter or thinner. The same questions were also asked about L. A child with adult knowledge of UR would answer that neither B nor L could be rolled to look just like M', and that B would be fatter than M' if rolled to the same length, while L would be thinner. Although knowing about the changes in length and width resulting from rolling was not part of the definition of UR, it was expected that children who knew about UR would also know about these changes. (iv) *Item 2*. A fourth thin sausage, $M'+$, was then introduced. The child agreed that it was just as thin as B', M' and L', but not the same length as any of them. He was asked 'Which of these fat sausages (B, M and L) could we roll to look *just* like this one ($M'+$)... Is there one?' He was then asked about each of B, M and L, as in (iii) above. It was expected that some children who passed item 1 would fail this item, in that they would think B or M could be rolled to look just like $M'+$, since the

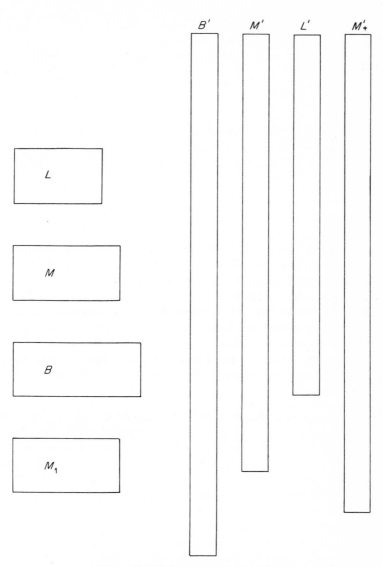

Figure 11.1. Materials used in the UR test

difference in length between B' or M' and $M'+$ was small. This expectancy was based on an assumption that learning about UR involves a gradual narrowing of the range of thin sausages which it is believed a particular fat sausage can be rolled to look like. (v) *Item 3.* Finally, a fourth fat sausage, M_1, was introduced. The child agreed that it was just the same to eat as M. He was asked 'If we roll this one (M_1), can we make it look *just* like this one (B'), just as long and just as thin?' The same question was applied to M' and L'. This final item was included to see whether any difference in difficulty between items 1 and 2 was due simply to differences in the reasoning involved. In both items 2 and 3, the child had to move outside the bounds of the original series; there was a greater memory load and a longer sequence of reasoning than in item 1. It was hoped that there would be no difference in difficulty between items 1 and 3, showing that such reasoning and memory factors could be ignored.

Subjects

The subjects were 67 children aged from $6\frac{1}{2}$ to $7\frac{1}{2}$ years, and five children aged between 5 years, 11 months and 6 years, 2 months. There were about equal numbers of boys and girls, and they all attended an infants' school near Southampton.

Treatment of Results

1. Pre-test. There were four types of reply to the question 'How could you make it so we've both got the same to eat . . .?'. (i) References to adding and/or subtracting. (ii) Suggestions of cutting the big ball in half, to give half to E. These children were questioned further, and they seemed to be using 'half' correctly. Usually they did not know how to deal with E's small ball, although two of them suggested cutting that in half too, to take half themselves. These two were placed in category (i). The children had been learning about halving and quartering in school; this probably accounts for the large number of unexpected (ii) responses. (iii) Suggestions of rolling or squashing the big ball. (iv) Finally, some children made no suggestions.

2. The conservation test. A score from 0 to 3 was given to each child for his performance in each of the three tasks. A score of 0: nonconserving judgments both before and after the countersuggestion; 1: nonconserving judgment before, but a conserving judgment after the countersuggestion; 2: a conserving judgment, followed by a nonconserving one after the countersuggestion; 3: conserving judgments both before and after the countersuggestion.

Statements of uncertainty and changes of mind about a particular judgment were noted and classified as 'uncertainty'. Reasons given for judgments were coded, but they proved redundant bases for classifying children into groups.

On the basis of his overall performance in the three tasks, each child was placed in one of six groups:

Group 1: score 3 in each task, with no uncertainty.
Group 2: score 3 in each task, but with uncertainty.
Group 3: score 1 in the first task, and 3 in the other two.
Group 4: scores not accommodated by any of the other groups, e.g. scores of 1 or 2 in each task; a score of 3 in the third task only, etc.
Group 5: score 0 in all three tasks, but with uncertainty indicating consideration of the possibility of conservation.
Group 6: score 0 in all three tasks, with no uncertainty.

3. Test of UR. Separate scores were given for items 1, 2 and 3. In item 1, the maximum score was 3: one mark for judging $M \rightarrow M'$; $B \rightarrow M'$; $L \rightarrow M'$. As expected, most children either thought B or L could be rolled just as long and just as thin as M', or they gave correct judgments about the width difference. Only two children fell into neither of these categories; they both thought L would be fatter than M'. These two were not penalized. In item 3, the scoring was similar: one mark each for judging $M_1 \rightarrow B'$; $M_1 \rightarrow M'$; $M_1 \rightarrow L'$.

In item 2, the maximum score was 5 marks: one for saying 'No' in reply to the question 'Is there one?'; one for always saying 'No' when first asked about the possibility of rolling B, M and L to look just like $M'+$; and one each for judging, by the end of questioning, that $B \rightarrow M'+$; $M \rightarrow M'+$; $L \rightarrow M'+$. Hence scores 3, 4 and 5 indicated that the child said, by the end of questioning, that none of the fat sausages could be rolled to look like $M'+$. A score of 2 indicated that he thought one of them could, a score of 1, that he thought two of them could, and a score of 0 that he thought all three of them could be rolled to look just like $M'+$.

Two criteria were used for dividing children into those who did and those who did not know about UR. According to the stronger criterion, a child knew about UR only if he scored three each in items 1 and 3, and 5 in item 2 (6–5). According to the weaker one, he knew about UR if he scored at least 6–3 (three each in items 1 and 3, and 3 in item 2).

Results and discussion

1. Pre-test. It was hoped that performance in the pre-test would allow non-conservers to be divided into more and less advanced groups. Unfortunately, only three children gave the 'less advanced' response of suggesting rolling/squashing the larger ball to make it the same amount as the smaller one. A much more common response was to suggest halving the big ball, while ignoring the little one. Children who gave this response were not clearly indicating that the amounts should be changed by addition/subtraction, rather than by deformation. The pre-test results could not, therefore, be used in the way anticipated.

Nevertheless, there was a significant relationship between conservation level and suggesting addition/subtraction in the pre-test. Children of higher conservation levels (groups 1, 2 and 3), were more likely to suggest addition/subtraction than were those of lower conservation levels (groups 4, 5 and 6): 28 of the children in groups 1, 2 and 3 did so, compared with 19 of the 39 groups 4, 5 and 6 ($\chi^2 = 8.76$. $p < 0.01$). Also, suggesting addition/subtraction seemed to be developmentally prior to the acquisition of full conservation, since 19 of the 39 group 4, 5 and 6 children made this suggestion, whereas only 5 of the 33 group 1, 2 and 3 children did not (Binomial test, $p = 0.006$).

2. Test of UR.   It was predicted that items 1 and 3 would not differ in difficulty, but that item 2 would be more difficult. The results provide strong support for both these predictions. Of the 72 children, 56 (77.8%) gained the same score in items 1 and 3, 12 (16.7%) gained scores differing by one mark, and 4 (5.5%) gained scores differing by two marks. Of those who did not gain the same score in both items, 9 scored higher in item 3, and 7 higher in item 1. It can be concluded that differences in reasoning and memory load between items 1 and 3 are unimportant, and hence these factors can be ignored in the comparison of items 1 and 3 with item 2.

To make that comparison, each child's scores for items 1 and 3 were summed, giving a maximum score of 6. The relationship between the (1 + 3) and the item 2 scores is shown in Table 11.1. Of the 44 children who scored 6 in items (1 + 3), 11

Table 11.1. UR test: relationship between scores in items 1 and 3, and scores in item 2

Score in items 1 + 3	5	4	Score in item 2 3	2	1	0	Total
6	26	2	5	10	1	0	44
5	0	0	2	2	2	1	7
4	0	0	0	4	5	2	11
3	0	0	0	2	1	2	5
2	0	0	0	0	0	5	5
Total	26	2	7	18	9	10	72

nevertheless failed item 2, whereas of the 35 who passed item 2 (i.e. scores of 3, 4 or 5), only two scored less than 6 in items (1 + 3). Both of these made a single error, and in item 2 they at first selected M, only to reject it on further questioning. This contrast between 11 children who passed only items 1 and 3, and two who passed only item 2, supports the prediction that item 2 would be the most difficult (Binomial test, $p = 0.02$).

In item 2, these 11 answered in the following way: six selected M as the only sausage which could be rolled to look like $M' +$, three chose B, one chose M and B, and one child chose L. That is, of the 44 children who knew that $B \nrightarrow M'$, $L \nrightarrow M'$, $M \rightarrow M'$ and $L \nrightarrow M' +$, ten nevertheless thought that $B \rightarrow M' +$ and/or $M \rightarrow M' +$. Knowledge of UR does indeed seem to be acquired through a gradual narrowing of the range of thin sausages which it is believed a particular fat sausage can be rolled to look like.

3. *Conservation and Knowledge of UR.* Table 11.2 shows the relationship between conservation groups 1–6, and scores in the UR test. The UR scores are presented in three ways: firstly, the separate (1 + 3) and item 2 scores; secondly, for easier statistical treatment, the summed (1 + 2 + 3) scores; and thirdly, for statistical comparison of scores spread throughout the range, grouped scores—the (1 + 2 + 3) scores were divided into four UR groups, A, B, C and D, as shown in Table 11.2. Group A includes all those who passed all the items by at least the

Table 11.2. Frequencies of children in each conservation group who gained each UR score

G	Sum	UR scores Item 1+3	Item 2	1 cons.	2	3	4	5	6 noncons.	Total
	11	6	5	13	6	4	1	2	0	26
A	10	6	4	1	1	0	0	0	0	2
	9	6	3	1	0	0	4	0	0	5
	8	6	2	2	1	3	1	1	2	10
B	7	6	1	0	0	0	0	0	1	1
	8	5	3	0	0	0	1	1	0	2
	7	5	2	0	0	0	1	1	0	2
	6	5	1	0	0	0	1	0	1	2
	5	5	0	0	0	0	1	0	0	1
	6	4	2	0	0	1	2	0	1	4
C	5	4	1	0	0	0	2	0	3	5
	4	4	0	0	0	0	1	0	1	2
	5	3	2	0	0	0	1	0	1	2
	4	3	1	0	0	0	1	0	0	1
	3	3	0	0	0	0	2	0	0	2
D	2	2	0	0	0	0	3	0	2	5
	Mean summed score			10·5	10·5	9·3	5·8	9·0	5·3	
	Total									72

weaker criterion; they gained summed scores of 9, 10 or 11. Group B includes those who gained summed scores of 7 or 8; Group C, 4, 5 or 6; and Group D, 2 or 3.

Three predictions were made from modified Model 4 about the relationship between UR scores and conservation level.

(i) The first prediction was that conservers would know about UR. Since conservation groups 1 and 2 did not differ in UR scores, both were considered conservers for the purpose of testing this prediction. Using the strongest criterion (6–5), 19 of the 25 conservers knew about UR (76%), while according to the weaker one (at least 6–3), 22 of them did (88%). The remaining three children (12%) thought that one of the fat sausages could be rolled to look like $M' +$, i.e. they were very close to knowing about UR. Although not perfectly in accordance with the prediction, these results strongly support the view that knowledge of UR is necessary for good performance in the conservation test.

(ii) The second prediction was that intermediate conservers would be ignorant of UR, i.e. that they would score less than 6–3. The performance of the group 3 children clearly does not support this prediction, since four of the eight children scored 6–5. A nonparametric trend test based on the statistic S (Ferguson, 1965) was used to compare the summed scores of those in groups 1 and 2 with group 3, and it failed to show a significant difference ($z = 1.49. p = 0.14$). However, group 3 contains children whose only nonconserving judgment was their very first one, and it is reasonable to take group 4, rather than group 3, as representative of intermediate conservers.

Table 11.2 shows that only one of the 22 group 4 children gained the maximum UR score, although by the weaker criterion, four others did know about UR. An S test performed on the grouped scores showed a highly significant drop from groups 1 and 2 to group 4 ($z = 4.65. p < 0.00006$). Hence, although five of the intermediate conservers (22.7%) did not behave in accordance with the prediction, the results do allow the conclusion that intermediate conservers are much more likely than conservers to be ignorant of UR.

(iii) Thirdly, it was predicted that knowledge of UR would be rare among nonconservers. Table 11.2 shows that none of the group 6 nonconservers knew about UR, although two of the five group 5 children did know about it. The UR scores of the group 5 children were not significantly different from those of the group 1 and 2 conservers (summed scores: $z = 1.67. p = 0.09$), while those of the group 6 children were very significantly lower (grouped scores: $z = 5.2. p < 0.00006$). There was no significant difference between the UR scores of the group 6 and the group 4 children (grouped scores: $z = 0.36. p = 0.7$). The fact that the only two nonconservers (groups 5 and 6) who knew about UR were uncertain, rather than strict, nonconservers (i.e. group 5 rather than group 6), supports the argument presented earlier concerning knowledge of UR among nonconservers.

The account of conservation acquisition being tested here requires that the nonconservers who knew about UR should, as soon as they accepted the possibility of perceptual compensation, move rapidly to a strong belief in conservation, rather than linger at intermediate stages. Unfortunately, the further conservation tasks necessary to test this were not given.

Summary and conclusions

The aim of this experiment was to test the predictions from modified Model 4 concerning the relationship between knowledge of the uniqueness of reversibility and performance in the conservation test. The model predicts that nonconservers are likely to be ignorant of the uniqueness of reversibility, intermediate conservers are ignorant of it, and conservers know about it. The results supported these predictions: 88% of the conservers knew about UR, 77·3% of the intermediate conservers did not, all the strict nonconservers were ignorant of UR, and two of the five uncertain nonconservers were not.

These results point to the importance in conservation acquisition of two relatively independent factors: knowledge of the uniqueness of reversibility, which is necessary but not sufficient for the attainment of full conservation, and a second factor which is sufficient for the child to reach intermediate levels. While the present experiment does not allow any conclusions to be drawn about the precise nature of this second factor, the results are consistent with those from the experiments reported in Chapters 9 and 10, which identify it as perceptual compensation.

Since UR can, logically, be discovered by the child, it is assumed that he does in fact discover, rather than invent, it. The idea that a long thin sausage can look equal in amount to a short fat one must, however, be invented rather than discovered. According to this view, therefore, the child invents the idea that amount conservation is *possible*, and the discovery of UR can then lead to a belief in the *necessity* of conservation.

CHAPTER 12

Overview and Conclusions

12.1 Summary of the models and the experimental results

The experiments presented in Chapters 7–11 were intended to investigate how adequately each of the four models describes the child's route to the acquisition of conservation. The models refer specifically to judgments of amount when a short fat plasticine sausage is rolled longer. It was assumed that an early stage on the route to conservation involves use of a single one-dimensional perceptual criterion, such as 'If it is longer, then there is more'. It was also assumed that any subsequent changes in perceptual judgments would derive from an increasing ability to take into account more than one dimension when making a particular judgment. The four models ascribe different roles to such perceptual changes:

According to Model 1, consistent with Bruner's theory, the child changes directly from using single one-dimensional perceptual criteria to using the NAS criterion; changes in perceptual judgments are irrelevant to conservation acquisition although they may occur as a consequence of it.

Models 2, 3 and 4, however, assume that if the child is to conserve, he must become aware of contradictory judgments of pre- compared with post-deformation amount, judgments based on alternative one-dimensional perceptual criteria. For example, when a short fat plasticine sausage is rolled longer, the contradictory judgments would be 'More now because it's longer' and 'More at first because it was fatter'. In the standard conservation test, in which a comparison object is used, there would be contradictory judgments of the post-deformation amount: 'More in the longer sausage' but 'More in the fatter sausage'. Model 2 proposes that awareness of this contradiction leads the child to cease using perceptual criteria in these situations, and to use instead an already developed NAS criterion.

Model 3, consistent with Piaget's theory of conservation acquisition, states that the child resolves the contradiction between alternative perceptual judgments by interpreting the changes in dimensions as exactly compensating each other at each point in the deformation, and simultaneously he constructs the NAS criterion.

The child might, however, resolve the contradiction between alternative perceptual judgments by developing a more complex perceptual criterion, involving a coordination of dimensions, and hence acquire the ability to make perceptual compensation judgments. As a result of making perceptual compensation judgments, he could develop the NAS criterion. This is the route to conservation proposed by Model 4.

As shown in Chapter 6, the models predict different answers to the following questions, which were investigated in the experiments.

(i) *At what stage in conservation acquisition does the child become unsure of AvB' perceptual judgments?* According to Model 1, uncertainty in AvB' perceptual judgments develop as a result of using the NAS criterion, whereas Models 2, 3 and 4 hold that such uncertainty is a necessary prerequisite for use of the NAS criterion in the standard conservation test. A comparison of performance in standard and reverse conservation tests (Chapter 7) provided evidence that even children who were only just beginning to conserve were able to distinguish between reliable (AvB) and unreliable (AvB') perceptual judgments. As soon as their performance in the conservation tasks suggested that they had begun to use the NAS criterion, children appeared to know that in the standard conservation test they should stick to their pre-deformation amount judgment, while in the reverse test they should correct this, if necessary, after seeing the post-deformation appearance. This supports Models 2, 3 and 4 rather than Model 1.

(ii) *Which situations make it easier for the child to use the NAS criterion?* Since Model 1 states that children continue to use one-dimensional perceptual criteria until for some reason the NAS criterion dominates, it should be possible to provide evidence that the NAS criterion is available to children before they begin to use it in the standard conservation test. Model 2 makes the same prediction, since it assumes that awareness of contradictory perceptual judgments of pre- compared with post-deformation amount is necessary if the child is to use the NAS criterion in the standard test, although this criterion is already available.

Both these models predict, therefore, that if the potential conflict between perceptually and NAS-based judgments were reduced or removed, some nonconservers should demonstrate their possession of the NAS criterion. In contrast, Models 3 and 4 state that the child has no tendency to conserve before he accepts that the pre- and post-deformation amounts can *look* the same; there is no potential conflict between judgments based on appearance and on the NAS criterion, and so putting the child in a 'reduced conflict' situation should not make it any easier for him to apply the NAS criterion.

In Chapter 8, performance in two reduced conflict situations was examined. In the 'rolled' situation, the child was screened from the pre-deformation appearance, but he knew that nothing had been added or subtracted and he saw the post-deformation, AvB', appearance. In the 'choice' situation the child was screened from the post-deformation appearance; again, he knew that nothing had been added or subtracted, but this time he saw only the pre-deformation, AvB, appearance. The results of these two studies gave no indication that the NAS criterion was easier to use in the reduced conflict situations than in the standard conservation test. In Chapter 9, performance in a third reduced conflict situation was investigated. In this, the child was screened from the post-deformation appearance, although in detail this situation differed from the 'choice' one. Again, the reduced conflict situation made the NAS criterion no easier to apply.

These results conflict with Bruner's (1966c) interpretations of the results of Frank's screening experiment, which were discussed in Chapters 3 and 5. But it was suggested there that Bruner's interpretations were not particularly credible given the methodological inadequacies of Frank's experiment.

A further opportunity to provide evidence supporting Models 1 and 2 arose in the experiment on 'Reverse conservation' (Chapter 7): the correcting strategy might have been easier to apply than the sticking strategy, since in the case of the former the child can accommodate his NAS-based judgment to one based on immediate appearance, whereas in the case of the latter, the child has to stick to his earlier judgment in the face of the immediate appearance. No difference in difficulty was found.

The results of all these studies support Models 3 and 4 rather than Models 1 and 2. In the absence of clear evidence that the NAS criterion is available to children who fail to use it in the standard test, Models 1 and 2 are not tenable.

(iii) *At what stage in conservation acquisition are deformational and perceptual information each sufficient for the child to make an equality amount judgment?* In the experiment on 'Compensation and screening' (Chapter 9), the child was given the opportunity of making an equality amount judgment on the basis of perceptual compensation in the absence of deformational information, and also of making one on the basis of the NAS criterion in the absence of perceptual information (the appearance). In the standard conservation test, both perceptual and deformational information are provided, and the models make different predictions about the child's use of the two kinds of information. Models 1 and 2 predict that deformational information alone should be easier to use than perceptual information alone. According to these models, the child accepts the possibility of perceptual compensation only as a result of using the NAS criterion in the standard test. Model 3 predicts that it should be equally easy to use either kind of information on its own, since the child acquires the operation of compensation simultaneously with developing the NAS criterion. Model 4, however, predicts that it should be easier to use perceptual information alone than to use deformational information alone, because this model states that the ability to make perceptual compensation judgments is a necessary prerequisite for development of the NAS criterion.

The results of the experiment on 'Compensation and screening' clearly supported Model 4 in this respect: it was common for children to make a perceptual compensation judgment while failing to make an equality amount judgment on the basis of deformational information alone. On the other hand, it was very rare for children to use the deformational information alone while failing to make a perceptual compensation judgment.

The models also make different predictions about the relationship between the child's use of the two kinds of information alone, and his performance in the standard conservation test. Models 1 and 2 predict that the child can apply the NAS criterion when given only deformational information before he can apply it in the standard test. Models 3 and 4, in contrast, predict that being given only deformational information may make the NAS criterion more difficult to apply than in the standard test. On the other hand, Models 1, 2 and 3 agree that to make perceptual compensation judgments should be more difficult than to apply the NAS criterion in the standard test, while Model 4 predicts that it should be easier.

Again, the results supported Model 4; the use of deformational information alone to make an equality amount judgment appeared too late in conservation acquisition to support Models 1 and 2, but the ability to make perceptual compensation judgments appeared too early to support Models 1, 2 and 3.

(iv) *Does the child make perceptual compensation judgments which are always consistent with his judgments about the effects of deformation on appearance?* According to Models 1 and 2, the child accepts that entities different in shape can look equal in amount only as a result of applying the NAS criterion. Model 3 states that the ability to make perceptual compensation judgments develops along with the NAS criterion. These models predict, therefore, that any child who makes a perceptual compensation judgment should reason consistently with the NAS criterion. Model 4, in contrast, allows the child to make a perceptual compensation judgment while reasoning inconsistently with the NAS criterion, since this model states that the ability to make perceptual compensation judgments precedes development of the NAS criterion.

In the experiment on 'Compensation and the NAS criterion' (Chapter 10) it was found that a number of children confidently selected from a set of long thin sausages, the one which they thought was the same amount as a given short fat sausage, and judged that the other thin sausages were not the same amount as the fat one. They then went on to judge that the fat sausage could be rolled to look like several of the thin sausages—the one judged to be equal in amount to the fat one, and also others. Furthermore, when provided with the information sufficient for them to reject their judgments that the chosen thin sausage was the same amount as the fat one, a number of children who did reject these judgments still continued to judge that the fat sausage could be rolled to look just like that thin sausage. These children were making judgments about amount which were inconsistent with their judgments about the possibility of deforming the judged amounts to look alike. If Models 1, 2 and 3 are correct, then such children should not exist; only Model 4 can accommodate their responses.

(v) *Does the child make perceptual compensation judgments only if he knows about the uniqueness of reversibility?* Model 3 states that the child resolves the contradiction between alternative perceptual judgments of pre- compared with post-deformation amount by interpreting the changes in dimensions as exactly compensating each other at each point in the deformation. This interpretation logically requires knowledge of one aspect of the uniqueness of reversibility, the knowledge that a given short fat sausage can be rolled to look just like only one of a set of thin sausages, equal in width but different in length. Models 1, 2 and 4, on the other hand, allow the child to make perceptual compensation judgments while being ignorant of this aspect of the uniqueness of reversibility.

The results of the experiment on 'Compensation and the NAS criterion' were inconsistent with Model 3 in this respect. A number of children who made perceptual compensation judgments (A = X) thought that the short fat sausage (A) could be rolled to look like several of the thin sausages (A → X, X+ and X−). Moreover, when a short fat sausage identical to A (B) was rolled to be just as thin as the thin ones but not the same length as any of them (B'), many children who made perceptual compensation judgments thought that A could be rolled to look just like thin sausages differing in length from B' (A → B', X and X+). Model 3 cannot accommodate these results.

Model 4 and its modification

The main findings of the experiments are accommodated best by Model 4, but there were some results which were not as expected by this model: those obtained in the experiment on 'AvB' amount judgments in a perceptual test', and certain results obtained in the one on 'Compensation and the NAS criterion'. Model 4 states that the ability to make perceptual compensation judgments is a necessary prerequisite for development of the NAS criterion. But in the experiment on 'Compensation and the NAS criterion', there were children who failed to make a perceptual compensation judgment while giving a conserving judgment in the compensation test (i.e. they judged B' = A but not X = A). A further problem for Model 4 was the absence of children who, when confronted with the choice of rejecting a perceptual compensation judgment or a contradictory conservation judgment, decided to reject the conservation judgment. This, combined with the small number of children who even hesitated before accepting that their compensation judgments had been wrong, suggests that the relationship between compensation and conservation is not so loose as is allowed by Model 4. Moreover, although Model 4 states that perceptual compensation precedes development of the NAS criterion, in the experiments presented in Chapters 9 and 10, it was rare for nonconservers to make perceptual compensation judgments. The ability to make perceptual compensation judgments seemed to develop along with the NAS criterion, rather than before it.

A modification of Model 4 was put forward in Chapter 10; it appeared to accommodate the deviant results of the experiment on 'Compensation and the NAS criterion' and it made further predictions which were supported in the experiment on 'Conservation and knowledge of the uniqueness of reversibility' (Chapter 11). According to modified Model 4, children classified as intermediate conservers on the basis of their performance in standard conservation tests do not have available the NAS criterion. Rather, they make amount judgments which on occasion are consistent with the NAS criterion although they are based on different reasoning. These judgments are not based on deformational information alone ('Nothing added or subtracted'); information about the appearance of the entities to be judged is necessary for the child to make his judgment. The child accepts the possibility that greater length in one sausage can be 'balanced' by greater width in the other: the two sausages can look equal in amount. 'Balance' implies that if there were a rearrangement of the compared shapes, so that the lengths were made equal, then the widths would also be equal. Hence deformational information may be relevant to the child's judgment; he can be described as using the rule 'If A = X, then A → X'. Learning about the uniqueness of reversibility could be necessary and sufficient for the child at this stage to develop the NAS criterion: to develop the ability to judge amount on the basis of deformation information alone. Children who perform perfectly in standard conservation tests seem able to do this: they can be described as using the NAS criterion. When the child learns that A can be rolled to look just like only one of a set of sausages the same width as X but different in length, he could decide that amounts which are equal cannot necessarily be deformed to look alike, i.e. he could abandon his rule 'If A = X then A → X', or he could decide that *only* amounts which are equal can be deformed to look alike, i.e. he could develop a new rule 'If A → X, then A = X', which is equivalent to the NAS criterion. It has been argued that it is more plausible that he should take the second decision, which allows knowledge about amounts to be integrated with knowledge about the effects of deformation.

If this suggestion is correct, then intermediate conservers should be ignorant of the uniqueness of reversibility, and conservers should not be. In the experiment on 'Conservation and the knowledge of the uniqueness of reversibility', this prediction was supported.

12.2 Wider application of modified Model 4

In Chapter 6 it was specified that the models applied only to the rolling of a short fat plasticine sausage into a long thin one. It is worth considering now whether, in principle, modified Model 4 might have a wider application: to shapes other than sausages, to materials other than plasticine, and to attributes other than amount.

Modified Model 4 is specified partly in terms of changes in the attention paid to lengths and widths of sausages. In the case of some shapes, dimensions would be difficult to specify, if, for example, a ball of plasticine were deformed into a ring or an irregular lump. Modified Model 4 would seem not to be applicable to these cases. However, it is still possible to think of the child as either confident or not in his perceptually based judgment of pre- compared with post-deformation amount, and as willing or not to accept that although the shapes are different, the amounts could look the same. Hence modified Model 4's route to conservation can be respecified as follows: at first the child makes confident perceptually based judgments of both AvB and AvB' comparisons, and does not accept the possibility of an AvB' equality amount judgment. Next, he becomes dissatisfied with perceptually based judgments of AvB' comparisons; he comes to accept the possibility that A and B' could look equal in amount. Finally, he develops the NAS criterion. It is not, therefore, crucial to modified Model 4 that particular dimensions such as length and width can be specified.

There seems to be no reason why modified Model 4 should not apply to the acquisition of conservation of amount of materials other than plasticine. One prediction made by the model is that if the comparison of pre- with post-deformation appearance were not necessarily an AvB' one, then the acquisition of conservation should be more difficult. This could be the case if the material used were sponge rubber, which can be squashed into a smaller volume. Similarly, in the case of non-compressible materials such as plasticine or liquid, it would be expected that the concept of conservation could be made more difficult to apply by presenting a deformation which did not result in an AvB' comparison. In the case of liquid, a trick container could be used so that pouring into what appeared to be a wider container resulted in an increase in level. Evidence that such a conservation task was more difficult than a standard one would provide support for modified Model 4, but also for the general view that awareness of changes in more than one dimension plays a role in conservation acquisition.

There is a reason why modified Model 4 might not be applicable to the acquisition of the conservation of some attributes of some materials. According to this model, learning of the uniqueness of reversibility follows the development of the ability to make perceptual compensation judgments; it is this feature which distinguishes Model 4 from Model 3. It is likely that materials differ in the extent to which they appear to the child to be expansible and contractible. Whereas plasticine is commonly deformed by squeezing or squashing, which perhaps give the impression of contraction, cardboard is more likely to be deformed in two dimensions just by rearrangement. If judgments of area of cardboard sheets were investigated, it might be found that by the time the child is prepared to make perceptual compensation judgments, he also knows about the uniqueness of reversibility. If so, then Model 3 would be more applicable than modified Model 4. (The relationship between these two models will be discussed in the next section.) It would also be expected, though, that there would be a very brief period of intermediate conserving performance, since once the child integrates knowledge about the uniqueness of reversibility with perceptual compensation, he should perform perfectly in the standard conservation test.

A series of experiments by Beilin (1964, 1966, 1969) is relevant to the question of the applicability of modified Model 4 to the acquisition of conservation of area, and also to the more general question of whether awareness of alternative perceptual judgments plays a role in the acquisition of conservation of area. Beilin used areas composed of either four or nine identical units, and the child was required to judge whether two areas covered the same or different amounts of space. In some tasks, the child saw deformation from configurational correspondence to noncorrespondence (conservation tasks). In others, called quasi-conservation tasks, the child saw no deformation and was required to compare two areas with equal numbers of units which were arranged differently. Beilin (1969) compared children's performance in conservation and quasi-conservation tasks, and he found that the quasi-conservation ones were more difficult: taking eight out of ten tasks correct as the criterion for passing, there were nine children who passed only conservation, compared with five who passed only quasi-conservation.

Beilin argues that the giving of correct judgments in quasi-conservation tasks required use of what he calls conceptual or 'infra-logical' strategies, involving either iteration (counting) or translocation (imagined or actual rearrangement). The reasons given for correct judgments suggested that translocation was most commonly used for the nine-unit areas, and iteration for the four-unit ones. Beilin also, apparently, assumes that identical or equivalent strategies were used in the conservation tasks, since he argues that these were easier because seeing the deformation 'triggered' the child to use an infra-logical strategy.

However, since Beilin in a similar experiment (1964) states that children who were classified as nonquasi-conservers did sometimes give translocation and iteration reasons, his conclusion that these strategies were easier to apply in the conservation tasks may not be valid. The children may have found it equally easy to apply the infra-logical strategies in both kinds of task, even though it was more difficult to give the right answer when the deformation had not been seen. In any case, a child who was using the NAS criterion should have no need to count the units in a conservation task. Neither is it valid to assume that use of the translocative strategy implies possession of the NAS criterion, since this strategy could be equivalent to modified Model 4's 'dynamic' perceptual compensation.

Beilin ignores the possibility that awareness of alternative perceptually based judgments was necessary for triggering use of an infra-logical strategy, but the results of his training experiment (1966) appear to support this view. Children were identified who failed to reach criterion (eight out of ten tasks correct) in quasi-conservation tasks, and also in similar tasks in which the areas to be compared were not equal; these children were then trained in one of three ways. The 'feedback' group was simply told whether their quasi-conservation judgments were correct or incorrect; the 'iteration' group was told to count the number of units in each of the compared areas; and the 'translocation' group was asked to rearrange one of the areas to make it look like the other. The subjects were given the pre-test, 21 training tasks and a post-test (identical to the pre-test) all in one half-hour session. Beilin found that only children in the feedback group gave significantly more conserving responses in the post-test than the children in a control group who had had no training. Of the 33 children in the feedback group 19 reached criterion in the post-test, compared with four of the 33 controls. The feedback training was found to be unsuccessful in improving the performance of a group of younger, kindergarten children, who presumably had not yet acquired the infra-logical strategies.

Beilin sees these results as supporting his argument that children who had infra-logical strategies available did not necessarily use them, and that the feedback served a function similar to the deformation in a conservation task, i.e. to trigger the child to use an infra-logical strategy. If this is the case, then it is odd that the translocation training was ineffective, since the children in that group did see deformation. An alternative interpretation is that the feedback encouraged the child to analyse the two areas more closely, made him realize that a perceptual judgment based on one aspect only was unsatisfactory, and led him to use translocation or iteration instead. If what encouraged the child to use translocation or iteration was the awareness that alternative perceptual judgments were possible, then the translocation and iteration training would be expected to be relatively ineffective compared with the feedback training.

There may be a similarity between the effects of Beilin's feedback training, and the effect on conservation performance of the compensation test used in the experiment on 'Compensation and the NAS criterion' (Chapter 10). As shown in Chapter 10, there was a highly significant improvement in performance in the fourth conservation task (which followed the compensation test) compared with performance in the first three conservation tasks (which preceded the compensation test). It was suggested that the experience of analysing the long thin sausages and comparing them with the short fat one may have made the child more aware of changes in both dimensions, and hence more likely to coordinate dimensions in subsequent tasks.

A similar interpretation can be made of Halford's (1971) experiment on the training of conservation of amount of liquid. In this, nonconservers were required to examine sets of containers which differed in either one or both dimensions (height and width), and to divide each set into particular subsets. In order to perform this task correctly, the child had to take both dimensions into account. Hence the apparent success of the training may have been due not to the child's learning to classify amounts (as Halford argues) but rather to increased awareness of changes in both dimensions, leading to increased coordination of dimensions in the post-test.

It appears, then, that the results of Beilin's experiments on the conservation of area, and Halford's on the conservation of amount of liquid, may be interpreted as supporting the general view that awareness of alternative perceptual judgments of AvB' comparisons is necessary for conservation acquisition, and they can be accommodated by modified Model 4 in particular.

12.3   General conclusions

As they stood originally, none of the four models did more than describe the route to the acquisition of conservation; none of them specified how the NAS criterion might develop. It has been found that the data support a modified Model 4 rather than Models 1, 2 and 3, and it is modified Model 4 which has been developed to provide a more complete account of conservation acquisition. But had the data supported Model 1 or Model 2, it would have been necessary to account for the origin of the NAS criterion while the child continued to judge amount on the basis of single one-dimensional perceptual criteria (or even before he developed such criteria). The author has no suggestions to make as to how this might occur (see Chapter 3). In the absence of any suggestion, Models 1 and 2 remain implausible, quite apart from the evidence against them.

Model 3, in contrast, does become plausible if it is compared with modified Model 4. According to Model 3, the child acquires the NAS criterion simultaneously with the ability to make perceptual compensation judgments, and he acquires knowledge of the uniqueness of reversibility either at the same time or before. How could this occur? It was suggested earlier that the information processing capacity to handle changes in both dimensions may be necessary both for the learning of the uniqueness of reversibility, and for acceptance of the possibility of perceptual compensation. Modified Model 4 states that the ability to make perceptual compensation judgments develops prior to knowledge of the uniqueness of reversibility, but the two developments could occur together. Modified Model 4 also states how learning about the uniqueness of reversibility could lead the child who accepts perceptual compensation to develop the NAS criterion. Hence if it were the case that acceptance of perceptual compensation did not develop prior to knowledge of the uniqueness of reversibility, the child could integrate these two faculties to develop the NAS criterion at about the same time that he came to accept perceptual compensation. It seems then, that Model 3 can be seen as a concertinaed version of modified Model 4. Model 3 was designed to be consistent with Piaget's theory of the relationship between compensation and conservation. It was shown in Chapter 5 that Piaget's account of conservation acquisition does not make clear how the operation of identity (equivalent to the NAS criterion) develops. Now, Piaget's theory becomes more comprehensible: the NAS criterion could develop in the way specified by modified Model 4, and Model 3 can be interpreted as providing essentially the same account of conservation acquisition as modified Model 4.

The method by which the four models were developed and tested has several features which should be emphasized, since they could usefully be incorporated into other work on intellectual development.

(i) As argued in Chapter 2, it is essential to analyse carefully the concepts to be investigated, and to develop operational definitions of these. The set-backs have been shown which arose from failure to make explicit the distinction between conservation and compensation (Chapter 2), qualitative identity and conservation (Chapter 3), or compensation and covariation (Chapter 4).

(ii) The advantages of pitting alternative models against each other are apparent in Chapters 7–10. The present study might have set out merely to test Piaget's theory, or to decide whether this was more or less adequate than Bruner's. Instead, four models were developed, the differences between which were clearly specified. This resulted in the derivation of precise predictions, and powerful tests of each of the models could be made. Had no distinction been made between Model 1 (consistent with Bruner's theory) and Model 2, or between Model 3 (consistent with Piaget's theory) and Model 4, less progress would have been made in the search for an explanation of conservation acquisition.

(iii) The value of discriminating finely between children at different stages in the acquisition of the concept in question has been demonstrated in the experimental reports. The relationships identified in the experiments presented in Chapters 7–11 could not have been found had the children simply been divided into 'conservers' and 'nonconservers'.

(iv) The experimenter knows he is on the right lines if finer and finer analyses of the results produce clearer and clearer relationships. In the experiments presented in Chapter 8, for example, children were divided into five groups on the basis of their performance in the conservation test. This allowed a thorough examination of whether or not the NAS criterion is easier to apply in reduced conflict situations. Had the children been divided into only two or three conservation groups, the conclusion that the NAS criterion is no easier to apply in these situations could not have been drawn so confidently. Similarly, in the experiments presented in Chapters 9, 10 and 11, the division of intermediate conservers into two or more subgroups allowed a more powerful test of the models.

(v) If each child is questioned adequately, there is little need for statistical analyses of grouped data. The assumption by many experimenters seems to be that data from children are necessarily messy, that children are likely to respond inconsistently. Statistical techniques are used, it appears, in order to try and ascertain what is really going on. Yet the muddle may lie in the experimenter's head rather than in the child's; statistics can be used to cover up a weak methodology and conceptual analysis as well as to make sense out of 'noisy' data. Many of the results given in Chapters 7–11 are surprisingly clear-cut; whether or not they are as expected by each of the models can readily be seen without the use of statistics. This is possible only because a variety of responses was gathered from each child.

(vi) This point may be taken even further to suggest that if we knew exactly what information one child had used in acquiring conservation, and how he had used that information, we could hope to develop a far more powerful account of conservation acquisition than we could if we had gathered a mass of superficial group data.

Apart from these methodological points, what other conclusions can be drawn from the present study about the investigation of intellectual development? In Chapter 1, it was promised that our understanding of a general process of invention would be reconsidered in the light of the suggestions made about the acquisition of conservation of amount. Whether or not it is valid to consider a general process of invention to underlie cognitive development has not been discussed; the aim here was to identify one concept which seemed to be a clear example of invention rather than discovery, and to investigate that. The question of whether it is sensible to try to identify general features of thinking, like Piaget's reversibility, has also been ignored. This is an issue which can be considered separately from the problem of explaining how certain basic concepts develop. Piaget attacks both of these problems on a grand scale—the process of equilibration is considered to be responsible for the development of concepts such as conservation of quantity, and also for the acquisition of the logical operations which structure the child's thought. But, as argued in Chapter 1, what is now needed is a detailed analysis of particular aspects of development.

On the basis of the present study, there seem to be three lines of investigation which it would be fruitful to pursue, either in the area of conservation acquisition (so that modified Model 4 could be tested further or developed into a more complete account), or of other concepts.

(i) The integration of discoveries with inventions could be investigated more fully than it has been here. As an extension of the work presented in Chapters 7–11, it would be interesting to identify children who had just begun to make perceptual compensation judgments and to teach them about the uniqueness of reversibility, to try and study the process of integration of knowledge about amounts with knowledge about the effects of deformation on appearance. It was suggested in Chapter 1 that discovery may play a more important role in the acquisition of other conservation concepts, conservation of number, for example. How does the child's discovery (by counting) of conservation of number interact with his invention of the concept? The concept of object permanence was presented as one in which it is difficult to draw a dividing line between invention and discovery. Can the child be trained to search for hidden objects like Etienne's chicks? If he can, how does the trained child differ from one who has acquired object permanence without being taught by the experimenter? Attempts to answer such questions as these may lead to an understanding of the psychological relationships between invention and discovery.

(ii) A second area which needs deeper investigation concerns the information-processing capacities which constrain the child's intellectual development. It has been suggested that unless the child can handle changes in both dimensions when a plasticine sausage is rolled, he cannot be expected to accept the possibility of perceptual compensation nor to learn about the uniqueness of reversibility. Yet, in a sense, a child who fails to do both of these may be able to handle both dimensions. For example, Piaget and Inhelder's level prediction task (1971; French edition, 1966) which was discussed in Chapter 4, was found to be much easier than the amount construction test of compensation. Children who judge amount of liquid only on the basis of level may nevertheless be able to use the width of the container to predict where the liquid level will come to. Can this be accounted for adequately in information processing terms? If not, what is happening between the time the child becomes capable of taking into account both dimensions when judging amount, and the time when he actually does so? In any study like the present one, it would be useful to have a specification of the information-processing requirements of each of the components of the concepts being investigated.

(iii) Perhaps the most interesting line of investigation concerns the role of conflict in intellectual development. As shown in Chapter 5, development by the resolution of conflict is central to the cognitive developmental approach to intellectual development, but there has been hardly any research which focuses directly on conflict. Even the designers of training experiments supposed to demonstrate the validity of the idea of development by the resolution of conflict have not seriously attempted to show whether the child is experiencing conflict during training (e.g. Smedslund, 1961d; Inhelder and Sinclair, 1969). It would be valuable to carry out a study designed to identify conflict in children just before they produced more advanced responses.

It was mentioned in Chapter 7 that a 'perceptual test' was designed to try to identify children who were aware of alternative judgments of an AvB′ comparison: judgments of 'More in the fatter sausage' but 'More in the longer sausage'. In this test, the child made an amount judgment of two sausages equal in width but clearly different in length (an AvB comparison), and then of one of those sausages compared with a shorter, fatter one or a longer, thinner one (an AvB′ comparison). The child was then asked 'Which was the easiest to tell, when I asked you about these (AvB) . . ., or these (AvB′) . . . or were they both just as easy?' If the child said one of the comparisons had been easier to judge, he was asked to give reasons. Each child was given three tasks like that.

In general, the results were as expected; all eight conservers said that the AvB comparisons were easier to judge and gave adequate reasons, and seven of the eight nonconservers said both the AvB and the AvB′ comparisons were just as easy. However, it was rather difficult to distinguish between two kinds of uncertainty in AvB′ perceptual judgments: uncertainty due to awareness of alternative judgments based on one-dimensional perceptual criteria, and uncertainty based on the knowledge that 'You can't tell'. It is this second kind of uncertainty which an adult would have; he would know that in order to be sure of the judgment, he would have to deform one of the sausages to make an AvB comparison. He might, for example, roll the fat sausage until it was just as thin as the other. While the child's reasons for his answer to the question 'Which was the easiest to tell . . .?' gave some indication of the basis of his uncertainty, a better way of identifying this needed to be found if confident conclusions were to be drawn about the existence of children who were aware of alternative judgments based on the criteria 'If it is longer, then there is more' and 'If it is fatter, then there is more'. A second difficulty with the study was that intermediate conservers had a tendency to say that the AvB', rather than the AvB, comparisons were easier to judge, although their reasons were not clear. Asking the child to verbalize his confidence in his judgments is probably not the best way of investigating the incidence of conflict between judgments based on alternative criteria. It would be interesting to try difference techniques for attacking this question.

It has been assumed that the child develops by making hypotheses which are then shown to be inappropriate: conflicts occur both between two hypotheses and between a hypothesis and external events. The child progresses by making mistakes. It has been suggested how this could happen in just one area, conservation acquisition, but it is unlikely that the processes at work in that area do not occur elsewhere. This suggests a return to the comparison made in Chapter 1 between the child and the scientist: both must resolve contradictions inherent in their theories and concepts if they are to achieve their aim of increasing their understanding of the world. Why should not the best means of achieving this aim be the same for both of them? What the philosophy of science has to say about how science progresses may be applicable to cognitive development in the child. If it is assumed that the child develops adaptively, then the way in which he abandons old concepts and accepts new ones may be based on the principles which the philosophy of science recommends. Popper (1959, 1963, 1973) points out that to be acceptable a new theory must be both conservative and revolutionary, in that it accommodates what was accommodated by the old theory, but also goes beyond that to account for even more.

When this is applied to the acquisition of conservation, it is clear that a child who developed in the way specified by Model 1 or Model 2 would not be advancing as Popper considers science should; at the time when he first accepts that amounts remain the same unless material is added or subtracted, he has not conserved what he already knows, that amounts look different when the compared entities are changed in shape. On the other hand, a child who acquired conservation in the way specified by Model 3 or modified Model 4 (now interpreted as essentially the same) would be developing as science should: the newly accepted concept of conservation of amount explains what the child already knows.

Perhaps when deciding on the acceptability of a theory about intellectual development, we should consider not only whether the theory is itself both conservative and revolutionary, but also whether it depicts the child as progressing like science: 'For the growth of scientific knowledge may be said to be the growth of ordinary human knowledge *writ large* . . .' (Popper, 1963, p. 216).

Appendix I

Experimental details

Five groups of children (groups I–V) took part in the experiments presented in Chapters 7–11, and also in Experiments A, B and C described in Chapters 2, 3 and 4. The children attended eight schools (schools 1–8), six in the London area and two near Southampton. The relationships between the experiments, the groups of children and the schools were as follows.

Children	Experiments	Schools
Group I (47 Ss)	Reverse conservation (Ch. 7) Perceptual test (Chs. 7 & 11) Experiment C (Chs. 2, 3 & 4)	1 & 2 London
Group II (34 Ss)	'Rolled' situation (Ch. 8) 'Choice' situation (Ch. 8)	3, 4 & 5 London
Group III (50 Ss)	Compensation and screening (Ch. 9) Experiment B (Chs. 2 & 4)	6 Southampton
Group IV (46 Ss)	Compensation and the NAS criterion (Ch. 10)	7 London
Group V (72 Ss)	Conservation and knowledge of the uniqueness of reversibility (Ch. 11) Experiment A (Ch. 2)	8 Southampton

Appendix II

Rough translations of the french quotations

p. 44

'Are they still the same amount of clay?' 'Is there the same amount of stuff in them both?'

'Did the two round balls have the same amount of clay before?' 'But then where has the clay gone from this one if there's less than before?' 'And if I roll it up and make it into a ball again?'

p. 57

'It's the same clay.' 'You didn't add any on or take any away.'

p. 60

'. . . the capacity to carry through a particular action in both directions, while being aware that it is the same action.'

p. 64

'The fact of being able to carry through the same action in two directions thus corresponds in a sense to the physical definition of reversibility . . ., whereas the awareness of the identity of this action in spite of the difference of directions, confers on reversibility an operational significance.'

p. 82

'. . . henceforth, in addition to the characteristics A and B, the child considers the actual actions which transform a pair A_n B_n into another A_{n+1} B_{n+1} .'

p. 85

'. . . a *de facto*, but not a necessary, conservation for certain cases . . .'

References

Beilin, H. (1964). Perceptual-cognitive conflict in the development of an invariant area concept. *J. exp. Child Psychol.*, **1**, 208–226

Beilin, H. (1965). Learning and operational convergence in logical thought development. *J. exp. Child Psychol.*, **2**, 317–339

Beilin, H. (1966). Feedback and infralogical strategies in invariant area conceptualization. *J. exptl. Child Psychol.*, **3**, 267–278

Beilin, H. (1969). Stimulus and cognitive transformation in conservation. In D. Elkind and J. H. Flavell (Eds.), *Studies in Cognitive Development*, New York: Oxford Univ. Press

Berko, J. and Brown, R. (1960). Psycholinguistic research methods. In P. H. Mussen (Ed.), *Handbook of Research Methods in Child Development*, New York: Wiley

Berlyne, D. (1965). *Structure and Direction in Thinking*, New York: Wiley

Beth, E. W. and Piaget, J. (1966). *Mathematical Epistemology and Psychology*, Dordecht, Holland: Reidel

Bever, T. G. (1970). The cognitive basis for linguistic structures. In J. R. Hayes (Ed.), *Cognition and the Development of Language*, New York: Wiley

Bower, T. G. R., Broughton, J. M. and Moore, M. K. (1971). Development of the object concept as manifested in changes in the tracking behaviour of infants between 7 and 20 weeks of age. *J. exp. Child Psychol.*, **11**, 182–193

Bower, T. G. R. and Wishart, J. G. (1972). The effects of motor skill on object permanence. *Cognition*, **1**, 165–172

Braine, M. D. S. (1962). Piaget on reasoning: a methodological critique and alternative proposals. In W. Kessen and C. Kuhlman (Eds.), Thought in the young child. *Monog. Soc. Res. Child Dev.*, **27**, 41–60

Braine, M. D. S. and Shanks, B. L. (1965a). The development of conservation of size. *J. verb. Learning verb. Behav.*, **4**, 227–242

Braine, M. D. S. and Shanks, B. L. (1965b). The conservation of a shape property and a proposal about the origin of the conservations. *Canad. J. Psychol.*, **19**, 197–207

Brainerd, C. J. and Allen, T. W. (1971). Experimental inductions of the conservation of 'first-order' quantitative invariants. *Psychol. Bull.*, **75**, 128–144

Brison, D. W. (1966). Acceleration of conservation of substance. *J. genet. Psychol.*, **109**, 311–322

Bruner, J. S. (1964). The course of cognitive growth. *Am. Psychol.*, **19**, 1–15

Bruner, J. S. (1966a). On cognitive growth I. In J. S. Bruner, R. R. Olver, P. M. Greenfield *et al.*, *Studies in Cognitive Growth*, New York: Wiley

Bruner, J. S. (1966b). An overview. In J. S. Bruner, R. R. Olver, P. M. Greenfield *et al.*, *Studies in Cognitive Growth*, New York: Wiley

Bruner, J. S. (1966c). On the conservation of liquids. In J. S. Bruner, R. R. Olver, P. M. Greenfield *et al.*, *Studies in Cognitive Growth*, New York: Wiley

Bruner, J. S. (1966d). On cognitive growth II. In J. S. Bruner, R. R. Olver, P. M. Greenfield *et al.*, *Studies in Cognitive Growth*, New York: Wiley

Bruner, J. S., Olver, R. R., Greenfield, P. M. *et al.* (1966). *Studies in Cognitive Growth,* New York: Wiley

Bryant, P. E. (1972). The understanding of invariance by very young children. *Canad. J. Psychol.,* **26,** 78–96

Cohen, G. M. (1967). Conservation of quantity in children: the effect of vocabulary and participation. *Quart. J. exp. Psychol.,* **19,** 150–154

Craig, G. J., Love, J. A. and Olim, E. G. (1973). Perceptual judgments in Piaget's conservation-of-liquid problem. *Child Dev.,* **44,** 372–375

Curcio, F. *et al.* (1972). Compensation and susceptibility to conservation training. *Dev. Psychol.,* **7,** 259–265

Décarie, T. G. (1965). *Intelligence and Affectivity in Early Childhood,* New York: Int. Univ. Press

Donaldson, M. and Wales, R. (1970). On the acquisition of some relational terms. In J. R. Hayes (Ed.), *Cognition and the Development of Language,* New York: Wiley

Elkind, D. (1966). Conservation across illusory transformations in children. *Acta Psychologica,* **25,** 389–400

Elkind, D. (1967). Piaget's conservation problems. *Child Dev.,* **38,** 15–27.

Elkind, D. (1969). Conservation and concept formation. In D. Elkind and J. H. Flavell (Eds.) *Studies in Cognitive Development,* New York: Oxford Univ. Press

Elkind, D. and Schoenfeld, E. (1972). Identity and equivalence conservation at two age levels. *Dev. Psychol.,* **6,** 529–533

Engelmann, S. (1967). Cognitive structures related to the principles of conservation. In D. W. Brison and E. V. Sullivan (Eds.), *Recent Research on the Acquisition of Conservation of Substance,* Educ. Res. ser. No. 2. Toronto: Ontario Institute for Studies in Education

Etienne, A. S. (1973). Developmental stages and cognitive structures as determinants of what is learned. In R. A. Hinde and J. Stevenson-Hinde (Eds.) *Constraints on Learning,* London: Academic Press

Feigenbaum, K. D. and Sulkin, H. (1964). Piaget's problem of conservation of discontinuous quantities: a teaching experience. *J. Genet. Psychol.,* **105,** 91–97

Ferguson, G. A. (1965). *Nonparametric Trend Analysis,* Montreal: McGill Univ. Press

Flavell, J. H. and Wohlwill, J. F. (1969). Formal and functional aspects of cognitive development. In D. Elkind and J. H. Flavell (Eds.), *Studies in Cognitive Development,* New York: Oxford Univ. Press

Fleischmann, B., Gilmore, S. and Ginsburg, H. (1966). The strength of nonconservation. *J. exp. Child Psychol.,* **4,** 353–368

Furth, H. G. (1968). Piaget's theory of knowledge: the nature of representation and interiorization. *Psychol. Rev.,* **75,** 143–154

Furth, H. G. (1969). *Piaget and Knowledge,* Englewood Cliffs, N.J.: Prentice-Hall

Gelman, R. (1972). Logical capacity of very young children: number invariance rules. *Child Dev.,* **43,** 75–90

Gelman, R. and Weinberg, D. H. (1972). The relationship between liquid conservation and compensation. *Child Dev.,* **43,** 371–383

Green, R. T. and Laxon, V. J. (1970). The conservation of number, mother, water and a fried egg chez l'enfant. *Acta Psychologica,* **32,** 1–20

Griffiths, J. A., Schantz, C. A. and Sigel, I. E. (1967). A methodological problem in conservation studies: the use of relational terms. *Child Dev.,* **38,** 841–848

Gruen, G. E. (1965). Experiences affecting the development of number conservation in children. *Child Dev.,* **36,** 963–979

Halford, G. S. (1968). An experimental test of Piaget's notions concerning the conservation of quantity in children. *J. exp. Child Psychol.,* **6,** 33–43

Halford, G. S. (1969). An experimental analysis of the criteria used by children to judge quantities. *J. exp. Child. Psychol.,* **8,** 314–327

Halford, G. S. (1970a). A theory of the acquisition of conservation. *Psychol. Rev.,* **77,** 302–316

Halford, G. S. (1970b). A classification learning set which is a possible model for conservation of quantity. *Aust. J. Psychol.*, **22**, 11–19

Halford, G. S. (1971). Acquisition of conservation through learning a consistent classificatory system for quantities. *Aust. J. Psychol.*, **23**, 151–159

Hall, V. C. and Kingsley, R. (1968). Conservation and equilibration theory. *J. genet. Psychol.*, **113**, 195–213

Hooper, F. (1969). Piaget's conservation tasks: the logical and developmental priority of identity conservation. *J. exp. Child Psychol.*, **8**, 234–249

Inhelder, B. (1962). Aspects of Piaget's genetic approach to cognition. In W. Kessen and C. Kuhlman (Eds.) Thought in the young child. *Monog. Soc. Res. Child Dev.*, **27**, 19–34

Inhelder, B. and Sinclair, H. (1969). Learning cognitive structures. In P. Mussen, J. Langer and M. Covington (Eds.) *Trends and Issues in Developmental Psychology*, New York: Holt, Rinehart & Winston

Koshinsky, C. and Hall, A. E. (1973). The developmental relationship between identity and equivalence conservation. *J. exp. Child Psychol.*, **15**, 419–424

Larsen, G. Y. and Flavell, J. H. (1970). Verbal factors in compensation performance and the relation between conservation and compensation. *Child Dev.*, **41**, 965–977

Lovell, K. and Ogilvie, E. (1960). A study of the conservation of substance in the junior school child. *Br. J. ed. Psychol.*, **30**, 109–118

Lumsden, E. A. and Kling, J. K. (1969). The relevance of an adequate concept of 'bigger' for investigations of size conservation: a methodological critique. *J. exp. Child Psychol.*, **8**, 82–91

Lumsden, E. A. and Poteat, B. W. S. (1968). The salience of the vertical dimension in the concept of 'bigger' in five and six year olds. *J. verb. Learn. verb. Behav.*, **7**, 404–408

McManis, D. L. (1969). Conservation of identity and equivalence of quantity by retardates. *J. genet. Psychol.*, **115**, 63–69

Mehler, J. and Bever, T. G. (1967). Cognitive capacity of very young children. *Science*, **158**, 141–142

Mermelstein, E. and Shulman, L. S. (1967). Lack of formal schooling and the acquisition of conservation. *Child Dev.*, **38**, 39–52

Miller, P. H. (1973). Attention to stimulus dimensions in the conservation of liquid quantity. *Child Dev.*, **44**, 129–136

Miller, S. A. (1973). Contradiction, surprise and cognitive change: the effects of disconfirmation of belief on conservers and nonconservers. *J. exp. Child Psychol.*, **15**, 47–62

Miller, S. A., Schwartz, L. C. and Stewart, C. (1973). An attempt to extinguish conservation of weight in college students. *Dev. Psychol.*, **8**, 316

Moynahan, E. and Glick, J. (1972). Relation between identity conservation and equivalence conservation within four conceptual domains. *Dev. Psychol.*, **6**, 247–251

Northman, J. E. and Gruen, G. E. (1970). The relationship between identity and equivalence conservation. *Dev. Psychol.*, **2**, 311

O'Bryan, K. G. and Boersma, F. J. (1971). Eye movements, perceptual activity and conservation development. *J. exp. Child Psychol.*, **12**, 157–169

Overbeck, C. and Schwartz, M. (1970). Training in conservation of weight. *J. exp. Child Psychol.*, **9**, 253–264

Papalia, D. E. and Hooper, F. H. (1971). A developmental comparison of identity and equivalence conservations. *J. exp. Child Psychol.*, **12**, 347–361

Peill, E. J. (1972). *Changes in Perceptual Judgments of Amount leading to the Acquisition of Conservation*, unpub. Ph.D. thesis, University of London

Piaget, J. (1952). *The Child's Conception of Number*, London: Routledge & Kegan Paul

Piaget, J. (1954). *The Construction of Reality in the Child*, New York: Basic Books

Piaget, J. (1957). Logique et équilibre dans les comportements du sujet. In *Etudes d'Epistemologie Genetique. Vol. 2. Logique et Equilibre*, Paris: Presses Univ. France.

Piaget, J. (1960). In J. M. Tanner and B. Inhelder (Eds.), *Discussions on Child Development, Vol. 4*, London: Tavistock

Piaget, J. (with McNeill, D.) (1967). Cognitions and conservations: two views. *Contemp. Psychol.,* **12,** 530–533

Piaget, J. (1968a). *On the Development of Memory and Identity,* Heinz Werner Lecture Series. Vol. II. Mass.: Clark Univ. Press

Piaget, J. (1968b). Quantification, conservation, and nativism. *Science,* **162,** 976–979

Piaget, J. (1970). Piaget's theory. In P. H. Mussen (Ed.) *Carmichael's Manual of Child Psychology,* 3rd ed., New York: Wiley

Piaget, J. (1971). The theory of stages in cognitive development. In D. R. Green, M. P. Ford and G. B. Flamer (Eds.), *Measurement and Piaget,* New York: McGraw-Hill

Piaget, J. and Inhelder, B. (1941). *Le Développement des Quantités Physique Chez l'Enfant,* Neuchatel: Delachaux et Niestlé

Piaget, J. and Inhelder, B. (1961). *Le Développement des Quantités Physique Chez l'Enfant,* Introduction to 2nd ed. Neuchatel: Delachaux et Niestlé

Piaget, J. and Inhelder, B. (1969). Intellectual operations and their development. In P. Oleron, J. Piaget, B. Inhelder and P. Greco (Eds.), *Experimental Psychology, its scope and method, Vol. 1: Intelligence,* London: Routledge & Kegan Paul

Piaget, J. and Inhelder, B. (1971). *Mental Imagery in the Child,* London: Routledge & Kegan Paul

Popper, K. R. (1959). *The Logic of Scientific Discovery,* New York: Basic Books

Popper, K. R. (1963). *Conjectures and Refutations,* London: Routledge & Kegan Paul

Popper, K. R. (1973). *Herbert Spencer Memorial Lecture* delivered at the University of Oxford

Pratoomraj, S. and Johnson, R. C. (1966). Kinds of questions and types of conservation tasks as related to children's conservation responses. *Child Dev.,* **37,** 343–353

Price-Williams, D. R., Gordon, W. and Ramirez, M. (1969). Skill and conservation: a study of pottery-making children. *Dev. Psychol.,* **1,** 769

Rothenburg, B. B. (1969). Conservation of number among four and five year old children—some methodological considerations. *Child Dev.,* **40,** 383–406

Rothenburg, B. B. and Orost, J. H. (1969). The training of conservation of number in young children. *Child Dev.,* **40,** 707–726

Schwartz, M. M. and Scholnick, E. K. (1970). Scalogram analysis of logical and perceptual components of conservation of discontinuous quantity. *Child Dev.,* **41,** 695–705

Sigel, I. E., Roper, A. and Hooper, F. H. (1966). A training procedure for acquisition of Piaget's conservation of quantity: a pilot study and its replication. *Brit. J. ed. Psychol.,* **36,** 301–311

Silverman, I. and Schneider, D. S. (1968). A study of the development of conservation by a nonverbal method. *J. genet. Psychol.,* **112,** 287–291

Sinclair, H. (1967). *Acquisition du Langage et Développement de la Pensée.* Paris: Dunod

Sinclair, H. (1969). Developmental psycholinguistics. In D. Elkind and J. H. Flavell (Eds.), *Studies in Cognitive Development,* New York: Oxford Univ. Press

Sinclair, H. (1973). Some remarks on the Genevan point of view on learning with special reference to language learning. In R. A. Hinde and J. Stevenson-Hinde (Eds.), *Constraints on Learning,* London: Academic Press

Smedslund, J. (1961a). The acquisition of conservation of substance and weight in children: vi. Practice in problem situations without external reinforcement. *Scand. J. Psychol.,* **2,** 203–210

Smedslund, J. (1961b). The acquisition of conservation of substance and weight in children: iii. Extinction of conservation of weight acquired 'normally' and by means of empirical controls on a balance. *Scand. J. Psychol.,* **2,** 85–87

Smedslund, J. (1961c). The acquisition of conservation of substance and weight in children: ii. External reinforcement of conservation of weight and the operations of addition and subtraction. *Scand. J. Psychol.,* **2,** 71–84

Smedslund, J. (1961d). The acquisition of conservation of substance and weight in children: v. Practice in conflict situations without external reinforcement. *Scand. J.*

Psychol., **2,** 156–160

Smedslund, J. (1962). The acquisition of conservation of substance and weight in children: vii. Conservation of discontinuous quantity and the operations of adding and taking away. *Scand. J. Psychol.,* **3,** 69–77

Smedslund, J. (1964). Concrete reasoning: a study of intellectual development. *Monog. Soc. Res. Child Dev.,* **29**

Smedslund, J. (1966). Les origines sociales de la décentration. In F. Bresson and M. de Montmollin (Eds.), *Psychologie et Épistémologie Génétiques: Thèmes Piagétiens,* Paris: Dunod

Smith, I. D. (1968). The effects of training procedures upon the acquisition of conservation of weight. *Child Dev.,* **39,** 515–526

Sonstroem, A. M. (1966). On the conservation of solids. In J. S. Bruner, R. R. Olver, P. M. Greenfield *et al., Studies in Cognitive Growth,* New York: Wiley

Strauss, S. and Langer, J. (1970). Operational thought inducement. *Child Dev.,* **41,** 163–175

Uzgiris, I. A. (1964). Situational generality of conservation. *Child Dev.,* **35,** 831–841

Waghorn, L. and Sullivan, E. V. (1970). The exploration of transition rules in conservation of quantity (substance) using film mediated modeling. *Acta Psychologica,* **32,** 65–80

Wallach, L. (1969). On the bases of conservation. In D. Elkind and J. H. Flavell (Eds.), *Studies in Cognitive Development,* New York: Oxford Univ. Press

Wallach, L. and Sprott, R. L. (1964). Inducing number conservation in children. *Child Dev.,* **35,** 1057–1071

Wallach, L., Wall, A. J. and Anderson, L. (1967). Number conservation: the roles of reversibility, addition-subtraction, and misleading perceptual cues. *Child Dev.,* **38,** 425–442

Wohlwill, J. F. and Lowe, R. C. (1962). Experimental analysis of the development of the conservation of number. *Child Dev.,* **33,** 153–167

Woodward, W. M. (1961). Concepts of number in the mentally subnormal studies by Piaget's method. *J. Child Psychol. Psychiat.,* **2,** 249–259

Name Index

Subject Index